AF477656

Islamic Literature in
Contemporary Turkey

Islamic Literature in Contemporary Turkey

From Epic to Novel

Kenan Çayır

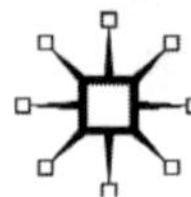

ISLAMIC LITERATURE IN CONTEMPORARY TURKEY: FROM EPIC TO NOVEL
Copyright © Kenan Çayır, 2007.

First published in 2007 by
PALGRAVE MACMILLAN™
175 Fifth Avenue, New York, N.Y. 10010 and
Houndmills, Basingstoke, Hampshire, England RG21 6XS.
Companies and representatives throughout the world.

PALGRAVE MACMILLAN is the global academic imprint of the Palgrave Macmillan division of St. Martin's Press, LLC and of Palgrave Macmillan Ltd. Macmillan® is a registered trademark in the United States, United Kingdom and other countries. Palgrave is a registered trademark in the European Union and other countries.

ISBN-13: 978-1-4039-7756-4
ISBN-10: 1-4039-7756-9

Library of Congress Cataloging-in-Publication Data

Çayir, Kenan.
Islamic literature in contemporary Turkey : from epic to novel / Kenan Çayir.
  p. cm.
Includes bibliographical references (p.) and index.
ISBN 1-4039-7756-9 (alk. paper)
1. Islamic literature, Turkish—History and criticism. 2. Turkish literature—History and criticism. I. Title.
PL207C39 2007
894'.350938297—dc22
2007060391

A catalogue record of the book is available from the British Library.

Design by Scribe Inc.

First edition: August 2007

10 9 8 7 6 5 4 3 2 1

Printed in the United States of America.

*For the two wonderful women
in my life, Ayda and Bade*

Contents

Acknowledgments

This book owes its life both to the workshops of Nilüfer Göle on Islamic movements at Boğaziçi University and to the guidance of my doctoral adviser Yeşim Arat. I consider myself privileged to have been Nilüfer Göle's student and to participate in her inspiring and illuminating workshops in İstanbul. I owe more than I can say to her. In like fashion, Yeşim Arat has been a supportive, wise and encouraging mentor. I am greatly indebted to her for invaluable comments and advice in planning the research and in thinking through some of the manuscript's key points. I would also like to thank Binnaz Toprak, Zeynep Gambetti, and Gül Sosay, whose criticisms on an earlier version of the text helped to finalize the key arguments I wanted to present in the book.

I wish to express my particular gratitude to Arus Yumul, Head of the Sociology Department at Bilgi University, not only for her personal loyalty but also for providing all of us in the department with a supportive and happy atmosphere conducive to good teaching and good research. Christopher Houston also deserves mention. He not only refined my English but also has always been a source of inspiration for me on social science and anthropological research in our long conversations during his visits to İstanbul. Chris made many invaluable suggestions during the writing of the book. I cannot thank him enough for sharing his expertise and insights into Islamic movements and social sciences.

Several friends assisted me with the translation of excerpts from novels. I would like to thank Rahim Acar, Seda Çiftçi and Tahsin Özcan for their poetic good sense. Ali Köse was always ready to lend a hand in providing necessary links to people at various stages of the study. And of course many other friends kept me motivated. In particular, I would like to let my dear friend Oya Dağlar know how much I appreciate her intellectual and emotional support. I am also indebted to Gülçin Gülelçe for her friendship and technical assistance throughout the study.

Last but not the least, I would like to thank my wife Ayda and my daughter Bade for their love, moral support, and encouragement. Will you let me back into your lives again now that the task of writing this book is over?! I would not have been able to write this book without the gifts of all these wonderful people … *Minnettarım*.

Introduction

Islam: A Global Phenomenon

Islam has become a global political and cultural phenomenon. Especially after the attacks of September 11, 2001, Islamist-appropriated signs have been increasingly politicized in the process of their deterritorialization (Roy 2002). The Islamic headscarf, for instance, is now considered a symbolic threat to progress and order by secularist regimes from Tunisia to France (Esposito 1999, 94). In Britain in late 2006, the leader of the House of Commons famously appealed to Muslim women to take off their veils, expressing his worry about the apparent communication of separatism. At the same time, terms like *jihâd*, *hijâb*, *sharia*, and *fatwa* have infiltrated Western languages, and it has become a common trend to refer to "bad" Muslims with shorthand terms like "Islamic terrorism," "Islamic fundamentalism," and "Islamic fanaticism." Clearly, the visibility of Islam and Islamic actors is no longer confined to the borders of the Muslim majority countries.

Islam's increasing global presence has led to a proliferation of books about the religion and its apparent convulsed state. Bookstore shelves in countries around the world are filled with books written for people with all levels of background knowledge on the subject, ranging from popular to semi-academic works on Islamic basics (Emerick 2002; Clark 2003). Intellectuals, too, have entered the information frenzy. In response to "the pressing need to inform about Islam" after September 11, 2001, John Esposito, a prominent expert on Islam, published a book for worried Americans titled *What Everyone Needs to Know about Islam: Answers to Frequently Asked Questions* (2002). The nature of the questions he constructs reveals the level of concern about Islam in the United States and the way experts both pander to and profit from it: in addition to questions like "What do Muslims believe?", the book asks "Why are Muslims so violent?"; "Does Islam permit suicide bombers?"; "Does the Koran condone terrorism?"; "Are women second-class citizens in Islam?"; "Why does Islam separate men and women?"; and "Is Islam compatible with modernization?" These queries exemplify a discourse on Islam informed by their writers' powerful identification with the West.[1] The way these questions are formulated demonstrates the way Islam-related issues are covered by the Western public agenda: the visibility of key symbols is often equated with fundamentalism, an alien culture, or a "threatening civilization."

Intimately related to this coverage is an increasing tendency to conceive of all facets of life in Muslim majority societies in civilizational or cultural terms. Despite its regional, political and ideological diversity, contemporary Islamic practices are explained through a general category of Islamic civilization that is thought to apply in all circumstances and geographies. In his introduction to an edited volume published in 1983, James Piscatori notes the following consequences of studying Islamic politics in civilizational terms:

> Dealing with Islam at this [civilizational] level seems to invite a preoccupying comparison with the West and to distort both civilizations by pitting "us" against "them". It probably also obscures the dissimilarities among Muslims and, by concentrating on a cultural whole, it makes short work of underlying economic and social realities (Piscatori 1983, 8)

Yet since Piscatori made his rather tame critique over twenty years ago, culturalist approaches, with their totalizing logic vis-à-vis contemporary Islamism, have flourished. People refer to Islam as a distinct culture with a common set of valuesand patterns, from Turkey to Indonesia. Those who think in cultural terms promote models of homogenous civilizations that are presently claimed to be in conflict, as exemplified by

Huntington's thesis (Huntington 1993). Of course, approaching Islam in cultural terms is not confined to those who conceive of Islam as a holistic civilization that threatens the West. Many radical Islamic groups also share this binary vision, producing a confrontational Islamic discourse that totalizes the Muslim world against a homogeneously perceived West. Thus the debate on Islam today is locked, as Roy notes, in a culturalist paradigm that posits the existence of distinct Western and Islamic cultures, each based on religion (Roy 2002, 328). The post–September 11, 2001, atmosphere has provided fertile ground for the dissemination of such an approach, favored by both conservative circles in Western societies and radical circles in Muslim contexts.[2]

Against the ideological simplicities of the culturalist approach to Islam and its reasonable, democratic other (the West), studying Islamic movements today is a complex matter due to their multiple or plural manifestations. There is no single party, institution or nation state that encompasses all the meanings and practices of contemporary Islamic movements. Islamic action involves plural forms in different national contexts (Göle 2006, 6). Contemporary Islamic movements today are associated not only with suicide bombers, but also involves the appropriation of Western public spaces by immigrant groups, the pursuit of identity and distinction through modern consumption by young Islamic actors, and veiled female actors challenging the subjugation of women in Muslim contexts. The new Muslim politicians of Turkey's Justice and Development Party speak a democratic and liberal discourse, especially in comparison with the confrontational modes of politics pursued by earlier Islamic activists. The middle class professionals who broke off from the Muslim Brotherhood to found Egypt's Wasat Party do not emphasize an explicit political dimension but rather highlight Islam's cultural and daily aspects (Ayoob 2004). Recent research on Islam demonstrates that new interpretations are challenging the collective voice of Islamists from the 1970s and 1980s, so that contemporary Islamism involves a "clash within Islam" in Middle Eastern Muslim countries (Sivan 2003). New interpretations of Islam renounce earlier

Islamist arguments for the unity of religion and politics in Islam and problemize conspiracy theories in which the West is equated with the source of degeneration for the Muslim world. New voices reveal the polyphonic and complex nature of contemporary Islamism.

Nevertheless, the denial of an essential Islamic culture that naturally produces Islamic politics does not mean that we cannot historicize the possibility of a shared imaginary among Islamist actors across regional or national boundaries.[3] Islamism as a social and political practice involves the production of a shared imaginary on transnational lines, disseminated through newspapers, cassettes and translations, particularly during Islamic movements' early years in the 1970s and 1980s. Contemporary Islamism refers to a new social and political stance that emerged in Muslim contexts in this period, along with a call for a reconceptualization of Islam in the face of Western modernity. The relationship of Islam to Western modernity has always been central for the Islamic agenda, from the first generation of Islamists in the late-nineteenth century to the contemporary Islamic actors of the 1970s and 1980s. This is because Muslim societies, either through their oppression under colonial power or through the voluntary action of local modernist elites, have adopted Western institutions, customs, and manners. This process of modernization involved the weakening and often the replacement of older Islamic institutions with "modern" organizations. It also resulted in the marginalization of a religious tradition that in many contexts was considered an obstacle to the success of modern civilization. Islamic movements emerged as a response to the challenges posed by the modernization process in Muslim majority countries. Islamism, then, is about "the problematization of the history of modernization in Muslim countries and its disruptive effects on religious memory and traditions" (Göle 1996, 20). This suggests that the Islamic imaginary did not develop in isolation from, but rather in intimate interaction with modernization processes. Islamic actors themselves were products of the modernization process since key activists were typically university students and children of newly urbanized families. They not only problemized modernization in the form of Westernization but also sought to develop an alternative Islamic response to the modern world.

Since the three decades following the rise of the Islamic movements in the 1970s, new Islamic actors have appropriated the products of modernity. In Muslim-majority societies that have been exposed to long state projects of modernization and secularization, Islamic movements emerged through a myriad of political, social, and cultural manifestations ranging from political parties and intellectual critiques, to new cultural and literary production, all of which reflected Islamic actors' intentions to formulate a new Muslim stance to the modern world. The dominant Islamic responses of the 1970s and 1980s were characterized by a reconceptualization of Islam as a system of thought and practical/political values that presented a model for both state and society. Islam was argued to provide a comprehensive way of life as set out in the Koran and as exemplified by the Prophet in his personal life (Esposito 1995). With the conviction that the Muslim world was losing its Islamic particularity because of modernization/Westernization, the Islamist response was formulated in opposition to Western frames of reference. The writings of influential intellectuals of the period such as Sayyid Qutb of Egypt, Abul Al'a Mawdudi of Pakistan, and Ali Bulaç of Turkey all sought to reconceptualize Islam as an alternative stance to contemporary Western ideologies such as capitalism, socialism, democracy, and secularism.[4] Islamic intellectuals produced a new politicization and ideologization of Islam, comparing Islam with capitalism or socialism rather than with other world religions. Contemporary Islamism in this sense can be conceived as a new consciousness that posits Islam to be a belief and action system that puts forward certain rules and regulations for reordering both public and private modern life.

Given the confrontational stance of at least this strain of contemporary Islamism, one important debate—despite the intensely self-interested motivations of many of its participants—revolves around the "compatibility" of Islam with democracy and human rights. Much of the literature on Islamism targets the Middle East where the lack of democracy—since at least the imposition of modern states by colonial powers—and existing gender inequalities provide polemical resources for the "compatibility" debate. At its most simplistic level, the "compatibility" debate polarized those who claim that Islam is totally incompatible with democracy and human rights and those who claim that true democracy and human rights can only be achieved by Islam.[5] Both sides, however, make culturalist arguments that attribute a homogenizing and static nature to Islam and modernity. Here, culturalism confines Islamism to "political expressions" in which actors are driven or fated to seek state power in the name of Islam. These culturalist or civilizational approaches disregard the temporality and relationality of Islamic movements and their interactions with secular contexts and values. Further, they pay little attention to the cultural manifestations such as film, music, and fiction through which the varying and variant narratives of Islamic actors can be followed.

Islamism and Islamic Literature in Turkey

This study explores Islamism and Islamist narratives in modern Turkey since the rise of Islamic social movements in that country in the late 1970s. Turkey offers key advantages for studying Islamist politics. In the first place, it diverges from most Middle Eastern countries through its constitutionally secular and democratic character.[6] Further, Turkey is the only Muslim nation considered viable for entry into the European Union. On the other hand, Turkey displays certain parallels with other Middle Eastern societies in terms of the relatively simultaneous emergence, interaction, and influence of contemporary movements. Turkey has also had the most radical of secularist (Jacobin) regimes in the region—perhaps along with the Pahlavi monarchs. The continuing role of Islamic movements in Turkish political and social life and Turkey's current candidacy to the

European Union present an invaluable setting for exploring relations between Islamism and modernity. Lastly, Turkish Islamic groups do not speak with a single voice: anti-Western Islamic groups that voice a polarizing discourse exist in contradistinction to new critical Islamic actors. A younger generation of Islamic politicians has broken away from their old party to form the ruling Justice and Development Party (JDP). Publicly criticizing the polarizing discourse of their old party colleagues, the JDP politicians argue that Islam promotes no particular type of regime. Their female and headscarved activists question the older male-dominated discourse of Islamism through literary and non-literary works, stating that they have benefited from feminism. In new autobiographical accounts, Islamic intellectuals take a critical stance toward their earlier selves and their oppositional and revolutionary interpretations of Islam.

This study does not confine itself, however, to Islamic intellectuals' or politicians' accounts. Most importantly, it examines Islamism and the changing compositions of Islamic identities in Turkey via an engagement with the Islamic literary fiction of the 1980s and 1990s. It is oriented not to generalizing categories of Islam and modernity, but to the fictional or literary stories that Islamic actors tell about themselves and other actors. These stories illuminate conceptions of modernity and their experiences in the relational context of Turkey, and these novels are products of a particular kind of relationship between Islam and literature, as has been seen in other Muslim contexts as well. *İslami edebiyat* (Islamic literature) in Turkish, or *adab Islami* (Islamic literature) in Arabic, refers to a body of literature with a polemical Islamic stance. This literature emerged in tandem with the rise of contemporary Islamic movements. It involves novels, poetry, and drama written from "a consciously Islamic perspective" for Islamic goals, differentiating these works from their "more secular cousin" (Malti-Douglas 2001, 6–9). Almost invariably, as Malti-Douglas reminds us, specialists of Middle Eastern literature have limited themselves to secular literature since they find it more worthy of study (2001, 5). This has been the case for Turkey, too, despite Islamic literature constituting a vital source for the exploration of Islamism and Islamic actors. The range of activities partly explicable by the broad banner "Islamist politics"—including the wearing and banning of the headscarf, Islamic journals and pro-Islamic parties (such as the Virtue Party or the Welfare Party), and relations between Islam and minority ethnic Muslims—have come under the close scrutiny of the media and social sciences in Turkey for the last twenty-five years. However, notwithstanding a few works that briefly analyzed select Islamic novels, Islamism in Turkey has yet to be studied through the production of its literature and novels.[7]

In this study, I limit myself to an examination of Islamic fiction, one small part of a vast body of Islamic writing in Turkey. I focus on two periods in the production of Islamist fiction: the Islamic "salvation" novels of the 1980s and the self-critical and self-exposing novels of the 1990s, in order to elucidate Islamic actors' perceptions of self, other and the social milieu in which they live. Like all fiction, the Islamic novels that emerged in both of these periods are closely attached to a political context, addressing, reflecting, representing, and constituting writers' and activists' experiences of the time. For this reason, I need to examine in more detail the history of Islamic revival in Turkey so as to clarify the significance of such fiction and art in generating Islamic movements and identities.

Parallel with other Muslim contexts, contemporary Islamic movements in Turkey emerged in the 1970s. It was, however, in the 1980s that Islamism truly made its presence felt in both public space and in relationship to dominant political struggles, as its intellectual accounts took a polemical stance on the very legitimacy of the modernizing project initiated by Mustafa Kemal (named Kemalism in Turkey) in the form of Westernization and secularization and of established traditional Islam. Islamism also emerged as publicly visible in the demand of headscarved girls to attend universities and Islamic party politics, as well as through its cultural products such as films, music, and novels.

The fact that Islamic actors were generally university students who were the first or second generation of newly urbanized families suggests that Islamism was a result of modernization in the form of urbanization and the huge increase of educational facilities in Turkey. Turkish Islamism resulted from these self-constituting actors' reevaluation or reformulation of Islam. What differentiated Islamism from Islam, and Islamist from Muslim, was that the former referred to a new consciousness and agency with a desire to reshape the modern world according to Islamic principles, while the latter signified—at least in Islamist discourse—the assumed passive historical and cultural stance of a religion and its believer.

Islamic groups cannot be conceptualized in a monolithic form in Turkey in the context of the 1980s. Islamism as a political and social practice involved—and still involves—diverse and multi-layered groups, including radical circles (who reject Islamic party politics and voice a revolutionary discourse of Islamism), groups organized under a political party (different parties of the National Outlook Movement), members of traditional Sufi groups (some of whom usually vote for right-wing nationalist parties), and Kurdish Muslims who condemn Turkish nationalism within Turkish Islamist groups.

In the politicized context of the 1980s, however, varied Islamic groups shared a common concern that Turkey (and the Muslim world in general) was losing its Islamic essence due to Westernization and secularization. Islamic actors claimed that Islam underwent a process of decline in the modern world due to the "invasion of Western values" and a "departure from the true path of Islam." They identified modern society as "pathological" since it had been "colonized" by Western moral codes, leading to materialistic conceptions, an unbridled individualism and free interaction of the sexes in public spaces.[8] The "remedy" to this situation was to truly understand the message of Islam and implement it in both private and public life; those who understood the message of Islam were considered the "doctors of humanity," who would "cure morally degenerated society" (ünal 1986, 8). On the basis of such a diagnosis, different Islamic groups in the 1980s often voiced an overlapping discourse with respect to their demand for the remoralization of public and private life according to Islamic principles.

To revitalize an Islamic way of life, Islamic actors in Turkey sought to clarify and reinterpret certain Islamic concepts that were represented as having been derived from the time of the Prophet through several books titled *Kuran'da Temel Kavramlar* (Basic Concepts in the Koran) (see ünal 1986; Kerimoğlu 1985). This clarification of Islamic concepts via a return to the fundamentals for their reapplication in the modern world illustrated the longing of Islamic actors for an Islamization of the public and private life. New meanings given to certain concepts proposed not a withdrawal but an active involvement in worldly affairs in the name of Islam.[9] To this aim, every aspect of life was filtered and reconstructed from an Islamist perspective, a point emphasized by the publication of books titled *İslam'da Kadın* (*Woman in Islam*) (Topaloğlu 1977), *İslam'da Erkek* (*Man in Islam*) (Şenlikoğlu 1993), and *İslam Devlet Yapısı* (*The Structure of Islamic State*) (Eryarsoy 1988). In the course of the formation of an Islamic imaginary, translation of books by prominent Islamic thinkers from other Islamic contexts (such as Sayyid Qutb, Abul Al'a Mawdudi, and Ali Shariati) served to provide oppositional and revolutionary language for many Islamic groups. New counter-public spaces were created to read these books and discuss Islamic concepts such as the teahouses of mosques, student houses, and seminar saloons of Islamic civil associations and foundations.[10] This new generation of Islamists differed from the first generation of the late nineteenth century on one crucial point, according to a leading Turkish Islamic intellectual: while the question the first generation reflected upon was, "Why did Islam recede in the face of the West?", contemporary Islamism formulated the question in a different paradigm: "What should the response of Islam to the modern world be?" (Bulaç 1987, 14). This point underlines the fact that contemporary Islamism is much more assertive and proactive than the first generation of Islamists. This was materialized in Islamic actors' confrontational posture toward the West and the Western-centric Kemalist modernization process of Turkey.[11]

Novel Islam: Salvation and
Self-Reflexive Fictions

Literature, particularly a certain form of Islamic novel in the 1980s, helped Islamic writers develop their criticisms of the Western-centric modernization, imagine an ideal Islamic order, and negotiate an Islamic identity at an intersubjective level. The novel as a genre with an Islamic content emerged concomitantly with the rise of Islamist movements toward the end of the 1970s in Turkey. Fiction writing was a new phenomenon in Islamic circles since, as a literary genre, it had long been construed as having a "destructive impact" on communitarian morality on the basis of the novel's exposition of individual private lives and "immoral scenes" (Meriç 1994, 84–86). Therefore the appropriation of the novel signified an attitudinal change among Islamic actors in the context of the Islamic revival. Islamic novels emerged as part of what Islamic writers called "Islamic literature," a committed literature with the aim of propagating an Islamic vision of the world.

As novelists state, the major motivating factor in the emergence of Islamic novels was the critical stance of Islamic writers toward "Republican literature," which was accused of "not represent[ing] us [Muslims] adequately" (Yardım 2000, 169). Islamist novelists radically homogenized and simplified the literary narratives of Turkey's Republican period, accusing them of causing "moral degeneracy" by importing the "westernization disease" and leading to the decline of Islam by bad-mouthing and misrepresenting Muslims (Miyasoğlu 1999). In the context of Islamic revitalization, the novel was appropriated as a genre charged with representing the "real," with conveying Islamic messages, and with combating "the negative effects of republican literature."[12]

The earliest novels by Islamic writers were set mostly in rural or village contexts, and were structured according to a reversal of the narratives of mainstream social realist novels written post-1950s in Turkey. Besides these standard village novels, other novels with complex narratives focusing on pious characters in urban life and their interrogation of the problems of the modern age were also written.[13] Nevertheless, the vast majority of 1980s Islamic novels can be categorized as *salvation novels* (*hidayet romanı*), a self-description that emerged from Islamic circles. Salvation novels formed a coherent genre with identical narrative structures. With their easily read popular forms, many became best sellers in Islamic circles; a number of these novels have presently reached their 40th or 50th edition. For instance, Ahmet Günbay Yıldız's twenty novels have sold more than a half million copies, making him one of the best-selling writers in Turkey (Yardım 2000, 168).

What characterized salvation novels is their message-bearing narratives in which Islam is presented as the only solution to the "moral degeneracy" of the modern world. These novels' central plot is based on the struggle between Islamic and secular worldviews, the former represented by "stable" Islamic characters, the latter by "degenerate" Westernized secular characters. Nearly all salvation novels conclude the same way: confused or unfulfilled secular/modern characters attain enlightenment and/or contentment with the illuminating guidance of exemplary Islamic characters. The time frame and referential contexts of these novels are usually the 1980s and modern urban spaces such as universities. They regularly narrate the struggles of "faithful" headscarved girls who are excluded from universities, or of young, educated, decent male characters who lead "depressed" girls living a Westernized way of life to salvation; this is always represented by such girls' embracing of the headscarf. Through the words of Islamic characters, novelists convey their message about the role of women in Islam, the requirements of Islamic morality, the "negative effects" of Westernization, the problems of the modern age, and Islamic solutions to these problems.

However, Islamic salvation stories do more than simply signify the oppositional truth claims of Islamism. Their depiction of idealized Muslim characters studying in universities or performing modern professions represents another dimension of Islamic movements: Islamic actors' will to participate in public life. In its construction of oppositional claims of truth, the Islamic movements were "world-accommodating" rather than "world-rejecting" (Toprak 1995). In other words, rather than presaging an Islamist withdrawal from modern life, Islamism promoted Islamic mental strategies to selectively reappropriate religion and modern forms of life (Göle 2002). In the same vein, the titles of books published by Islamists in the 1980s were *İslami Antropolojinin Oluşturulması* (*Shaping and Islamic Anthropology*) (Davies 1991), *İslami Sosyoloji* (*Islamic Sociology*) (Yunus 1988), and *Bilginin İslamileştirilmesi* (*The Islamization of Knowledge*) (Faruki 1985). Accordingly, the revolutionary Middle Eastern Islamic literature was not the only source of textual inspiration for Islamism; Islamism interacted with many critical European thinkers such as Arnold Toynbee, Alexis Carrel, Ivan Illich and Carl Gustav Jung. Islamic publishing houses first translated these writers' works into Turkish, and their books became best sellers in Islamic circles during the 1980s. Moreover, the inclination of headscarved girls to attend university did not abate, despite the call of some Islamic groups for the girls to leave school in the face of the headscarf ban. Indeed, when the ban was strictly enforced, many girls wore wigs or sought to study abroad. Islamist intellectuals' plea for a "revolt against industry and technology" (Toprak 1993, 171) was influential only at the rhetorical level and did not find an echo among Islamic groups who sponsored the training of their own engineers, journalists, and economists through scholarships or boarding houses as the 1980s moved into the 1990s. As a result, Islam in the 1990s appeared more and more in the public agenda via debates over Islamic companies, luxurious Islamic hotels, Islamic beauty parlors, and fashion shows that reflected the formation of an Islamic middle class and a pluralization of Islamic actors' life experiences.

Islamic actors' interaction with secular values, secular "others," and their theorization of new experiences has led to the emergence of new voices that challenge the collective and oppositional Islamic discourse of the 1980s. Although some Islamic groups still maintain a collectivist discourse, several self-critical Muslim actors have publicly taken a critical stance toward their old revolutionary interpretation of Islam. It is in this context that more self-reflexive narratives of Islamic actors, revealing aspects of conflicted inner selves, began to emerge. Islamic actors in these novels, which in this study I will call *self-reflexive and self-exposing* Islamic novels, are depicted as squeezed between their Islamist identities and religious ideals of the 1980s, and their new life experiences in the context of the 1990s. Several female novelists created Islamist characters that were educated but frustrated headscarved housewives, directing their criticism toward the male Islamic actors who had become "insensitive to their situation." Male characters, on the other hand, were allowed scope to explore the dilemmas of "illicit" love, their unhappiness in Islamic marriages, and their attendance in non-Islamic spaces like bars. These new Muslim characters resisted the stereotypes of secularism and collective Islamism with their self-reflexive and self-exposing narratives. The very act of self-exposition and reassessment of Islamist ideals violated collective definitions of Islamism.

Despite these developments—the internal diversity of Islamic groups, newly emerging self-critical Islamic actors and the changing narratives of Islamic identity—current intellectual and political polemics in Turkey, parallel to the global agenda, often work through totalizing the category of Islam(ism). The appearance of headscarved girls in urban spaces and universities, Islamic actors' will to participate in public life through proliferating cultural, educational and commercial initiatives, and the transportation of Islamic demands into the political arena via party politics are often radically homogenized and treated as a threat to basic tenets of the secular republic by some secularist groups. The historicity lying behind such a perception of Islamic practice is the Kemalist project of modernization, which in its most radical form aimed to cut all ties with the old Islamic (Ottoman) order on the basis that Islam as a way of life promoted a backward and particularistic vision of the world in the face of contemporary Western civilization (Mardin 1989; Kasaba and Bozdoğan 1997). In the new Turkish Republican political context, Islam was simultaneously

disestablished and re-established, leading to the marginalization of Islamic visibilities and symbols as "residues of the old
system" that had been and should be left behind (Göle 1997b).
Thus the rise of Islamist movements and the public assertion of
religiosity in the context of the 1980s has been constructed
and feared as "the intervention of an anachronistic predeces-
sor" (Davison 1998, 27) by many secularist groups whose narratives stress that overt manifestations of Islam should be
construed as impediments to civilization and modernity.

Despite these polarized potential subject positions, homogenous groups of Islamists did not clash with monolithic secular
groups in Turkey (Toprak and Çarkoğlu 2000). Some secular,
liberal, and leftist groups have defended headscarved girls'
right to education and expression of Islamic demands via politics. Nevertheless, influential secularist circles, including many
members of the mainstream media, military and bureaucratic
elites, and related NGOs, still treat unauthorized manifestations of Islamism—especially the headscarf—as a challenge to
secular democratic values, considering them "conscious steps"
taken toward realizing an Islamic order.[14] These groups are
skeptical about new critical actors, including younger Muslim
politicians who seem to bracket out their religious convictions
when deliberating about politics. For many Kemalist critics,
the moderate tone of Muslim politicians and headscarved
actors is no more than cosmetic.

What underlies such essentialist interpretations of Islamism is a conviction that Islam possesses certain inherent characteristics (such as the imposition of the headscarf on women)
that are incompatible with democratic and secular values since
they require believers to implement an Islamic rule of law in
public life. This kind of reading assumes that Islamism is
informed by prediscursive meaning structures that determine
all subjective positioning. Accordingly, the narrative varia-
tions of Islam among different Islamic groups are considered
means to disguise real intentions and demands posited by these
prediscursive or metalinguistic meaning structures.[15] This
essentialist reading of Islamism focuses on the category of

Islam, thereby constituting the Islamic self as a dependent variable. In other words, Islamic identity or subjectivity seems to have no reality independent of key concepts of Islamic *jihâd* or Islamic order into which it has to conform. Such a reading then considers Islamic agency impossible since it is determined by the ontological primacy of Islam.[16] In the last instance an essentialist reading of Islamism denies the historicity and relationality of Islamist movements. Further, it disregards the intersubjective creation of social meanings, relational agency, and Islamic social action.

By contrast, in this study I will consider Islamism as a social and political practice that is subject to constant reevaluation by Islamic actors in the relational context of the last twenty-five years in Turkey. I consider the novel a genre that has served Islamic actors as an important tool to develop and imagine a collective identity as well as to reconsider and renarrativize their experiences. In my analysis, I will explore Islamic meaning-making strategies and identities as constructed in fiction in the 1980s and 1990s.

Studying Islamism through Novels

Exploring a social movement or a social identity through literature—Islamism and Islamic identity in the context of this book—entails an interrogation of the very nature of fictional texts. It is crucial to clear the ground to understand the nature of literature and its relation to "nonfictional reality" since literary texts have long been identified as the repository of rhetoric, subjectivity, and fantasy. Employing literature—especially novels—for social scientific research necessarily involves a discussion of the relation between the "factual" and "fictional" implications of literary texts.

By definition, literary texts are regarded as fictional. The term "fiction" carries a double connotation. A more negative meaning suggests that fiction is false, contrary to fact, and concerned with the non-existent, while another understanding implies that fiction is constructed or imagined (Lamarque 1994, 139). Literature has long been regarded in conformity with such connotations, and thus has been treated with some suspicion in the realm of the social sciences[17] Literature is thought to appeal to fictional images, subjective feelings, and emotions that cannot easily be incorporated into the rational epistemology of sciences (Mendus 1996, 54). Underpinning this contention is the claim that literature stands as a separate domain from scientific writing, since the latter is objective, unambiguous, and non-metaphoric, while the former is associated with imaginative and subjective language. This division has been shaped by a modernist scientific presumption positing that there are facts "out there" and that they can objectively be reflected by "transparent" scientific writing (Eagleton 1996, 2).[18]

To advocate the importance of literature in understanding and interpreting society entails questioning this assumed distinction between literature and science. In his book *Literary Theory*, Eagleton (1996) does so by asking "if literature is 'creative' or 'imaginary,' does this imply that history, philosophy and natural science are uncreative and unimaginative?" (1996, 2). He goes on to question the constructed boundary between literature conceived as a domain inherently connected to value-judgments on the one hand, and scientific accounts characterized by "plain" and "objective" language on the other. Scientific, objective and descriptive statements, Eagleton notes, often involve invisible value categories, without which people would have nothing to say to each other at all. He gives the example of a statement one may make to a foreign visitor: "This cathedral was built in 1612." According to Eagleton, this seemingly "value-free" sentence presumes a number of value judgments such as "classification of buildings according to dates is valuable" and "this cathedral is worthy of mention" (Eagleton 1996, 12). Based on this example, Eagleton argues that there are no statements, scientific or otherwise, that reflect "reality" transparently without involving value-judgments. Indeed, the contention that "facts" exist and are "objectively representable" implies a belief in essences and carries its own political baggage.

What this contention implies is that there is no essence of literature. As Eagleton states, "some literature is fictional and some is not. Some literature is verbally self-regarding, while some highly wrought rhetoric is not literature. Literature, in the sense of a set of works of assured and unalterable value, distinguished by certain shared inherent properties, does not exist" (1996, 9). This suggests that the nature of literature, as with any field of knowledge, is determined relationally and institutionally within the context of relations of power in a given society (1996, 14). In other words, there is no literature outside of the boundaries of what Bourdieu (1995) calls power relations operating in the cultural field.

In this book I will consider the salvation novels of the 1980s and the self-reflexive novels of the 1990s as valuable cultural texts for interrogating Islamic understandings of the period. One might object that this claim confuses the "fictionality" of literature with the "factuality" of real contexts. However, following Eagletonian, Bourdieuan and Bakhtinian conceptualizations of literature, I argue that Islamic novels are not "true" or "fictional" *representations* of the 1980s and 1990s, but are themselves material and discursive aspects of the context of this period.[19] In other words, Islamic novels are not fictional creations of meaning, but rather create particular views of reality. They cannot be thought to exist outside of a given political and cultural context since the author (and readers) operates within a linguistic and cultural tradition—a field in a Bourdieuan sense (1995)—from which the texts' signs are derived and interpreted. This suggests that the novel is itself a construct, but one which is anchored in a historical and cultural context.[20] It is the work of a narrator who imagines, observes and describes herself and her milieu from a particular cultural perspective (Evin 1993, 95). In this sense, Islamist novelists, to use the analogy coined by Schutz, are like "the audiences in the theater" (Embree 1998, 10). They are authors who have attended "the play," or the context of the 1980s and

1990s, and reported afterward what they have seen. Thus analysis of Islamic novels involves the interrogation of Islamic novelists' representations of Muslims, others, and their surrounding world during the last two decades.

Studying Islamism through Islamic literary narratives introduces issues of change, space, historicity, and an analytical relationality into such an enterprise, concerns excluded by the essentialist reading of Islamic identity. This is because what differentiates narrative from essentialist accounts is that narratives embed characters and events in time and space, and order them according to a causal "emplotment." In this study I will use the terms "narrative" and "novel" interchangeably in order to make use of narrative theory that conceives of narrative not only "as a mode of representation but also a mode of reasoning" (Richardson 1990, 2).[21] Underlying this is the contention that people produce meanings through a narrative that allows them not merely to make sense of events but to partially constitute happenings as "events" in the first place by locating them in temporal and sequential plots. This argument is made by a number of social theorists who argue that narrative is an important component of an adequate understanding of self and identity since identity is partially constructed through the relational telling of stories—individual or collective—that order one's self in sequential plots (MacIntyre 1985; Taylor 1992; Benhabib 1996; Nussbaum 1992). By representing individuals as political agents who make choices or possess intentions and motives, the novel brings several aspects of human life to the fore for theoretical attention. It expands the scope of political investigation by presenting the particularities—emotions, ethical choices—of individual lives that resist political theorizing (Nussbaum 1992). Although it might be argued that the novel's individualistic perspective limits its usefulness for political analysis, the novel depicts individuals responding to other stories (again, individual or collective), and portrays individuals in relationship to other actors and to their social settings (Whitebrook 1996).

By drawing on the philosophical claim that there is an inherent relation between narrative, identity and politics,[22] this book argues that the Islamic novels of the 1980s and 1990s are not simply descriptional depictions but are representations that partially create the very realities to which they appeal. They are a means, then, through which Islamic readers, through their own "writing" of their acts and practices in relation to the novels, make sense of themselves and their social milieu. Salvation novels in this regard represent the project of Islamic actors' to develop a coherent sense of self in the context of the 1980s, a decade when a radical and oppositional discourse dominated Islamic circles. In this broader context, salvation novels appeared as an influential aspect of Islamic cultural criticism against Westernization. Novelists engaged in a discursive struggle against secular narratives of civilization and attempted to renarrativize the history of Turkish modernization and the current social scene from their own refracted angle. Novelists sought to develop a positive image of Islam and the Islamic self by debating the meaning of modernity, civilization, and secularism in the context of modern social relations. I argue that the narrative structures, the depiction of characters, and the identical closure of salvation novels signify a strand of Islamism, what I call *collective and epic* Islamism, which was dominant in the 1980s and maintained itself in the context of the 1990s. It is collective because it speaks with a language of "We," invoking a "them" and "us" discourse, and epic (in the Bakhtinian sense) because it voices a collective "epic absolute truth" derived from an "epic past," i.e., the period of *Asr-ı Saadet* (the age of happiness involving the period of the Prophet Mohammed and four Caliphs), to impose a unitary and singular Islamic worldview upon others. The identical conclusions of salvation novels in which all characters are blessed with Islam represent collective Islamism's ideal for a total Islamization of society.

Cultural narratives or stories, as Taylor notes, "feed directly into our identity by signaling valued attributes and behaviors and giving explanation for our past and present" (1991, 4). Moreover, stories provide us with an emotional repertoire since we learn our emotions from cultural stories (Nussbaum 1992,

287).[23] In this regard, I consider salvation novels cultural narratives that not only represented Muslims in a singular way, but also contributed to the formation of gender roles, emotions, and the affirmation of Islamism's claims for authenticity via stories and role models derived from Islam's "golden age." With their didactic and pedagogical narratives detailing "how Muslims should live in the modern world," salvation novels provided Islamists with a means to disseminate ideas in popularized form and to develop life strategies that paved the way for an assertive Islamic identity. Moreover, through the mediated language and imagery of literature, salvation novels served as a means of communication in Islamic circles, binding Muslim actors living in different part of Turkey to the formation of a collectively imagined Islamic community.

By contrast, the self-reflexive novels of the latter half of the 1990s diverged from the narratives of salvation fiction. While salvation novels depicted Muslims as a solid and homogenous collectivity and narrated the struggle and victory of Muslims against a "decadent" secular order and its representatives, the new novels of the 1990s portrayed Muslim agents with internal conflicts and contrasting desires, torn between their religious ideals and more worldly concerns in the face of modern urban relations. In these new novels, Islamic characters appeared no longer so sure of the virtues of the collective Islamic identity to which they were once committed. Two exemplary novels on which I will focus later in the book portray a headscarved woman's exploration of new modes of activity and a new sense of Muslim self through her process of unveiling, and the sinful love of a married ex-Islamist man. Islamist protagonists' self-scrutinizing and self-exposing narratives brought the experiences of Islamist actors in the 1980s and the 1990s to the fore. In other words, the conceptualizations, ideals, marriages, and commitments of the 1980s Islamist movement were put under close literary examination via the mediating contexts of these self-reflexive novels in light of Muslim actors' new experiences in the changing context of the 1990s.

The narrative form of the novel in the 1990s provided Islamic actors with grounds for revising life histories and imposing new patterns on events in the face of changing social relations. New novels enabled Islamic actors to reevaluate the stories of an Islamic golden age and Islamist conceptions of the 1980s, paving the way for novel practices and interpretations of Islam. Importantly, these new self-reflexive novels do not signify the resignation from or disavowal of Islamic identities, but rather a search for a new, not necessarily "Islamist," Muslim self. In essence, Islamists' attempt to "Islamize the novel" during the 1980s has resulted in "the novelization of Islam" in the 1990s.

On the Approach and Organization of the Study

Working with literary data imposes distinct problems relating to sampling (or the exemplary status or otherwise of novels), reader responses, and how best to approach literary texts. One cannot, for instance, easily paraphrase novelists' words, as a survey researcher might do for her informants' sentences, since literary data rest on a deliberate and distinctive use of language. Similarly, focusing on a wide range of data in order to generalize limits the explication of exemplary texts and literary language, while it also risks the loss of the aesthetic and creative dimension of literary texts. On the other hand, drawing on selected novels allows an in-depth examination of literary data but leaves readers with a mass of quotation marks and potential sampling insufficiency. Nevertheless, sociologists of literature (and literary critics) usually favor "depth over breadth" (Rogers 1991, 16) by focusing on one novelist or a few novels.

In this book I have chosen to examine Islamic novels in depth by focusing on two salvation novels of the 1980s and two self-reflexive novels of the 1990s. The novels selected for discussion were chosen on the basis of their "canonical" status in

Muslim circles, and because they appear to have become prototypes for the narrative structure of each period. Moreover, I
have deliberately made a gender-sensitive sampling. Each of
the two sets of novels includes texts of male and female novelists who mainly narrate the story using characters of their same
respective genders. Besides these novels, I refer to many other
salvation and self-reflexive novels of the period to substantiate
my analysis. In order to examine my selected fictions not only
"in depth" but also "in breadth"—and thus to relate them to wider
contexts—I have tried to situate my exemplary novels within
the broader boundaries of Turkish and Islamic literary fields.

I will not attempt to present a literary analysis of Islamic
novels by only drawing on a literary technical terminology.
The novels of the period are relevant for me in as much as they
involve signs, characters and narratives for understanding
Islamic subjectivity in Turkey in the 1980s and 1990s. In other
words, this study aims to examine Islamic novels for sociological and political illumination (of the Islamic social movement)
rather than judge them according to their aesthetic qualities. I
consider Islamic novels to be what Eagleton calls the "signifying practices" of Islamic actors within a whole field of discursive experiences. Approaching literature not as an abstract and
isolated field (the aesthetic field of art and the sublime), but as
a practice of signification among other discursive practices
transforms the literary object by placing it in a wider context
(Eagleton 1996, 177–78). Following this line of thought, I read
Islamic novels as sites of Islamic actors' discursive struggle over
the representation of Islam, Islamic identity, secularism, secular
[mis]recognition of the Islamic self, and modernity in an inter-
active and intersubjective fashion. My analysis, in this respect,
extends beyond a text-centered approach to include literary
texts' relations with the social and political events partially
constituting them. It also involves reading Islamic novels in
intimate relation to other non-literary Islamic and non-Islamic
texts of the period.

I examine novels mainly with a qualitative textual analysis. This includes considering the style, characterization, and

narrative structure of salvation and self-reflexive novels. These more formal qualities of novels are read as part of the content of Islamic representations of the period. In other words, characters or the narrative form of novels were themselves claimed to represent the dominant Islamic perceptions and Islamic subjectivities of the 1980s and 1990s. Since I consider salvation novels to be a means of discursive struggle against secular narratives of universal civilization and civility, and self-reflexive novels as narratives that convene a debate amongst Islamic circles over Islamic identity, my analyses involve examining the struggle over meanings, conditions, and consequences of telling a story in a particular way. My major concern is to search for how Islamic identity is narrated in novels, how Islamic actors tell stories about themselves and respond to stories told by others about themselves, how Islamic actors interact with other actors and contexts, and finally to consider whom the story is told to and for what purpose. These are all pertinent questions to political and sociological processes of identity construction and vital in understanding Islamism and Islamic identities in the context of the 1980s and 1990s.

The first chapter aims to situate Islamic literature within the field of Turkish literature while relating the emerging salvation novels to the context of the 1980s. It demonstrates how the literary field is construed by both Islamist and secularist writers as a space of struggle over narration. The chapter explores Islamist novelists' conceptualization of literature by drawing on published interviews with Islamist novelists, and gives examples of the narratives of early salvation novels. It also addresses the politics of literary translation that reveal how struggle over narration is not only limited to novel writing but also extends into the field of translation.

Two exemplary salvation novels will be examined in the second chapter, constituting one of the central parts of the study. I will focus on their narrative structure in order to elucidate the context through which Islamist novelists emplot their characters, the stories they respond to and develop, and the conclusions they reach. I will specifically focus on the nature of the

Islamic messages, on the representation of Islamic and secular identities, and the gender dimension of the novels. I will argue that these novels, with their identical messages and narrative closure, are indicative of collective and epic Islamism of the 1980s, the dominant strand of Islamist politics.

The next chapter, chapter 3, aims to develop a more general understanding of salvation novels and to relate them to non-literary Islamic writings of the 1980s. This involves analysis of how these novels provided Islamists with a repertoire of action and emotion that paved the way for the emergence of assertive and collective Islamic subjectivities.

The other central part of the study is chapter 4, in which the much more self-reflexive and self-doubting narratives of the 1990s are examined. These novels will also be read in relation to the context of the 1990s that witnessed the rise of Islamic middle classes, the incorporation of Islamic actors into commercial and cultural life, and the emergence of self-critical Islamic voices over the excesses of Islamist politics rather than of Muslims' lack of commitment. I will contend that these narrative voices expose the inner conflicts of Islamic characters that challenge the collective Islamic definitions of the previous decade while reflecting and expressing the changing perceptions of Muslim actors and the emergence of new Muslim subjectivities in the context of the 1990s. The book concludes by arguing that these changing Islamic narratives reveal two currently coexisting and conflicting strands of Islamism.

The Turkish Literary Field: A Space of Struggle Over Islam, Secularism, and Modernity

Literature, Politics, and Islam in the Context of Turkish Modernization

Literature does not refer to a category that is historically invariant and aesthetically determined by its "good writing" (Eagleton 1996, 170ff).[1] What this contention implies is that literature exists not because of its intrinsic aesthetic properties, but rather through established cultural, political and institutional relations. In other words, literature cannot be isolated from the context in which it arises and from the way people comprehend and consume a given text. What gives literature its meaning or value is its historically situated existence in a certain epoch.[2] More precisely, literary texts gain their meanings within the web of social relations operating in what Bourdieu calls the cultural field (1995).[3] The meaning and social value of a literary work is not determined outside of the habitus, or the institutions of a cultural or literary field (Bourdieu 1996). The literary field involves actors struggling over cultural and symbolic resources.[4] The meaning of literary activity, in this sense, is in symbolic struggle within the literary field in relation to other fields, including material resources.[5] In other words, the literary field is a site of struggle over the definition of meaning. Literary works are "the tools and stakes of

[that] struggle" (Bourdieu 1995, 183). In sum, literature and its producer do not exist independently of a literary field that involves a complex set of institutional frameworks making sense of both literature and the producer.

Exploring Islamic literary writing with this understanding entails an examination of the cultural and political field in which it emerged. Islamic literature in particular and Turkish literature in general refer to discursive practices taking place within existing relations of power in a cultural field and an overall field of power. In this sense, there is no pure "Islamic literature," removed from what Islamic and other actors say about it. Islamic fiction gains its meaning within a Turkish literary field that is constituted on the basis of a struggle between different positions.

It should be emphasized that the history of Turkish literature from the late Ottoman period to the present has proceeded hand in hand with Turkish Republican political history. Although it is impossible to explore a hundred years of the novel in Turkish literature as a space of struggle between various political ideologies in any detail here, in this section I will gesture to some of the main fault lines in the Turkish literary field in terms of the representation of Islam, civilization, and modernity. My focus will be on the depiction of religion and modernity in several influential novels before the 1980s and the emergence of Islamic salvation novels.

In the Ottoman context, the novel did not emerge in tandem with a developing bourgeoisie or with social and political changes instigated by this class, as was the case for the Western novel.[6] The genre was imported from the West at the end of the nineteenth century with the gathering momentum of modernizing movements in the late Ottoman society. Early novelists such as Namık Kemal, Şemsettin Sami, and Ahmet Mithat argued that the novel revealed a "civilizational problem," praising the Western novel while treating traditional Ottoman narrative techniques as "unsuitable to the contemporary age" (Moran 1983, 9–11). For these writers, the novel was considered an "integral part of the modern civilization," adapted to the Turkish context "not as a literary form but as a requirement of contemporary civilization" (Evin 1993, 96).[7]

These early novelists were indeed political thinkers and reformers of their period—Namık Kemal and Şinasi, for instance, were important figures of the Young Ottoman movement.[8] Their literary narratives emerged as part of their political activities. As reformers seeking to synthesize traditional Islamic values with the material progress of Western civilization, they construed the novel as a means "to disseminate their ideas," "to educate people," and thus to civilize the nation (Evin 1983, 16–20). Accordingly, the novels of the late nineteenth century involved themes derived from the social issues of the period. They sometimes gave voice to the problem of the traditional arranged marriage and took a stance in favor of free marriage choice.[9] The themes of free marriage choice and love signify the early novelists'/reformers' more liberal reconsideration of interaction between the sexes. However, these novelists were also critical of the "undesirable" effects— both materialistic and individualistic—of westernization on Ottoman society. As Jale Parla notes, despite the westernizing efforts of the late nineteenth century, the dominant cultural code was still based on a traditional cultural epistemology. The early novels in this vein were critical of the unveiledness of women and the exposition of sexuality and worldly desires (Parla 1993, 79–87).[10] The so-called "super-westernization" of some sections of society, represented by a degenerate-westernized social type, was ridiculed and criticized in these novels (Mardin 1974). In brief, the Young Ottomans responded to the sociopolitical transformation of the Ottoman polity by employing literary narratives to suggest alternative changes.

Besides Young Ottoman thought, but various syntheses or distillations of other ideologies were also introduced via literature to Ottoman society during the late nineteenth and early twentieth century. Beşir Fuat, for instance, was an influential positivist thinker of the period who saw the novel "as a branch of sociology." Fuat employed literature to introduce the Turkish intelligentsia to Comtean positivism and social Darwinism in contradistinction to traditional vision of the world (Evin 1983, 96). Indeed, literature proved a vital field in which concepts and ideologies were debated.[11] In the context of major social and political transformations of the late nineteenth century, the Turkish literary field emerged as a space of struggle between various political ideologies.[12]

The literature of the period of nation-formation and nationalism in the first quarter of the twentieth century is not exempt from these close relations between literature and politics. In this period, the modernizing nationalist elite criticized and rejected *divan edebiyatı* (Ottoman court poetry) since it was "difficult" and belonged to the "corrupt Ottoman court." The literature of the new nation, for them, would be based on a "simple" Turkish vernacular, purified from Arabic and Persian terms (Hallbrook 1994). According to the nationalist elite, the absence of modern literary forms in Turkish culture (until the modernizing efforts) was due to the traditional Islamic structure of Ottoman society. In other words, modern genres that expose private lives, inner worlds, and the loves of individuals could not develop in Ottoman society since these revelations were considered "immoral" by the traditional Islamic order.[13]

In the early republican period, Turkish literature developed in intimate contact with the official ideology for the narration of the nation. Many novels aimed to support and spread the modernizing efforts and the ideology of the nation state (Köksal 2003).[14] Some canonical novels of the period such as *Vurun Kahpeye* by Halide Edip Adıvar (1999 [1926]) and *Yeşil Gece* by Reşat Nuri Güntekin (1995 [1926]) depicted religion and religious figures extremely negatively and as the sources of the Anatolian people's backwardness, in line with the secular narratives of Kemalist modernization. Religious personalities in these novels were portrayed as dishonest, intriguing, and lecherous characters who cooperated with enemies during the independence war. They instrumentalized religion for their own interests and deceived the ignorant masses with religious dogmas.[15] What is striking is that these novelists depicted religious figures as social types rather than as individual characters, and they generalized religion to be the main source of narrow-mindedness and obscurantism. These examples cannot be extended into all canonical literary works of the early republican period. Nevertheless, the major theme of the republican novel until the 1950s was westernization and the conflict between the East and West as represented by opposed binary categories such as *ala turca/ala franga* (traditionalist/westernist), *mahalle/apartman* (traditional quarter/apartment), and *imam/öğretmen* (preacher/teacher) (Moran 1983, 324). It can be argued that the negative representation of religious figures in various novels of the period still functions, to use Charles Taylor's terminology (1991), as cultural narratives that feed directly into secularist imagery and secularist identities in their approach to religion.

In the post-1950s, a certain type of village novel emerged that portrayed village life and its dramas via a social realist stance. These novels were written mostly by graduates of the village institutes founded in the 1940s. Many of these novels, such as Mahmut Makal's *Bizim Köy* (1950) and Fakir Baykurt's *Onuncu Köy* (1975), narrated the struggles of idealist teachers to modernize the village against forces of the status quo. The idealist teachers in these novels were depicted as "representatives of civilization" seeking to alleviate the village's miserable conditions and to transform the power relations that subordinated ignorant villagers (Karpat 1962, 61–66). Once again, one major source of rural backwardness appeared to be religious figures who promoted superstition and maintained the status quo, in alliance with landlords, by a certain self-interested construction of Islam. Thus, as progressive characters, idealist teachers fought religious personalities in order to liberate villagers from bigotry.[16]

An alternative literary construction and use of Islam was produced by other literary figures such as Necip Fazıl and Sezai Karakoç, whose works stressed the importance of religious values in post-1950 period. Here, poetry allowed a focus on supposedly essential conservative-Islamic or Turkish-Islamic values. Their stress on Islamic values differed from the Islamic literary stance that emerged in the 1970s. Novels with an Islamic content came out in the 1970s along with a new conceptualization of the novel by a generation of Islamist novelists.

The Appropriation of the Novel by Islamism in the Context of Modernity

The emergence of Islamic literature and Islamic novels embodying a clear Islamic stance occurred in tandem with the rise of Islamist movements at the end of the 1970s and the beginning of the 1980s. Until this period, the novel as a genre with a Western origin was severely criticized by Muslim circles in the name of its project to explore and expose private lives in detail. According to Cemil Meriç, a thinker widely read in Islamic circles, the novel is a sign of "social sickness" since it emerged as a result of a class conflict in Western societies. The novel, according to Meriç, is an "exposition (*ifşa*).... [The Western novel] opens the roofs of houses and takes us to the bedroom." While the nationalist novelists of the early republican period condemned the absence of the novel in the Ottoman society due to an Islamic social order that precluded the depiction of interaction between the sexes, Meriç argues that the novel did not exist in the religious Ottoman society because its order was far removed from the anarchy of the West and thus did not constitute the conditions for novel writing (Meriç 1994, 84–86). What lies at the core of his criticism is the "expository quality" of the novel that is thought to be in conflict with Islamic communitarian morality.

This critical stance toward the novel is both maintained and extended by several prominent Islamic intellectuals of the 1980s, such as Ali Bulaç.[17] Bulaç conceives of modern literature as a "trap" that misguides believers by keeping them away from the realities of current societies. With its focus on "artificiality and abstraction," literature for Bulaç constitutes one of the "dangers of modern experience." He does not deny the importance of literature, but argues that an Islamic literature should be based on an Islamic vision of the world and reflect the realities of social life. For literature to achieve this, he contends, "we need first to develop an Islamic thought based on the Koran and Islamic history that will take us to unity (*tevhid*)" (Bulaç 1995, 115–16). Bulaç, thus, advocates deferring literary endeavors until Muslims develop their own social and theoretical concepts.[18] His position signifies Islamists' intellectual search for a claim of truth during the 1980s that paid no attention to or even disparaged the importance of artistic expressions of Islam.

Despite these criticisms of the novel, a group of Islamist novelists emerged in the 1970s that included Hekimoğlu İsmail, Ahmet Günbay Yıldız, and Şule Yüksel Şenler, all of whom believed that the novel was an important way to narrate Islam to the masses. Hekimoğlu İsmail, whose novel *Minyeli Abdullah* (2003 [1968]) has presently reached its seventy-fifth edition with total sales of 275,000 copies, was one of the first novelists in Islamic circles. He states his motivation for writing fiction in a recent interview:

> There were three important strains of thought during the 1960s: nationalists (*türkçüler*), religious people (*dindarlar*) and those who were against religion (*dine karşı olanlar*). The ideas of each were being propagated through books during those years.… The books of religious people, however, consisted only of *ilmihals* (essential Islamic teaching books). They were repeatedly publishing *ilmihals*. Yet *ilmihal* is a book that is read by people who have already adopted Islam. Actually, the most important thing was a concern with 'how might we lead people to believe in Islam?' I mean the way (*usul*) was wrong … we had to talk to the man in the street. (Kalyoncu 2002)

Thus, novel writing in the context of the Islamic revival of the 1970s referred to a generation of Islamist novelists' new Islamic consciousness to disseminate their ideas in a popularized fashion through the narrative form of the novel. As another Islamic literary figure, Mustafa Miyasoğlu stressed, their new literary activities were a result of the political process after 1960s in which Muslims in general gained some freedoms: "Islamic literature had developed under the repression of the existing order. This order treated us more intolerantly than socialists.... [Yet] the 1961 Constitution that presented advantages to socialists, also allowed Muslims to gain freedom of expression in some matters" (1999, 42).[19] In this context of relative freedom, Miyasoğlu goes on to say, "Rescued from repression, Muslims began to think and produce (1999, 42). The Islamic literary stance in this sense is part of a broader Islamist movement, and it displays a close parallelism with Islamist intellectual discourse, specifically in its critical posture toward westernization and contemporary modern culture. This will be explored below.

Islamist novelists were aware that the modern novel had a Western origin, and its incorporation into an Islamic frame was not self-apparent, since as a genre it did not exist in the Islamic tradition. It even had "conflicting expository qualities" with Islam. The new generation of novelists, however, stressed that "the contents of the words are more important than [the words] themselves" (Miyasoğlu 1999, 31). In other words, even though the novel is a Western genre, it was conceived as a tool that could be employed for Islamic purposes. As Miyasoğlu argues,

> in a time when everything is imported from the West and adapted to our life, it is futile to take a critical stance to the novel.... We have the different narrative techniques of a genre. We have to make use of it and we have to endure some difficulties in order to develop a narrative that is most appropriate for our people. (1999, 146)

He also presents an Islamic measure for the appropriation of the novel in an Islamic context:

> In our works in which we reflect Islam's worldview, we can be like Westerners, in conformity to the Prophet's saying that advocates "getting the arms of the enemies."

> In order to be different from them, our old culture provides us with rich examples. (1999, 270–71)

This quotation is indicative of the broader Islamist movements' stance toward key products of modernity. The Islamist movements that emerged toward the end of the 1970s in Turkey have never been anti-modernist in nature. Rather, Islamist agents sought to tailor influential products of modernity to an "Islamic garment." The 1980s, in this sense, witnessed the endeavors of Islamists to develop an "Islamic science," an "Islamic sociology," or an "Islamic anthropology."[20] Similarly, the novel began to be seen as a genre that could be used for Islamic purposes. Islamist actors who problemizes Western modernity sought to appropriate its products in order to respond to it by using its "own arms." They legalized novel writing by invoking the Prophet's saying that authorized Muslims to act like their opponents while simultaneously seeking an Islamic alternative. Miyasoğlu's reference (in the quotation above) to "rich examples of our culture" as a source of Islamic narratives signifies the Islamist novelists' ideal of developing an original and alternative Islamic narrative based on Islamic history and traditional narratives.[21] In brief, the novel in the context of Islamic revival was regarded as a genre that could be "Islamized."

The Emergence of Islamic Novels

In tandem with the appropriation of the novel as a tool that could be used for Islamic purposes, several novels emerged during the 1970s that "derived from Muslim imagery" (Eroğlu 1982, 218).[22] Several novels by Islamist writers such as Rasim Özdenören and Mustafa Miyasoğlu appeared, their authors claiming that they were also concerned with the aesthetic quality of literary texts. For instance, in his novel *Kaybolmuş Günler* (1975), Miyasoğlu narrates the difficulties of pious Anatolian characters who migrated to big cities. In *Dönemeç* (1980), he narrates the struggle of pious intellectuals in

Anatolia to defend Islam as a political system against socialism and liberalism. These novels are not easily read and do not involve simple plots, as was the case for Islamic popular salvation novels—the object of this study.

The Islamic literary field was dominated in the 1980s by salvation novels (*hidayet romanları*). The first two Islamic novels, *Minyeli Abdullah* by Hekimoğlu İsmail in 1968 and *Huzur Sokağı* by Şule Yüksel Şenler in 1970 were prototypes for these novels. In *Minyeli Abdullah*, Hekimoğlu İsmail[23] narrates his Islamic views in a narrative form through his protagonist Abdullah. Abdullah lives in Minye (a province of "westernizing" Egypt) during the time of King Faruk when "Islamic activities" are strictly monitored and suppressed by the regime. In the course of the novel, Abdullah is taken to jail and tortured because of his religious thoughts and behavior. The plot of the novel revolves around his struggles and teachings. Through his protagonist, the author narrates his views on socialism and westernization, and delineates his solutions point by point through the concepts of Islamic *jihâd*, the Islamic economy, and the social order. He takes his characters on a journey to Muslim countries including the Balkans, Turkey, Iraq, Saudi Arabia, and Pakistan, evaluating each nation in the light of his Islamic worldview. Islamic principles and the way of *jihâd* are presented to the readers with long quotations from the Koran and the writings of Said Nursi.[24] After its publication, the novel received a great deal of attention among Islamic circles and was later adopted for the cinema.[25] *Minyeli Abdullah*, according to an Islamist literary critic "demonstrated that the Islamic way of life was not a utopia. It exemplified the transition from an individual to a collective Islamic life style" (Yardım 2000, 126). This novel, in this regard, can be treated as an imaginary scenario describing what happened to Muslim people in this century and how Muslims should react to events.[26]

This first novel was followed by *Huzur Sokağı* by Şule Yüksel Şenler (2003), which has presently reached its 85th edition.[27] In *Huzur Sokağı*, Şenler narrates the story of poor but pious Muslim people living in a "peaceful street" (as the title of the novel suggests) in Istanbul. "The peaceful lives" of the people are disturbed when a new apartment is built on the street. This apartment brings with it new people living a "luxurious and westernist" life. The male protagonist of the novel, Bilal, lives on this street and studies at the university where, as a student living an Islamic life, he is in a constant conflict with other students. The author is very harsh in her portrayal of university youth, presenting them as immoral characters concerned with flirting, making-out, dancing, and drinking. The female character, Feyza, who comes to the street when the new apartment is built and later falls in love with Bilal, is portrayed as one of the decadent youths. The narrative of the novel revolves around Feyza's adoption of headcovering and Islamic precepts, her new struggles as a covered woman, as well as Bilal's endeavors to narrate Islam to his friends. As in *Minyeli Abdullah*, *Huzur Sokağı* uses Said Nursi's writings to narrate Islamic precepts through the speech of the characters. One striking point is sufficient to demonstrate the kinship of the two novels. Both novelists, at different places in their novels, make their characters speak with the same sentences:

> O sons of this land! Do not try to imitate Europeans! How can you reasonably trust in and follow the vice and invalid, worthless thought of Europe after the boundless tyranny and enmity it has shown you? No! No! You who imitate them in dissoluteness, you are not following them, but unconsciously joining their ranks and putting to death both yourselves and your brothers. Know that the more you follow them in immorality the more you lie in claiming to be patriots! Because your following them in this way is to hold your nation in contempt, to hold the nation up to ridicule! (İsmail 1986, 173; Şenler 2003, 107)

This paragraph is a quote from Said Nursi's *The Flashes Collection* (2000, 166). Hekimoğlu İsmail does not cite the source but employs it as Abdullah's words in one of his speeches given in a conference. In *Huzur Sokağı*, on the other hand, Yüksel Şenler allows one of the young characters to read this paragraph by citing its source and then using it to question himself. The result is his adoption of an Islamic way of life. Besides several Koranic references, both novelists interweave their narratives with quotations from Said Nursi in order to disseminate his ideas. The above paragraph also gives a clear indication of the content of salvation novels: they revolve around the problems brought about by Westernization and the presentation of Islamic solutions. In both novels, Islamic characters engage in a struggle with secular characters over the representation of Islam and the process of westernization, and they both end up with a "happy ending" represented by the salvation of all characters.

Some of these early salvation novels in the 1970s were "village novels" written in response to the social realist novels of the post-1950 period. The first Islamic village novel was *Yanık Buğdaylar* (1974) by Ahmet Günbay Yıldız. He states the following reasons for his writing of this novel in an interview:

> In [social realist] village novels I read, I have seen that the village did not exist. I was a villager. These novels were not narrating us.... Moreover there were indecent scenes in these novels. As if all villagers were indecent. I could not stand that. I wrote *Yanık Buğdaylar* to represent the village in a real sense. (Yardım 2000, 169)

This novel opens with an earthquake scene after which some villagers become rich by looting the whole village. They then began to exploit villagers, selling at high prices and employing at low wages, while the village men gamble and drink in the village café. Conflicts within the village are sharpened when Dikçe, a pious character, returns to the village as a teacher. Dikçe teaches people to read and write, and narrates Islam. With his endeavors, the café is transformed into a library and the playing cards are burned in the village square. At the end of the novel, all characters are blessed with "true faith."

This narrative signifies Islamist novelists' discursive struggle over the representation of village or rural religion in contrast to its portrayal by Turkish social realist writers. The resemblance between the two kinds of narratives is remarkable. While social realist novels depicted religious characters of the village negatively and "civilized" the village through the "illuminating" role of teachers, Islamist novelists employed an Islamist civilizing project via pious teachers. They replaced the socialist/secular teacher with a pious one who raised the Islamic consciousness—as opposed to the class consciousness—of the villagers. This feature of salvation novels indicates the dialectical nature of Islamic and secular literature. As Malti-Douglas notes, for Arabic contexts, Islamic literature "sits alongside the more canonical secular literary tradition and functions in a dialectic way with it.... The religious writer swims in a textual universe in which he or she is surrounded by the more secularized members of the writing profession. The secular corpus functions almost as a gauge against which Islamic literature measures itself" (2001, 5–6). This is also the case in Turkish Islamic literature. Islamist novelists in Turkey who both appropriated the novel yet claimed to have developed an original and distinct narrative are not outside the boundaries of the broader Turkish literary field. Presenting an inverted version of social realist novels, salvation novels are indicative of an infusion of secular tradition into Islamic imagery. In their aim to present the "real village" (and "real Islam") Islamist novelists engage in a dialectic relation with secular narratives. Islamic novels in this sense refer to literary narratives that emerged as a result of a dialogic relation between Islamists, socialists, and secularists.

These early attempts to narrativize an Islamic worldview and belief in a particular narrative form paved the way for the emergence of many Islamist novelists in the 1980s. Among this new generation of Islamist authors were Ahmet Günbay Yıldız, Şerife Katırcı Turhal, Raif Cilasun, Emine Şenlikoğlu, Şerif Benekçi, Mehmet Zeren, Sevim Asımgil, and several others. The novels published by these novelists in the 1980s were often reprinted numerous times and became best sellers among Islamic circles. For example, the twenty-five novels by Günbay Yıldız have sold over 500,000 copies in twenty-five years

(Yardım 2000, 170). These novelists, with their identical salvation narratives, formed a coherent Islamic literary stance that was conceptualized in Islamic circles as *Direniş edebiyatı* (resistance literature), *Kuran edebiyatı* (Koran literature), or *Davet Edebiyatı* (invitation literature) (Çalışkan 2002).

One outstanding characteristic of the new generation of Islamist novelists is that most of them were born during 1945–1955 and have a rural origin. Almost half of them do not have a literary profession. The biographies of several others, on the other hand, display an interesting similarity: they studied literature and worked as high school teachers of literature. The targeted reader, according to the novelists themselves, is high school and university youth (Aksoy and Kaplan, 1997). As Ian Watt has shown, there is a close link between the rise of the novel and the growth of a reading public (1995). The huge sale of Islamic novels, in this sense, suggests that the books themselves generated a book-buying public that numbered in the millions. It can be argued that the emergence of Islamic novels coincided with the emergence of an urbanized and educated young population with Islamic concerns in the 1980s, which accounts for the strength of Islamist movements in the same decade.

It is, however, difficult to talk about an institutionalized Islamic literary field in the Bourdieuan sense. Despite the appearance of numerous salvation novels, literary journals, and a literary almanac during the 1980s, Islamic literature could not give an institutional form to its practices. Many salvation novelists published only one novel through publishing houses that did not have a long life. Accordingly, it is hard to follow the genealogy (first and later edition dates) of salvation novels since they were reprinted by different publishing houses. Nevertheless, Islamist authors' desire to respond to secular narratives of civilization led to the writing and publishing of hundreds of salvation novels.

What is common to Islamist novelists is their instrumentalist approach to literature in which literature is not treated as an end itself, but as a means to develop an Islamic consciousness.

Literature, as in the case of post-revolutionary Iran, is viewed not as "a mere source of aesthetic enjoyment … but as an effective means of politicizing, educating and inspiring" (Milani 1992, 232).[28] According to Islamist writer Hekimoğlu İsmail, a novel cannot be "devoid" of social context and responsibility. Today's problem, he argues, "is the collapse of the family.… We have to create a hero, as a believer and self-sacrificing volunteer who will scream the truth to all people" (Yardım 2000, 133). Conveying Islamic messages is prioritized over the literary quality of the texts.[29] Accordingly, most of them are not interested in any theory of the novel or in literary aesthetics. Günbay Yıldız as the most prolific author of salvation novels refuses to develop a theory and definition of the novel. In an interview, he replies to such a question by saying that "literary critics should tackle that. The most important thing for us is to give a message to people" (Yardım 2000, 172). In keeping with such an understanding, the novels of many Islamist writers are written quickly with simple sentences, under-developed characters and plots, and sometimes with glaring inconsistencies. Artistic concerns therefore are minimalized by these novelists for whom the fundamental aim of writing a novel is to convey the message of Islam to their readers.

In response to criticisms of the message-conveying narratives of his novels, Günbay Yıldız notes that "there is no novel in the world without a message, for a novel depicts either good or evil. If narrating Islam as the source of all goodness is to convey a message, depicting falsehood is also a message. Those who criticize our messages want us not to narrate Islam" (Yardım 2000, 171). Günbay Yıldız also replies to critics in one of his novels, *Benim çiçeklerim Ateşte Açar* (*My Flowers Blossom in Fire*), in an indirect way through the words of his pious character, a professor of literature. The professor helps one of his female students who tries to write a novel. When they meet in his office, the professor asks the student:

—What do you want to tell people with this novel?
—Should a novel convey a message, professor?

—Can you tell me any sentence that does not bear any meaning? ...

The Professor continues:

—You seem to be against a message but with your story you actually send a message. You narrate the story of two young people. The girl's father does not permit them to marry. Then to force him to accept their marriage, they violate one of the moral pillars of society [they engage in an extra-marital sexual relationship].
—But these are all in the imagination professor.
—When your novel is published, will you put a footnote and tell people 'these are wrong, do not use them as guide'? (Yıldız 2000, 40–42)

These quotations are indicative of a dominant Islamic discourse that posits that Islam as a message and lifestyle should permeate all spheres of life. Islam is posited as the basis of every act, vocation, and position. Hence, the act of writing a novel is not thought of as outside one's religious commitment. Islamic novelists construct every scene to convey their Islamic messages and principles to readers. When in this novel the professor meets with his female student, for instance, he warns her not to close his door. The student cannot understand the meaning of this warning. But later she is made to learn the Islamic principle that being alone with the other sex in private spaces is unacceptable to Islamic morality. This scene signifies Islamist novelists' sensitivity to never depicting a "falsehood." This refers to an Islamic motto that states, "the depiction of falsehood corrupts pure minds (*batılı tasvir saf zihinleri idlal eder*)," that, according to Fatih Andı, a professor of Turkish literature, has influenced the Islamic perception of art and literature throughout history (Andı 1996, 41). In another conversation in the same novel, Günbay Yıldız concludes his messages about the place of literature in Islamic imaginary through the mouth of a pious professor. The professor tells his student: "The writer does not have a right to play with words as he wishes. Literature derives from the term *edep* (decency).[30]

Start from there" (Yıldız 2000, 44). *Edep* here signifies a morally appropriate Islamic attitude and serves as the basis of an Islamic imagery that outlaws the narrative depiction of scenes outside the limits of Islamic morality.

In line with their appropriation of the novel as a means to narrate Islam, Islamist novelists are very careful to emphasize that what they write is not a product of the imagination. In replying to a question asking "whether his novels are fiction or not," Günbay Yıldız answers that: "[my novels] are the results of what I have seen in the society and of my investigations of lived lives. I mean, all are real."[31] Accordingly, Islamist novelists stress that their novels are not written for and cannot be read as a means of entertainment. Ahmet Lütfü Kazancı, in the introduction to his novel *Kaynana,* writes that "there does not exist even one word in this novel to entertain the reader." He goes on to say that he himself did not dare to presume a literary concern while he was writing the novel, as he did not have a literary profession. He asserts that the only merit of his novel is to guide people (Kitap Dergisi 1989, 12). These accounts suggests that the novel in Islamic circles has meaning not because of its extrinsic aesthetic qualities but, to use Eagleton's term, because it represents a "signifying practice" of Islamists within the political context of the 1980s, a period when Islamist movements dominated the public agenda with alternative claims to truth about the secular narratives of civilization. Parallel with the "Islamic literature" of other Muslim contexts, the novel, for Turkish Islamists, draws on a "committed literature," (Malti-Douglas 1994, 119), or a literature committed to Islamic political goals. The Islamic salvation novel can be considered a kind of *roman à these* that is primarily didactic in its aim to demonstrate the validity of Islamic political propositions.[32]

As part of the cultural politics of 1980s Islamism, the narratives of salvation novels are based on a negotiation between Islamic and secular/westernized orientations toward the world. These two different worldviews are inscribed into novels through "idealized" Muslim and westernized characters. Through these characters, Islamic novels relate a dialectical interplay of secular and Islamic visions of the world. Muslim protagonists who feel themselves "alien" and "victimized" in the hegemonic secular order are made to retain their peaceful-ness, stability, and assertiveness in the face of problems they confront throughout the narratives. On the other hand, west-ernized protagonists, mostly girls who are deemed to live a deeply distressed life, are made to fall in love with pious Muslim characters. Their encounter, in the corridors of a uni-versity or in an urban quarter, provides novelists with the opportunity to explore the edifying mission of the novel. On the basis of their relations, novelists both teach and present an Islamic way of life to westernized characters as the only remedy for their wretchedness.

These two social types, representing two "incompatible ways of life," are not allowed to get together until the process of the Islamization of the westernized character is complete. Their relation is never taken out of the boundaries of an Islamic imaginary. For instance, with regard to the representa-tion of love affairs, Islamic narratives differentiate themselves from popular romances in their determination to not depict Muslim characters in non-Islamic spaces (such as pubs), in non-Islamic relations (Muslim characters are not portrayed alone in private spaces with the other sex), or even with non-Islamic thoughts. Rather Islamist authors construct every scene to convey their messages and articulate their Islamic positions on current issues in a popularized form. Westernized characters are made to learn and to adopt ways of conduct, love, and moral-ity appropriate to Islamic life. Basic moral premises are presented to "others" with simple analogies. Novelists transmit basic Islamic precepts and engage in a discursive struggle with secular idioms by interweaving their narratives with quotations from the Koran, religious books, and journalistic or academic texts.

A general focus of the message, in conformity with the pol-itics of 1980s Islamism, revolves around the position of women. Almost all salvation novels—regardless of the gender of the author—involve dialogue that emphasizes and exemplifies the importance of women's modesty and chastity for an ideal Islamic order. Accordingly, the adoption of the headscarf is promoted as the moment of "fulfillment" for female subjects. Headcovering is presented as an "emblem" that saves women from becoming a source of *fitne* (disorder) and allows them to become keepers of Islamic order. A rhetoric of domesticity (especially illustrating the motherhood role of women) goes hand in hand with a will to attend university and acquire a modern profession. This desire for a modern profession is legitimate only in so far as it provides women with the means to serve Islam for the greater collective purpose.

Lastly, salvation novels adopt an identical narrative closure in which Muslim characters are always vindicated and secular characters are led to salvation—the reason these novels are called salvation novels in Islamic circles. The focus on Islam and westernization, the emplotted Islamic and secular characters, and the relational context of salvation novels suggest that these narratives signify Islamists' endeavor to retell the story of westernization in Turkey in a different way. In this sense, these novels symbolize the responses of Islamist novelists to secular narratives of civilization, as represented through the novels of the republican period. Narratives of salvation novels develop in a dialectical and confrontation way with what Islamist novelists call "the republican novel."

Novel Contra Novel:
Islamic and Republican Literature

In Islamist novelists and literary commentators' recounting of the history of literature in Turkey, the key measure appears to be fictions' adoption or rejection of Western values. Thus, novelists of the late Ottoman period, such as Ahmet Mithat and Namık Kemal, are praised for their handling of the conflict between Ottoman tradition and Western values, especially for the way that they "humiliated imitators of a Western life style and exalted Ottoman and Islamic values" (see Miyasoğlu 1999; Yardım 2000). The second period of literary work, beginning with the movement named *Servet-i Fünun* and followed by the classic period of Republican literature, is represented as a rupture symbolized by the adoption of Western values by literary figures. They sometimes cite Ahmet Hamdi Tanpınar and Yahya Kemal as positive literary figures in terms of their approach to religious manifestations. Except for a very few exemplary figures, Islamist novelists have a monolithic perception of republican fiction on the basis of their characters' adoption of Western lifestyles and values. For example, Hurşit İlbeyi, a novelist from Islamic circles, argues that "the novelists of the republican period have totally disregarded this conflict [between Islamic and Western values] and embraced and approved Western culture." He takes Nuri Güntekin's novel *Gökyüzü* (*Sky*) as an example and asserts that "the major theme of this novel is a revolt against God represented by *Gökyüzü*" (Yardım 2000, 287). In this vein, Islamist novelists accuse the novels of the Republican period of having negative effects on society. This is because these novels "represent human types and familial relations that are totally alien to our society.... [And the novels of the Republican period] caused degeneration in familial and social ethics since they encouraged sinful love and decadent social relations" (Miyasoğlu 1999, 250). Miyasoğlu labels Republican novelists such as Halide Edip, Yakup Kadri, and Nuri Güntekin, as "speakers of official ideology," since they slander religious personalities in parallel with official historiography. Their novels, he argues, are "ideological and diseased" (Yardım 2000, 218).

Those novelists that cause "moral degeneration" consist not only of the "westernist Republican" writers. Social realist novelists of the post-1950 period, too, are considered by Islamist novelists a group that "exploited the tradition and values of Anatolian people for their own ideological agenda" (Yardım 2000, 287), using novels as a means to propagate Marxism. Social realist novelists indeed are regarded as having close links with republican writers since "[in the conflict between the West and Islam] they have taken their place in the Western camp" (Yardım 2000, 288). Beşir Ayvazoğlu, a literary critic, similarly contends that "the only point that differentiates Marxists from non-Marxists is their anti-capitalist stance. Both are in a deep agreement on all other issues because their cultural base depends on cultural sources imported from the West" (Ayvazoğlu 1982, 222–23). Islamist novelists thus homogenize all other actors in the literary field on the basis of their supposed adoption and dissemination of Western values, which leads to the "moral degeneration" of society.

As their emphasis on the negative effect of the republican novel on society reveals, Islamist novelists attribute to the novel an important role not only in representing but also in constituting reality. Şerif Benekçi regards novels as tools that are "more disruptive (*sarsıcı*) and more re-orienting (*yönlendirici*) than revolutions" (Yardım 2000, 255). In a parallel vein, Günbay Yıldız considers literature "the most important means to construct and demolish a nation." He goes on to say,

> several circles have made use of literature in the service of indecency, our society and family structure have been shaken, and bars (*meyhaneler*), jails and gambling saloons are full. In order to stop this, we have to take action on behalf of our cultural tradition and use literature to strengthen the family and decrease dissoluteness. (Yardım 2000, 170)

As mentioned above, and ironically in agreement with Bourdieu's own approach to literature, fiction as a pure artistic form does not exist for the Islamist novelists. It appears as a conscious political activity and the criticism it imparts derives from the novelists' political agenda. Actually, all criticisms, as Eagleton argues, are in this sense political. They differ from each other on the basis of their values, beliefs, and goals. Feminist criticism, for instance, focuses on the relations between writing and sexuality, while social realism considers the relation between the text and ideology (Eagleton 1996, 184–85). In this sense, the values and goals held by Islamists shape their criticism of other literary works. The content of Islamist criticism indicates the critics' values and beliefs. When the criticisms of Islamist novelists are taken into consideration, what constitutes the Islamic literary stance is a preoccupation with the "moral and social degeneration" brought about by secular and socialist novels. Islamist novelists emphasize the "ideological and practical effects" of these novels in modeling an "indecent" way of life. Aware of the transformative capacity of novels, Islamist novelists aim to employ literature for disseminating Islamic belief and practice and in constructing Islamic social relations. Islamic novels thus emerge as an alternative to and critique of "secular Republican literature" whose themes and concepts are represented as the "real source of moral degeneration."

Similarly, Islamic novelists regard the literary field as the most important site for a counter-hegemonic struggle. They assert that the "current degeneration" caused by Republican literature can only be cured by "real" literature. As Islamist novelist Galip Boztoprak succinctly summarizes,

> we are struggling against the novel with the novel. Novel contra novel. Where the child falls it can also rise up (*çocuk düştüğü yerden kalkar*). Against the novel, we protect ourselves with the novel. We are restoring the damage wrought by novels with the novel. (Boztoprak 1982, 231)

As this account demonstrates, the novel means much more than an expression of a literary imagination for Islamist authors. It appears as a means of "cultural war" in the Turkish political and literary fields.

Interestingly, alongside this radical simplification and rejection of republican literature, Islamist novelists also feel that they are marginalized and do not possess cultural capital in the literary field. They claim that the literary almanacs published by "the westernist circles" deliberately exclude Islamic artistic works. With this "blindness," Miyasoğlu argues that "they [the westernists] try to prove that we did nothing in those years and even that we did not exist.... They call their works 'Turkish literature' yet they only mention westernist literature" (Miyasoğlu 1999, 160). This feeling of exclusion has led Islamist novelists, as part of their literary activities, to publish an alternative almanac in 1982, the *Suffe Kültür Sanat Yıllığı*, in order to form "the first collective voice of Truth and God (*Haqq*) in artistic and cultural life" (Miyasoğlu 1999, 65). This almanac, published annually between 1982 and 1988, was intended to provide a space in which "writers sharing the same belief" could be introduced to each other and discuss literary topics.[33] *Suffe Kültür ve Sanat Yıllığı* was, then, an important attempt by Islamist novelists to publicize their thoughts on certain topics each year and to explore the category of Islamic literature. It not only consisted of articles relating to work published in Turkish, but also covered literary works from other Muslim countries. With titles like "Afghan Literature," "Egyptian Literature," and "Fraternal Literatures" (*Kardeş Edebiyatlar*), Islamists attempted to form connections with literary works from other Muslim contexts in accordance with the bounded universalism of Islamic discourse. Each edition of the almanac consisted of articles evaluating the Islamic literary works of the year and proposals to determine the agenda of the coming year. Yet typically, Islamist novelists who contend that "they are excluded" from the literary almanacs of the secular republicans are equally excluding in relation to novelists outside of Islamic circles.[34] In brief, these almanacs represented Islamists novelists' attempts to institutionalize an Islamic literary discourse as a tool of "cultural battle" against secular literature.

Islamic Politics of Literary Translation

Islamic circles treated both the writing of novels and the translation of literary works from other languages as an activity of struggle. Indeed, the act of translation itself cannot be understood unless it is connected to political choices and orientations, not only for Islamists but for secularists and socialists too. In her study on translation activities in the Republican period, Şehnaz Gürçağlar demonstrates how translation during the early years of the Turkish Republic was consciously used as a means of "culture planning" (Gürçağlar 2001). She argues that especially in publications commissioned by the state-sponsored Translation Bureau between the years 1940 and 1946, the choice of works and their preferred terms were chosen or supported by the Republican elite as part of the modernization efforts of the Republican regime. The translation of several Western classic philosophical and literary texts in this period was part of conscious politics that emphasized the importance of establishing a humanist cultural tradition in Turkey.

Translation involves politics not only in the selection process of the works, but also with the interpretation, the deliberate mistranslations, conscious omissions, and additions by translators. Several striking examples in Turkish literature demonstrate that literary translation represents and constitutes a "cultural battleground" for different groups, particularly between secularists and Islamists. The most interesting is the translation politics surrounding Antoine de Saint-Exupéry's *The Little Prince*, a well-known book in world children's literature, which has been translated into Turkish by at least twelve different publishing houses (Neydim 1998, 34–41). Necdet Neydim, a literary critic, compares different Turkish translations of *The Little Prince* in terms of the inadequacy of mistranslation in children's literature. However, these translations also reveal an Islamist and secularist politics of translation.

In this short story, the asteroid known as B-612 where the Little Prince lives is first seen by a Turkish astronomer in 1909. This astronomer presents his discovery to the International Astronomical Congress, yet nobody believes what he says since he wears a traditional Turkish costume. Saint Exupéry then writes,

> Fortunately, however, for the reputation of Asteroid B-612, a *Turkish dictator* made a law that his subjects, under pain of death, should change to European costume. So in 1920 the astronomer gave his demonstration all over again, dressed with impressive style and elegance. And this time everybody accepted his report. (1971, 14–15)[35]

Saint Exupéry, as a writer addressing children, concludes the above quotation with the phrase "Grown-ups are like that." What Exupéry wants to point out, as Neydim argues, is the way that how one is dressed is important in the adults world (Neydim 1998, 39). It might be argued that Saint Exupéry does not derive his reference from historical "facts" since the Kemalist dress code was legislated in 1925, not in 1920 as mentioned in the text. And, of course, the writer is not concerned with historical accuracies since his story is a work of fiction. Nevertheless, the phrase "a Turkish dictator" encourages the reception of this text in the Turkish context not as literary fiction but as a "history book," which allows translators from different circles to engage in a discursive struggle. Translators have accordingly treated the text in light of their ideological orientation rather than in keeping with the "plain" or most immediate meaning of the text.

Thus some translators prefer to translate "a Turkish dictator" with more "neutral" expressions like "a Turkish leader whose word was the law (*dediği dedik bir Türk önderi*) or "a Turkish leader" (*bir Türk yönetici*):

> Fortunately, in order to protect the honor of Asteroid B 612, a Turkish leader whose word was the law, ordered: "Henceforth, everyone will dress like Europeans. Those who do not obey this regulation will be sentenced to death." In 1920, the very same astronomer, this time elegantly dressed, appeared in front of the committee. Of course, all members accepted his point of view. (trans. Tomris Uyar and Can yayınları n.d.; quoted by Neydim 1998, 35–36)[36]

Similarly,

> For the sake of the reputation of Asteroid B 612, a Turkish administrator promulgated a law requiring his people to dress in the European style. Consequently, in 1920, the astronomer put forth his arguments dressed in such elegant garb and in an effective manner. Thus,

everyone accepted his report. (trans. Emine Erendor and
Barış Dağıtım 1984; quoted by Neydim 1998, 37)[37]

Another translator omits entirely the sentence involving "a
Turkish dictator":

> However, when the same astronomer put forth his thesis
> in European garb, everybody believed him. (trans. Filiz
> Borak and İnkılap Kitabevi, n.d.; quoted by Neydim
> 1998, 37)[38]

In some translations, translators make a specific intervention in
the text and inscribe "a Turkish dictator" as a "great leader"
in order to praise the dress code. They also omit the threat of
death to those who refuse to conform to the new dress code.
One translator even identifies this leader as Atatürk, the
founder of the Turkish Republic:

> Fortunately, the great commander Atatürk required that
> all Turks dress like Europeans. So later the Turkish
> astronomer dressed up like a European and restated his
> thinking. As a result, B 612 was accepted as a reality.
> (trans. Emel Tanver and Düşünen Adam yayınları 1994;
> quoted by Neydim 1998, 37)[39]

Most striking, perhaps, an Islamist translator extends these
original four lines into a huge paragraph by adding sentences in
accordance with his ideological agenda:

> Among the Turkish people a terrible blood-thirsty dicta-
> tor came to power. By law he forced people to dress like
> Westerners (Europeans and Americans). He sent those
> who disobeyed to their death. He tortured those who
> refused to wear a hat. He dismissed students and officers
> who did not wear a tie. He made the police and gen-
> darmerie remove the headcoverings of women in the
> street. After all these regulations were implemented, it
> was then accepted that B 612 was discovered by the

Turks. In 1920, the speech of the Turkish astronomer dressed in a tuxedo, sporting a bowtie around his neck and with clipped, neat hair combed back with brilliantine, accompanied with documents printed in the Western, not his own, alphabet was applauded enthusiastically. So this is what adults (westerners and imitators of westerners) are like. (trans. Muharrem Ekisçeli and Nehir Yayınları 1996; quoted by Neydim 1998, 37–38)[40]

This remarkable example demonstrates how the literary concerns of Islamists extend into the field of translation. In addition to several "ideological additions," the translator, in accordance with the general anti-Western stance of Islamic literature, transforms the phrase "grown-ups" in the original text into "Westerners and those who imitate them," to use the phrase for a very different meaning. These different examples of translation, moreover, demonstrate how certain literary fictions have been transformed into a space of struggle as they gain a new meaning among competing actors in the Turkish context. Contrary to the time frame of the original text, secularists consciously mistranslate the text to praise Atatürk and his reforms. Islamist translator, on the other hand, more clearly intrudes in the text and rewrites it to insert an Islamic agenda.

This insertion of an ideological agenda is also visible in the translation of several Western classics by Islamic publishing houses in the 1980s. Timaş, as a major publishing house of Islamic novels, has been publishing Western classics since 1982. Between 1982 and 2001 it published twenty-nine famous texts such as *Don Quixote*, *Les Misérables*, and *Robinson Crusoe*. İsmail Demirci, an editor for Timaş, claims that they introduced these Western classics to an Islamic reading public. Yet a close analysis of the translations demonstrates that they were not made with complete fidelity to the original work. Similarly to the example of *The Little Prince*, these translations involve additions and modifications in line with the "Islamic sensitivity" of the translators. Indeed, Demırci argues that the translators have a right to modify the classics since these classics, as he puts it, "are not sacred texts [of the West]" (Okay 2001).[41]

Even more explicitly, Ali çankırılı, translator of several of the works, notes that

> While translating, I cannot disregard my people's cultural values. Let's think of the Count of Monte Cristo. Except for his drinking, all the qualities of the protagonist comply with Islam. If, in the name of the fidelity to the text, I make the protagonist drink, I devalue him in the eye of my readers. His drinking actually is just background, not a major theme. While translating I either omit that sentence or make him drink water. This does not mean I deform the original text. (Okay 2001)

As a result of his approach, characters in European novels speak in Islamic phrases like "*Allah rahatlık versin*" ("May Allah have mercy on you") and "*fi sebilillah*" ("In the way of Allah"). This process has led to the "invention" of a "Muslim" Cervantes, Hugo, and Defoe in the Islamic literary sphere. In other words, Islamist publishing businesses that did not outright reject Western writers have appropriated them in an "Islamized" fashion, parallel with their instrumental use of the Western genre of the novel. This Islamization of Western classics derives from the socially committed position of Islamist actors who seek the realization of Islamic ideals in every sphere of life, the endeavor that also forms the basis of the course of all Islamic salvation novels throughout the 1980s.

Salvation Novels of the 1980s: The Islamic Ideal for a Total Islamization of Society

The emergence of Islamic salvation novels in the 1980s signifies both the relational and confrontational nature of Islamism toward key cultural products of modernity. These novels represent the appropriation of a modern literary genre by Islamic actors. The novel has been adapted by Islamic circles mainly to challenge what they call the "westernist novels" of the republican period. It has been instrumentalized to combat the narratives of "republican novels" that, according to Islamist authors, represent Islam and Muslims as obstacles to reaching the required level of modern civilization. Islamic salvation also involved the construction of a positive and assertive understanding of Muslimness along with their message-conveying contents. They embody a repertoire of instructions and norms about "what is to be done and not to be done" in life. Novel writing, as stated by an Islamist novelist, is a response to the basic human query, "why do we live and where are we going?" (Aksoy and Kaplan 1997). Therefore the novel in Islamic circles emerged, in the sense theorized by Nussbaum, as a crucial act in searching for the fundamental question of "how should one live?" (Nussbaum 1992, 95). As answers to this query, Islamic novels stand as a vital means for the construction of an Islamic imaginary and identity in the relational context of Turkey. They display the value judgments, goals, and intentions of Islamist actors writing (and reading) with an Islamic imaginary.

Salvation novels, like any other literary narrative, cannot be construed as abstract imaginary significations of isolated authors. They are not, in other words, only or even mainly the "fictional" creations of Islamist novelists. Islamic novels are literary narratives written by authors who operate within the linguistic, literary, and cultural worlds of contemporary Turkey. Their works consist not only of words as the expression of an individual, but involve a constellation of "quotations" originating in various sources of Turkish political culture. Further, the meaning that is generated by salvation narratives does not, to use Voloshinov's terminology, "reside in the word or in the soul of the speaker or in the soul of the listener" (1971, 102–3). Rather, Islamic literary texts, contexts, and readers are inextricably linked with each other in the formation of meaning.[1] Islamic salvation novels, then, are social creations that contain a selection of signs and issues from a variety of social, historical, and political processes in contemporary Turkey as referential fields for the texts, in accordance with Islamist novelists' claim to represent "reality" and their usage of real time frames. To put it differently, Islamist novelists' conception of literature as a space of struggle against secular narratives allows Islamists to engage in a dialogue with their opponents over Islam, civilization, modernization, westernization, secularism, and conceptions of morality in specific reference to Turkey's current context. In this regard, Islamic novels provide information about how Islamist actors contemplate their lives and actions as well as their perception of the "other" and surrounding events.

In this chapter, I will interrogate Islamists' presentation of the self and perception of the "other" by drawing mainly on two Islamic novels of the '80s—one by a female, the other by a male writer—but I will also give references to several other narratives on certain issues to sustain my arguments. Before going into detail, it will be useful to give a short summary of the selected novels.

Müslüman Kadının Adı Var and *Boşluk* as
Exemplary Novels

In *Müslüman Kadının Adı Var* (1999)—first edition in 1988—
Şerife Katırcı Turhal[2] narrates a story about a girl, Dilara, who
graduates from the faculty of medicine with honors and later
becomes a doctor in Ankara, the capital city of Turkey. At the
beginning of the novel, Dilara is portrayed as a very beautiful
and successful "modern" girl with "modern friends," all raised
in Ankara with the "necessities of modernity" (*çağdaşlığın
icapları*) such as dancing and flirting (11). Yet Dilara is presented as a character who expresses some criticism of this modern lifestyle. She begins to feel worthless in an environment
where women are perceived as the "commodities of males" (10).

The novel consists of two parts: In the first part, Dilara, as
a new graduate waiting for the graduation ceremony, goes to
Kayseri, a provincial town in Anatolia, to spend her summer
holiday. This town is where her father, a professor of biology
lives. During a walk with her father in Kayseri, Dilara witnesses
a traffic accident in which İbrahim, the pious male character of
the novel, and his child survive while his wife dies. Dilara and
her father take the man and the child to their house and let
them recover for a few weeks. During this period, Dilara is
heavily influenced by İbrahim's reading of the Koran and his
Islamic views on life and death. As is common in all Islamic
novels, the female protagonist falls in love with this pious
character. Her dialogue with İbrahim on religious issues leads
Dilara to reflect upon and investigate Islam. During her search
for books on Islam, she encounters a pious bookseller in
Kayseri. This bookseller and his wife appear as important figures in teaching Dilara basic Islamic precepts. At the end of
the summer Dilara adopts the Islamic way of life, symbolized by
her putting on the headscarf.

The second part of the novel narrates Dilara's "difficult
days" (81) of returning back to Ankara to get her diploma as an
Islamist figure. When she arrives in Ankara, she goes to the
dormitory she normally stays in. Her friends do not recognize

her and are surprised by her new headscarved outlook. Her close friends do not reject her, but some of her acquaintances take a critical stance and keep away from her because of her Islamic garment. The Directress of the dormitory expels her from the dormitory since her "headscarf is not suitable for an official institution" (83). Dilara meets a Muslim woman while she is in a park thinking desperately about what she should do. Dilara is invited by this woman to her house where she spends "peaceful days" (97) practicing an Islamic way of life until the graduation ceremony. However, despite having graduated with high honors, Dilara is not allowed to get her diploma on the stage while wearing her Islamic outfit. She defends her Islamic lifestyle against her professors who try to convince her that "her style of life was contrary to the contemporary age" (113–15). Then, as a self-assertive Islamic character, she begins to work as a pediatrician in a hospital where she narrates Islam to her patients. The novel closes with Dilara being assigned to Mecca as a doctor during the *hajj* (Islamic pilgrimage) as well as with a marriage proposal from İbrahim. She considers both "rewards" (149) for her patience and insistence on maintaining the Islamic way of life.

The second novel I will draw on, *Boşluk* by Ahmet Günbay Yıldız (2003), tells the story of a male character, Cihan, with a central plot revolving around his Islamization process. Cihan, as a young boy beginning to learn Islam from some of his friends, is frowned upon by his "civilized and modern" family and sent to Europe to study medicine. After his return to Turkey as a doctor, he appears as a character who humiliates his pious cousin Tuba, since he finds her Islamic way of life "primitive" and "uncivilized" (50–54). He not only mocks Muslim characters but also displays condescending attitudes toward the poor villagers that come to his office, where he refuses to examine them. Cihan is portrayed as a doctor examining the "hypochondriac people of high society" (57). Over time, he makes money and "searches for peace in materialism" (78). However without delving into any detailed psychology, Cihan begins to question himself as he sinks into a state of meaninglessness. He realizes that materialism does not bring happiness (79).

Cihan then proposes to his pious cousin Tuba who works as a primary school teacher. However, she refuses him since he does not live an Islamic way of life. Sometime later he marries Ebru who is depicted as a "modern and civilized woman" with worldly desires such as attending parties where she dances with other males (105). This marriage does not last long since Cihan still finds his life meaningless. At this moment of crisis, he recalls doctor Vedat, an old pious friend of his. The author employs doctor Vedat to present his Islamic views framed through the "Islamization process" of Cihan. At the end of the process, Cihan turns into an assertive Muslim character preaching Islam to his friends and neighbors. His new identity, however, disturbs some people who "curse" him for "advocating an Islamic order (*sharia*)" (203). Then he is taken to court, and as a result is exiled to a small province. While Cihan is working there as a "Muslim doctor" praised by the local people, he learns that his cousin Tuba is working in one of the local schools. Cihan convinces her that he has changed, and this time they marry. The novel, just like all salvation novels, closes with a happy ending.

Both novels, one narrating first the Islamization and then the stigmatization and exclusion of a young female university student, and the other focusing on the process of conversion to an Islamic way of life by a male character, can be taken as representative of Islamic novels of the 1980s. The stories of Dilara and Cihan involve dialogues, signs, and representations that are often replicated by Islamic novels of the period. As is common in all Islamic novels, their stories open up scenes in which pious and secular characters engage in a discursive struggle over the true meaning of civilization.

First Encounter: The "Civilizational Clash" Between Muslims and "Others"

The narrative structure of Islamic novels is organized around two competing value systems: Muslims and the other (secular/westernist). In line with the dominant Islamic discourse of the 1980s, Islam is presented as the source of a value system that is totally distinct from secular/westernist visions of the world. These two different value systems engage in a competitive dialogue via pious and westernized characters in novels. Importantly, it is hard to identify these characters in novels as "true" characters in novelistic terms, since Islamist novelists do not enter deeply into the ambiguous emotions of characters in order to develop psychologically complex characters. Rather, they portray stereotypical characters that represent the basic qualities of two social categories: Islamic and secular/westernist. Accordingly, the dialogue between Islamic and other value systems is conducted via idealized characters representing two competing and contradictory worldviews. These social types are represented as "stable and strong" Muslim characters on the one hand, and stereotypically "degenerate" westernized characters on the other. The central plot of Islamic novels revolves around the Islamization of these westernized characters who discover a solution to their problems in the message of Islam, conveyed to them by stable pious characters.

Cihan in *Boşluk* and Dilara in *Müslüman Kadının Adı Var* typify these westernized characters. Through these characters' dialogue and close circles, the authors give voice to a discourse of modernity and civilization that has a problematic relation with religion. This discourse is spelled out through the encounter of westernized and pious characters. When Cihan returns from Europe as a doctor and meets with family members for dinner and drinks, he asks about his pious cousin Tuba:

—Why is Tuba not with us?

His uncle replies:

—She keeps away from alcohol and those who drink alcohol. [...]
—Has she still not changed?
—Unfortunately civilization is not contagious. She still has primitive people's mind within such a family. A teacher's character should not be like this. (54)

When Cihan meets Tuba, he is surprised because she has begun to wear a headscarf. He shouts at her:

> Are you kidding? We are a family that has attained European civilization. How can you do that? (87)

These quotations are indicative of Islamist novelists' portrayal of the appropriation of civilization by their secular opponents. Secular characters who consider themselves "civilized," and who construe civilization as westernization or Europeanization, are usually depicted in scenes in which men and women freely socialize, flirt, and drink alcohol. Their approach to religion and religious manifestations are made explicit when they encounter Islamic characters, especially those who wear the headscarf. The headcovering, or a critical stance toward alcohol, as in the case of Tuba, is taken by westernized characters as a feature of "primitive" people in conflict with the European civilization. Thus, Islamic characters are situated and gain meaning in the context of Islamists' portrayal of a westernized vision of the world that considers religious belief and symbols retrograde manifestations that must be left behind.

In our second novel, Dilara, the protagonist of *Müslüman Kadının Adı Var*, receives a similar response from her professors in the faculty when she returns to Ankara wearing her new Islamic garments. The secular professors think in the following way:

> How could this be! This dress, in the twenty-first century? It is contrary to the contemporary age and civilization. Above all, a doctor's veiling in secular Turkish Republic. (104)

One of Dilara's professors tries to convince her to unveil in a way that exemplifies Islamists' representation of secular narratives of civilization:

> We have to be modern now! Look, Europe has been rapidly advancing in science and technology. We have to

catch up with their civilization. We cannot waste our time with rules made fifteen hundred years ago. (115)

These expressions that revolve around the identification of a civilization that excludes religious manifestations constitute the major framing device of nearly all Islamic salvation novels of the 1980s. In a Bakhtinian sense, the term "civilization" has a socially charged life and derives its meaning from a history within the contemporary context of Turkey. Islamist novelists, by making westernized characters speak with secular idioms, give voice to a historicity lying behind the concept of civilization in Turkey from their own perspective. What lies at the core of Islamic narratives is a conviction that Islam and Muslim characters have been silenced and excluded from modern public life by westernized agents' conception of civilization. Therefore they contest the meaning of civilization that is, to use Bakhtin's words, "populated with the intention of others" (Bakhtin 2000, 293). Islamist novelists make westernized characters' "intentions" explicit by making them speak a secular language that promotes the idea that Islam does not belong to the contemporary civilization.

"Civilization," then, is a key term for both Islamists and secularists in Turkey. Every word, as Bakhtin notes, involves a "social atmosphere" (2000, 277) in which it takes its meaning. Language, in general, is inherently social since it involves a shared sign system between people.[3] Words, thus, are not neutral; all words belong to someone (Bakhtin 2000).[4] One cannot, therefore, easily make a word their private property, since each word also belongs to someone else. This suggests that words are always used or secondhand, and their meanings are never singular, but plural and contested. Every word has a history behind it and the usage of each word positions the user with respect to this historicity. In the attempt to expropriate a word for oneself, one must engage in dialogue with other people. Individuals or groups have to struggle to adopt a word for their own expressive intentions. The fact that Islamic salvation novels revolve around the term "civilization" signifies Islamist novelists' aim to challenge secular narratives of civilization and to combat the negative representations of Muslims by contesting the meaning of civilization and modernity. To this aim, they necessarily engage in a discursive struggle with secular/westernized characters. Westernized characters are often positioned against Islamic figures along with a claim that associates civilization with Europeanization or westernization. Through such a frame, Islamist authors demonstrate how the equation of civilization with Westernization (in the form of de-Islamization) has reproduced negative representations of Muslim actors. This is made salient in the stigmatization of Muslim visibilities, as in the case of Tuba and Dilara, whose westernized professors, family members, and friends consider them "backward," "primitive," and "contrary to the age," as well as "conflicting with modern civilization" (Yıldız 2003, 54ff; Turhal 1999, 114ff).[5] By employing these "stigmatizing concepts," Islamist novelists struggle against secular narratives of civilization and the negative representations that they construct of Muslims in contemporary Turkey. They struggle for positive representations of Muslim social identities.

The self does not construct a story in isolation (Whitebrook 2001). People construct identities by locating themselves within "a repertoire of emplotted stories" (Somers and Gibson 1994, 38–39). And during this emplotment, various time frames, contexts, events, and dialogic relationships contributing to the construction of a narrative may be interrelated in a number of ways. Islamist novelists of the 1980s, however, emplot their narratives within a "civilizational discourse" in the political/cultural context of contemporary Turkey. Emplotment of Islamic novels within the dominant secular narratives of civilization is indicative of the nature of contemporary Islamic movements and of the ground on which these movements have arisen. As sociologist Nilüfer Göle puts it, the decisive realm of social inequality upon which Islamist politics is built "is neither the realm of economic deprivation nor that of political authoritarianism, but is rather a cultural model of hegemonic modernity, namely a higher form of life to be emulated and embodied personally and in everyday life" (Göle

2006, 19). The novels' depiction of Muslims as victims of this secular modernization project and their authors' aim to construct an Islamic identity via a challenge to secular conceptions of modernity illustrate the centrality of the theme of modernity in Islamic politics. Islamic salvation novels provide us with a case study demonstrating the contemporary search for an Islamic self that is based on the criticism of the equation of the modern self with the civilized West. The constitution of the central plot of Islamic novels via a discourse of civilization in which Islamic and westernized characters engage in conflict also signifies that Islamic novels are narratives of "the intimate encounter of Islam with modernity" (Göle 2002) in the context of Turkey during the 1980s.

The place of Islamic narratives within the contemporary context of Turkey allows Islamist novelists to present their criticisms of secular narratives of civilization. In this sense, Islamic literary discourse can be apprehended as an attempt to retell the story of civilization in Turkey in a particular way. To achieve this end, Islamic literary discourse seeks to "defamiliarize the familiar world" and to disturb the "habitualization" brought about by secular narratives of civilization. This suggests that Islamist novelists intend for the reader to reexamine the assumptions, conventions, and stigmatizations brought about by the secular framing of civilization and modernity. In other words, they aim to make people see the narratives of civilization differently and anew. Islamist novelists seek to make their readers feel that the process of modernization has taken Turkey not to the level of contemporary civilization, but to "moral degeneration" and "social disintegration." This is because, as Sevim Asımgil, an Islamist novelist, writes, "irreligion [atheism] has been injected into Turkish society in the name of contemporaneity and modernity" (*Dinsizlik, Türk toplumuna çağdaşlık ve modernlik adına şırınga edilmiş*)" (Asımgil 1993, 70). Islamist writers, as third person narrators, often intervene in their texts to present their views on the current situation brought about by the process of modernization in the form of westernization. For example, Katırcı

Turhal, in *Müslüman Kadının Adı Var*, depicts contemporary Turkey in a scene when Dilara, wearing her headscarf, is not allowed to get her diploma:

> That day, while they made a spiritual massacre and many innocent people were put through hard conditions, thousands of girls on the streets escaped their homes with hopes of becoming actresses, and ended up in brothels, because of the defective education they received.
>
> The number of call-girls has been increasing dramatically, and newspapers, which are behind the promotion of prostitution, announce that many of these girls are university students, as if they are proud of it.
>
> The young generation commits murders and robberies without hesitation, since they do not have the fear of God inside them. Because of the spiritual void, thousands of youngsters commit suicide in such a variety of ways....
>
> And bars, pavilions and Atari saloons, customers of gambling machines have been in rapid increase. So many families fall into ruin, so many children inhabit the streets. A jailhouse has been erected opposite each school building. (130)

This quotation is representative of Islamist novelists' critical depiction and perception of current Turkish society. Secular modernization, they write, led to "an age in which not civilization but de-civilization has been dominant," to a society where "obscene posters have proliferated" (Yıldız 2003, 286), and to "a mentality that rewards the bosses of brothels since they pay high taxes" (Turhal 1999, 131). What lies at the core of Islamist novelists' criticism toward the secular conception of civilization is that this secular mentality has led to "disastrous moral dissipation," especially for youth. As the above quotation makes explicit, this occurred because youths have grown up with modern secular values that exclude a religious idiom. Moreover, this mentality, as Islamist novelists commonly emphasize in their narratives, has led to a social context in which young people fall into meaninglessness and aimlessness.

Cihan and Dilara, the protagonists of the two novels, represent these types living in modern secular social contexts. The social milieu in Ankara, in which Dilara and her university friends grow up, is depicted as follows:

> All of them have grown up in the most privileged districts of Ankara, where relationships between genders are free from traditional bonds. They have enjoyed love, flirtation, being or having a mistress and unfaithfulness, all of which are included in what modernity requires [...] (11)
> concerning their family life, even the word Islam was not heard at all at home, let alone observing Islamic commands. Their life consists of eating-drinking, dressing as the fashion prescribes, drinking alcohol, gambling, flirtation and having a good time whenever they can. (88)

Characters living this modern way of life uninformed of Islam allow Islamist novelists to construct a social category of "the other" around the concept of modernity. "Modern characters" belonging to this social category are portrayed as those who are ignorant about—and often hostile to—Islam, due to their Western-centric conceptions of modernity and civilization. They are made to live according to the "necessities of modernity," represented as drinking, flirting, dancing, and enjoying "immoral" love affairs. Islamists, thus, envision a form of secular collective identity institutionalized by the secularization/modernization process. The wearing of mini-skirts, alcohol consumption, attending parties where men and women freely socialize and flirt, and displaying condescending attitudes toward Muslim characters characterize such a collective identity. These characteristics are commonly employed as the attributes of characters that are identified as "modern/secular/westernized" in salvation novels of the 1980s.

These modern characters, however, are represented as persons who do not have full control over their existence and way of life. Rather, they are depicted as inauthentic "imitators of Western modernity." To put this in Islamist novelist Raif Cilasun's own terms, modern characters are those who "think of civilization as imitating the West, deviating from their religion"; as a result, these modern characters "lose their essence, even their humanity" (Cilasun n.d., back cover).

Ebru, whom Cihan marries while living a modern/westernized way of life, exemplifies one of these modern characters. Novelists depict scenes in which modern characters are made to act according to the "necessities of modernity."[6] For instance, while Ebru and Cihan are dancing at a party, a man comes forward and offers to change dance partners. Cihan, as a character who has begun to adopt a critical attitude toward his environment, becomes both jealous and angry with that offer. Ebru criticizes Cihan and says to him, "[but] you are a civilized man." In response to Cihan's jealousy, Ebru takes recourse to civilization, stating, "I think you have contradicted European vision. This is civilization, whether you want it or not!" (Yıldız 2003, 106–7).

In a similar way, Dilara of *Müslüman Kadının Adı Var* accuses her professors, who do not allow her to attend the graduation ceremony with her headscarf, of being "imitators of Western civilization":

> You, who commit injustice by insisting on modern dress code, are you going to pronounce people old-fashioned, people whose dressing does not properly cover their bodies, if the Jewish designer Pierre Cardin, which creates such modern costumes of the world, designs a couture that properly covers the body? Does this nation deserve to be so base, is it apt for this nation to imitate others blindly? (129)

Thus what constitutes "the other" in contrast to Muslim identity is blind imitation of the West.[7] Further, characters depicted as "modern" are not permitted any self-consciousness about their lifestyle choices. Rather, they are employed by the novelists as objects of Islamic pedagogy that legitimize Islamic ideology as the only alternative to secular narratives of civilization. In the identification of opponents, Katırcı Turhal often cites Jews as symbolic of the generic category of "the other" of

Muslim identity. The term "Jew" is used to include the Western powers that support Zionist ideology as well as a materialism that, as professed by Islamic movements, alienated Islam and made Muslims lose their essence. This rhetoric of conspiracy leads Islamist novelists to construct modern characters—the category of "the other"—as "alienated subjects" of the process of westernization. Indeed, in a way they are presented as the victims of this process. Therefore, Islamists call out to them: "You are not the victim of Islam but de-Islamization" (Şenlikoğlu 1993, 17).

Islamist novelists then have a deep conviction that modern subjects are doomed to unhappiness in a social context from which Islam has been excluded. By contrast, Islamic narratives claim that what the age and modern people need is the true message of Islam. Cihan and Dilara are two modern but wretched characters employed to present an Islamic solution to the problems of modern age.

Construction of Islamic Identity

Islamist novelists presuppose that the modern conception of civilization has led to a "corrupt order" since it excludes religious morality, promotes an egoism, and seduces youth with its stress on the free interaction of the sexes. Cihan and Dilara represent two young characters living in such a "corrupt milieu" where Islam is not lived, talked about, or practiced. They are portrayed by their authors as falling into meaninglessness because of the "imitative and decadent" relations governing their circles. Their realization of the worthlessness of this secular way of life begins their process of Islamization.

Yet interestingly, despite their degenerated milieu, these westernized protagonists of salvation novels are also made to maintain their "purity" since they are later transformed into agents struggling for Islam. In particular, female characters, who are often depicted as beautiful, do not engage in any illicit relations with men. Katırcı Turhal, for instance, introduces Dilara to the reader by underlining her "decency":

She was a really very beautiful girl with jet black hair draping down from her shoulders. Her almond green eyes were shining like emeralds in her wheat colored oval face. Long and clipped eyelashes were giving a different style to her face. But her beauty has never spoiled her. She was always a serious girl. She never had an affair with her boyfriends that could lead her to the wrong path. There has always been a distance between Dilara and boys. (9)

Such an introduction, as will be illustrated later, exemplifies the central position of women in maintaining a communitarian morality in the Islamic framework. The key westernized characters, particularly females, are "saved" from the threat of degenerate relations and portrayed as "unspoiled" characters. It is this that facilitates their process of Islamization.

The Islamization of westernized characters begins when their feelings of meaninglessness arise in a context in which they meet Muslim characters. In almost all novels of the period, this encounter is connected with the experience of love. Westernized characters are made to fall in love with Muslim characters who take them on a "journey" to adopt an Islamic life. Dilara falls in love with the pious teacher İbrahim, who stays in her house after a traffic accident, while Cihan—inconsistent with his position in the novel—proposes marriage to his devout cousin Tuba. This love triggers secular characters' curiosity about an "Islamic way of life" that is alien to them. Westernized characters, however, are not allowed to be with Islamic characters until their Islamization—the construction of an Islamic identity—is complete. In the process of learning an Islamic lifestyle, novelists present Islamic ideas about how to think, behave, pray, and—logically—how to love.

For example, the pious male character of *Müslüman Kadının Adı Var*, İbrahim, stays at Dilara's house while recovering from a traffic accident in which he loses his wife. İbrahim reads the Koran in memory of his dead wife. Basic messages about the Koran and Islam are immediately conveyed to the reader from the first dialogue between İbrahim and Dilara. Dilara, who is influenced by İbrahim's reading of the Koran, asks: "Have these verses and the Koran been sent for dead people?" Through the mouth of İbrahim, the author conveys his Islamic message: "No, the Koran appeals to both worlds" (22–23). This message is indicative of the Islamist message that the relevance of the Koran is not confined to otherworldly events but is also a holy text holding prescriptions for this world. After several instructive dialogues and messages, Dilara says, "I accept. I wholeheartedly submit to this holy Koran" (23). This starts her process of learning about Islam, each point of which is constructed with a different manner of thinking, behaving, and acting with regards to the secular modern way of life.

Dilara is said to be drawn to İbrahim "not because of physical appearance, but because of his character." This Muslim man, the novelist writes, "was kind, polite and cultured. At the same time he was a conscious Muslim practicing God's orders. He had initiated a new epoch in a young girl's [Dilara's] life by giving her the Koran as a gift" (50). Dilara is made to qualify her love in contradistinction to the love of secular/Westernized people: "My love is totally different from theirs. Their love depends on sexuality" (70). Generating an Islamic politics of differentiation marked by a language of "us" and "them," Dilara is made to identify her love as "metaphysical love" (*ilahi bir sevgi*). Through Dilara's mind, the novelist presents what is required for "real love" in an Islamic frame:

> I love his personality.... It is the holy book that binds me to him.... I have heard it from him for the first time, and I was affected.... Are not these enough to bear love?... What if I get to know him closely, if I enter into his life in which he punctually observes Islam. Who knows, how much would I love him? (70)

To know İbrahim more closely, and to "satisfy her soul," Dilara decides to learn about Islam. Similarly, Cihan, as a result of his unhappiness with the secular way of life, decides to find one of his old pious friends, doctor Vedat. The edifying mission of the novels is worked out through dialogues between these two

characters and pious figures. The bookseller Dilara meets in
Kayseri when searching for religious books appears as one of
the "teaching figures" of the novel. He advises Dilara to start
by reading Islamic history. Dilara's response as follows signifies her first step in acquiring Islamic consciousness: "So far
we have read European history. From now forth let us read
Islamic history" (35).

As Dilara reads Islamic books, she begins to question her
upbringing, education, and the ignorance of her circle about
Islam. Via Dilara, the author takes every opportunity to criticize modern families and the Turkish education system that
disregard religious belief:

> Sometimes she wondered why she had not learned or
> heard these [Islamic teachings] before. While I was born
> in a Muslim family, I never learned about God while I
> learned other information, and I never loved God either.
> She was getting angry with her father about these mat-
> ters.... But her father was not knowledgeable on this
> [Islam].... He was more ignorant than she. He became a
> great professor, spent his life exploring insects, but he did
> not learn about God, his creator. Perhaps he will pass
> away not knowing God. (36–37)

Dilara's questioning represents her first step to the formation of
a critical consciousness and then to differentiation from her
secular family and environment.[8] Dilara goes on to ask the following questions about her past:

> Why did not they teach them a bit of spiritual knowledge
> additionally in those schools where she was taught
> knowledge of the material world for many years? Or was it
> not necessary?.... Or was religious education something
> meant for only a specific group? Or could not religion be
> reconciled with science? (29)

Dilara then engages in dialogue with Muslim characters to find
the answers to her questions. These questions and dialogues

are designed to present readers with basic Islamic precepts. *Müslüman Kadının Adı Var*, in this sense, is more didactic than *Boşluk*. Katırcı Turhal makes Dilara ask the pious bookseller several basic questions such as, "Why do we always turn to the direction of Ka'ba [to perform prescribed prayers]?" and "Why do we confirm our intention as we elevate our hands, when we perform prescribed prayers?" (40–41). Similarly, in *Boşluk* the dialogue of Cihan and the pious Vedat revolves around the question of "why one should believe" and serves the same end. These dialogues provide novelists with a way to not only present basic Islamic knowledge but also to clarify and speculate about certain issues like morality, polygamy, and the status of women in Islam.

What is going on in these novels? In the first instance, novelists connect events—Dilara's and Cihan's love, their search to learn more about Islam, etc.—in the form of narrative and reconstruct them in a signification process. Narrative here does not function as a linguistic activity but provides Islamic actors with a space to integrate events in a chain of cause and effect and thus make them understandable. Narrative, then, appears as the form through which people understand who they are and how they act. As Seyla Benhabib notes:

> Narrativity, or the immersion of action in a web of human relationships, is the mode through which the self is individuated and acts are identified. Both the whatness of the act and whoness of the self are disclosed to agents capable of communicative understanding. Actions are identified narratively.... To identify an action is to tell the story of its initiation, of its unfolding and its immersion in a web of relations constituted through the actions and narratives of others. Likewise, the whoness of the self is constituted by the story of a life. (1996, 127)

Islamic salvation novels, then, represent Islamic narratives through which an Islamic self is constituted, actions are identified, and events are made comprehensible. The stories of the protagonists of both *Boşluk* and *Müslüman Kadının Adı Var* can be read as Islamist authors' attempt to order and pattern the events surrounding them for the construction of a coherent Islamic self within the modern world. Each event in Dilara's and Cihan's story signifies the issues at stake in the construction of a coherent Islamic identity. To achieve this, Dilara's love for İbrahim, her questioning of the secular way of life, and Cihan's attempts to find answers to his feelings of worthlessness are refracted in a narrative form that emerges, in the sense that Richardson uses the term, not only as "a mode of representation but also a mode of reasoning" (Richardson 1990, 2). Dilara and Cihan appear as agents who need to make choices within the context of particular dilemmas to develop a narrative unity in the construction of a coherent Islamic identity. In their quest for narrative identity, characters are led to make choices between "metaphysical and material love," "European and Islamic history," and an "Islamic and secular/Western way of life." The answers that characters—or Islamist novelists—develop to these dilemmas constitute sequential plots of Islamic narratives through which Islamic identities are formed.

The theme of the West (or Europe, as novelists often employ) emerges as an important topic within the construction of an Islamic self. What characterizes salvation narratives and '80s Islamism more generally is their problematization of secular modernization in the form of westernization. Salvation novels, as mentioned above, challenge the exclusion of Muslim actors due to such a process of westernization. The Islamic questioning of the history of modernization, or the Kemalist modernization in a Turkish context, necessarily involves a negotiation over the meaning and representation of the West and Europe. The West, in other words, represents a site of conflict for Islamic actors in their debate on the meaning of civilization. The authors of both *Boşluk* and *Müslüman Kadının Adı Var* take every chance to challenge Kemalist westernist narratives of civilization.

Almost all westernized characters of salvation novels are made to have close contacts with Europe, represented as the source of their alienation and wretchedness. Dilara, for instance, is introduced to the reader at the beginning of the novel as someone who had "spent her youth in European cities due to her father's job" (Turhal 1999, 8). This is the only sentence referring to Dilara's relation with Europe; the author never again mentions Dilara's years in Europe. However, this small note signifies the centrality of the problematization of the West in Islamic imaginary. Several of Dilara's responses quoted above, such as "so far we have read European history. From now forth let us read Islamic history," are also indicative of an Islamic mentality that positions itself as distinct from Western frames of reference. Günbay Yıldız' *Boşluk*, on the other hand, involves a more direct reference to Europe as the source of evil. Cihan, who is sent to Europe to study medicine, returns to Turkey as an alienated character.

Significantly, then, Islamic salvation novelists nearly always create a homogeneous West in contradistinction to the Islamic world. They often employ a conspiracy theory that presents the West as the major source seeking the weakness of the Muslim world. However, it can be argued that there are two layers of this representation of the West. In some novels, authors gesture to a Western conspiracy, so that the West is presented as the source of all evil. In more oppositional narratives like *Müslüman Kadının Adı Var*, the West or Europeans are depicted as eternal enemies of Muslims:

> The grandchildren of those who divided our country into seven regions before the War of Independence, and who jailed Muslims into mosques, here are those Europeans. Now, they pretend to be our friends, and our fellow men take them to be our friends.... [These Europeans] have always attacked this noble nation, sometimes by crusades, sometimes by cultural imperialism, immorality and the illness of fashion. (120)

A second type of representation of the West (and this is more common in salvation novels than the first type) is based on a religious perspective. Europe or the West, in other words, is viewed in religious terms by the novelists. Novelists refer to the spiritual dimension of the West and argue that it is "us" who "misunderstood and appropriated it" only in the form of a secular and irreligious civilization. In *Boşluk*, Cihan is sent to Europe to become an "intellectual" yet returns to Turkey a "degenerate" man; this signifies a character that has misunderstood the West. This fact is spelled out in his dialogue with doctor Vedat, who asks him,

> —Were there not venerable fathers where you come from?
> —There were.
> —Did those illuminated people, among whom you got your education, urge you to follow the religion they follow?
> —They did.
> —And then?
> —I rejected. [...]
> —What did [those people] used to do on Sundays or Saturdays?
> —They used to go to certain places called Church or Synagogue.
> —What do they use to do there?
> —Probably, worship. Those days, we used to invite their daughters to parties, but they would not attend. [...]
> —Have you ever asked why?
> —They used to say simply "it is our holy day."
> —So, Europe is different.
> —Why?
> —As far as we are concerned, they call the people who worship "backward." But they observe things that their religious beliefs require. (163)

Moreover, the author, through the mouth of doctor Vedat, refers to and quotes from several Western thinkers such as Carl Jung and Alexis Carrel to emphasize the importance of belief in human life.[9] Such a representation of Europe, however, is again complemented with reference to a Western conspiracy. This is made explicit at the end of the dialogue by Vedat: "aaah

Europe. It is Europe which prescribed us irreligiosity while preserving its own church" (163). Therefore, the blame is again put on the West and the Westernizing agents in Turkey.

Yet the representation of Europe in religious terms performs a double function for Islamist novelists. It conveys the message that it is Turkish secular modernizing elite who misunderstood and mimicked Europe in the form of a secular and irreligious civilization. Novelists claim that they present the "real" meaning of European civilization in contrast to that of "imitative" westernist agents.[10] A perception of Christian Europe in this vein also serves Islamic actors' interests in arguing that scientific and technological development and religion do not necessarily conflict. An image of Christian Europe provides Islamists with a ground to claim that religion is not an obstacle to scientific development.[11]

At the end of this discussion, Cihan is transformed and declares that: "I BELIEVE ... GOD EXISTS. THIS UNIVERSE IS NOT ON ITS OWN. I WILL NOT LEAVE AND ABANDON THIS WELL SET-UP ORDER TO CHANCE" (capitals original). He is transformed into a character who will spend the rest of his life conveying the message of Islam to humanity. For male characters to transform into Islamic subjects, it seems to be enough to announce that "they believe." After their transformation they are not generally made to undergo any physical alteration such as wearing a beard. For female characters, on the other hand, being a believer requires a symbol, the *headscarf*, as emphasized by all salvation novelists without exception.

The Headscarf:
A *Sine Qua Non* for Islamic Salvation

The Islamic headscarf is today the most important and controversial manifestation of contemporary Islamic movements. It is the most visible symbol of Islamic identity. The headscarf controversy, i.e., the demand of headscarved girls to attend public schools and universities in both Muslim and Western contexts, has made this piece of cloth part of a global practice. It has been turned into a controversy through which sociologists, anthropologists, and political scientists debate the limits of democracy, human rights, and liberal political theory.[12]

In Turkey, the contemporary Islamic outfit is a headscarf that completely covers the hair and falls upon the shoulders, and a long coat that hides the body. It is a garment that emerged with the rise of Islamic movements in the 1970s in Muslim contexts. New veiling, generally called *hijâb* in Arab Muslim contexts, refers not to the hiding of the face but to the covering of the head. It is not a revival of some traditional clothes that involves covering the face (Badran 1995). In Turkey, too, this new Islamic headscarf is different from traditional veiling that is associated with uneducated, mostly rural women. The former represents a claim of educated urban classes to share modern urban spaces.[13] In line with the Islamic politics of distinction, the headscarf appeared in all Islamic texts of the 1980s as "the most powerful meta-political icon" (Göle 2002) differentiating Islamic identity from secular/westernized characters. This is particularly true for salvation novels that represent the headscarf as a *sine qua non* of Islamic identity. The position of Dilara in *Müslüman Kadının Adı Var* best exemplifies Islamic novelists' concern about the headscarf. Günbay Yıldız's *Boşluk*, too, which narrates the story of a male character, involves several instructive dialogues giving messages about women's headscarves.

Dilara, who turns into a devout character and begins to perform daily practices and praying, is presented as still lacking an important dimension in being a true believer. She is made aware of this dimension when she goes to a mosque with her mentor bookseller. While the bookseller enters the mosque, she realizes that she cannot since she is not covered. Then she feels guiltily: "I cannot here enter into God's home without veiling. How can I dare to enter paradise if I die in this situation?" (40). Dilara's life-altering moment arises when she is made to hear a "metaphysical voice" while she prays to God to reach fulfillment. This voice addresses her as follows:

> Look my daughter, look at this apple! It has a hull. Whatever living being, whatever fruit, whatever animal you take, all have shells on them. The shell of women is their clothes. Your veiling yourself will protect you from all kinds of danger. (47)

As a result of this "metaphysical moment" Dilara finds the commitment to acquire a full Islamic identity and asks herself: "Can a woman adopt the Islamic way of life without veiling?" (48). She discovers veiling as the cornerstone of Islamic female identity. At the end of this process, she adopts an Islamic head-covering and turns into a "true" Islamic character. Her headscarf is represented as "the flag of her chastity" by the author, who through the mouth of the bookseller warns Dilara about the headscarf as follows:

> Look my daughter, ignorant people of the day will first assault your headscarf. The headscarf is the flag of your chastity. When an enemy attacks a castle, the first thing they remove is the flag from the castle tower. You should carry this flag on your head with pride.... You should be aware of the importance of your headscarf. (78)

In another salvation novel, Günbay Yıldız identifies the head-scarf as the sign of Islamic identity. In *Benim Çiçeklerim Ateşte Açar* he warns a girl who states that she would like to cover her head in the following manner: "This dress is the symbol of an identity. Veiling has its own rules. Will you be able to apply them to your daily life? (Yıldız 2000, 120). Similar dialogues about the headscarf are replicated in almost all salvation novels. In one of the more influential novels of the 1980s entitled *Müslüman Savaşçı* (Tekin 1998), the Muslim character Abdullah falls in love with Selma, the daughter of a tyrant land-lord. Abdullah writes Selma a letter and invites her to become a Muslim. Selma asks herself "Am I not a Muslim? What does it mean to be a Muslim?" An old man she consults warns her, "you will cover your head. If you do not, everything is futile" (Tekin 1998, 145). What marks the narrative construction of Islamic identity, therefore, is the veiled woman. Women, not only in literary but also in all non-literary Islamic texts of the 1980s, function as the "boundary marker of Islamic difference" (Göle 2000, 101). Islamic difference via the woman's headscarf is supported by references to the Koran and sayings of the Prophet. After her veiling Dilara is informed of a saying that is replicated in many Islamic texts to sustain a politics of distinction: "If one imitates a nation, she belongs to it.... We have to take not Europe's but *Asr-ı Saadet*'s (the age of happiness) women as models (78). The headscarf, therefore, is presented as a symbol leading to fulfillment and distinguishing Islamic identity from secular Western culture. In line with Katırcı Turhal, Yıldız, the author of Cihan's story in *Boşluk*, makes the pious character Tuba question herself and adopt Islamic veiling.[14] Female characters after veiling are depicted as transformed: Dilara's "face is enlightened, an attribute that others do not have" (48) and Tuba "becomes like an angel" (87). Islamic veiling signifies not only their newly acquired Islamic consciousness and identity, but also appears as a curtain identifying insider and outsider categories.

Importantly, the category of the outsider in Islamic imaginary not only includes secular and non-Islamic identities but also extends to the supposed traditional Muslim identity. Islamic movements then take a critical stance not only to Kemalist modernization but also to traditional Islam, or a passive notion of Islam in Islamist discourse. Islamic identity is constructed in the various Islamist texts as differentiated from an ignorant or de-politicized Muslim identity. Dilara, who took her essential step in developing an assertive Islamic identity through veiling, is now led to her next step: to gain an awareness that the identity Islam prescribes is distinct from traditional understandings of Islam. This traditional Muslim character is Dilara's aunt, who helps her during her first phase of learning about Islam. Dilara asks several basic questions when she begins to learn about Islam. However, as Dilara possesses an Islamic consciousness, she asks her aunt: "You pray five times a day. What do the verses you read say about our Creator?" Her aunt is surprised about the question and replies as such: "How do I know? I cannot understand what I read. I do not know Arabic" (54). The author again intervenes in the text and writes a critical sentence against the secular modernizers as follows:

> The young girl [Dilara] suddenly came face to face with a reality: They [modernizers] tried to cut all the ties of that woman and thousands of Muslims with God. They even exterminated the language between man and God. But they could not manage it, with the help of God. She has been praying to her God with submission, even though she does not understand what she says. (55)

The author thus puts the blame on secularists in Turkey that, according to him, "tried to cut all ties" with true Islam, leading to a Muslim identity that believes and performs prayers without understanding the true message of Islam. Dilara's new critical position on her aunt's type of religiosity represents the point at which Islamist identity is differentiated from traditional Muslim identity. The author, in other words, draws a border between an Islamist and a Muslim. Being a Muslim (represented by Dilara's aunt) refers to an agency position in which one is born a Muslim, one learns about religion through traditional channels (from older generations) and one practices Islam without its political engagements. One becomes an Islamist (represented by Dilara), on the other hand, by revising this given Muslim identity, by endowing it with a new political will to apply Islam in private and public life and thus by a personal choice. Hence Islamism is reinterpreted by contemporary Islamic activists not as a continuation of tradition, but as what Eickelman and Piscatori (1996) call—with reference to Hobsbawn—an "invention of tradition." The idea of the Islamic state and the Islamic headscarf are all new inventions of Islamic actors in the context of modernity. Islamism refers to the re-appropriation and revision of Islam by Islamist actors in their engagement in worldly affairs in the name of Islam. It is with Islamism that a Muslim shifts to an Islamist and searches for an "agency position in modern political settings." Such a transformation from Muslim to Islamist is achieved by a social movement, the Islamic movement, and its production of collective agency (Göle 1996, 12). The way Islamic movements recruit their members displays a similar pattern to that of other Muslim contexts in which young actors take a critical stance to and differentiate themselves from the traditional Islam of their families. A young Moroccan Islamist woman, whom Hessini interviewed in her work, makes the same point as expressed by Dilara: "You must understand that our parents did not know much about Islam. We were not raised correctly, they did not teach us to follow the correct path" (1994, 49).[15] This transnational pattern can also be seen in other Muslim contexts.

In the Turkish context, too, Dilara represents a character born not into an Islamic family or environment but an agent produced by the contemporary Islamic revival. Her agency position is part of a shared Islamic imaginary and collective movement since, as it is noted in the introduction of the novel, Dilara's experience resembles "hundreds and thousands of other young people in our country" (6). Furthermore, the veiling adopted by Dilara and her newly acquired Islamic position do not simply refer to women's religiosity but also, as it is presented in these novels, appears as a signifier of communitarian morality as the basis of ideal Islamic society. There is therefore a certain gender dimension of literary Islamism that needs to be addressed.

Collective Islamic Morality
on the Basis of Gender

One point that should be elaborated about the Islamic literary sphere is that with few exceptions almost all authors of political Islamist texts were male actors of Islamism. This conforms to the context of the 1980s where the voice of males dominated the Islamic discourse of the period. These men, including Ali Bulaç, Abdurrahman Dilipak, and İsmet Özel, wrote books (even, or perhaps especially, on the position of women in Islam), gave lectures, and discussed religious issues in public spaces. All of the few outstanding female Islamists, on the other hand, were active in the literary field as novelists or short story writers. Islamist women novelists—such as Emine Şenlikoğlu, Mecbure İnal, and Şerife Katırcı Turhal—reflected upon social and political matters and transmitted their messages through literary narratives rather than "intellectual" books in the 1980s.[16]

The novels written by Islamist women do not differ from, but rather share a common discourse with, those of males since they also voice a "metapolitical narrative" of Islamism and problemize common social and moral issues. Emine Şenlikoğlu states: "I write my novels to give particular messages.... Being male or female makes no difference for me.... As far as belief is concerned, there should be no discrimination between men and women" (Çakır 2000, 110). This statement reflects the collective nature of Islamism of the 1980s. Islamic salvation novels, as part of a cultural politics of Islamism, represent collective Islamic identity through a collectivist discourse against homogeneously perceived secular narratives. In emphasizing collective harmony this collectivist discourse did not portray different and conflictual representations between the genders.

Women's position has always been central to representations of collective Islamic identity in Islamic writings, including the salvation novels of the 1980s. Women were the cornerstone of the agenda of the dominant Islamic discourse that revolved around creating an ideal Islamic order and morality. The centrality of women in the Islamic challenge to secular conceptions of civilization can be delineated by a close analysis of the process of Kemalist modernization in the context of Turkey. It should be noted that woman's visibility, body, and posture have always been political and social issues in modernist and nationalist movements. The body, particularly the female body, is considered a site that defines the parameters of a new modernist stance. The body is also often "metaphorically employed as a symbol of the nation." As Alev Çınar notes,

> targeting the body as the symbol of the nation, modernizing interventions involve the incriminations of the present condition of the body as that which is corrupt and impaired, thereby framing it as in need of liberation and transformation. The intervening subject, whether state or some other political actor with a modernizing agenda, can then project itself as the savior who will liberate the body from its present confines and take it toward its deserved feature. (2005, 54)

This quotation illustrates the case in Turkey where the modernizing elite during the first half of the twentieth century introduced many regulations relating to the body and dress in order to catch up with modern Western civilization. An example of one of these regulations is the Hat Law of 1925, which aimed at constructing a new modern male citizen who wore European style hats instead of traditional religious garb. Intervening in the female body during nation formation and the modernization process were much more important than transforming the male body, since women's rights and emancipation were considered an integral part of a country's modernization. According to the reformist elite, the modern world was "sexually integrated," in contrast to the sexually separated order promoted by Islam. This elite believed that the social backwardness of Turkey in the face of the civilized West was a result of social relations structured by Ottoman interpretations of Islam. In a speech in 1923, Atatürk said the following:

> Our enemies are claiming that Turkey cannot be considered a civilized nation because this country consists of two separate parts: men and women. Can we close our eyes to one portion of a group, while advancing the other and still bring progress to the whole group? The road of

progress must be trodden by both sexes together, marching in arm and arm. (Karal 1956, 54)

Thus for the Kemalist elite, national progress and modernization were inextricably bound up with the emancipation of woman.[17] The phrase "emancipation of woman" in a Muslim context meant the freeing of woman from her religious bonds and outlook. Within the modernization process women were carried into the public sphere through different occasions. Islamic veiling was discouraged.[18] Western type balls were organized where men and women danced, women were encouraged to go to restaurants and other urban spaces, different contests were organized making women's bodies, voices, etc. visible in the public sphere, and education was unified to make way for the compulsory co-education for boys and girls.[19] Kemalist modernist reforms therefore involved a project of "degendering" and "regendering" (Durakbaşa 1998).[20] Women's modern veil-less bodies and public visibility were considered the prime signifier of modernity in secular Turkey.[21]

In such a context, the increasing visibility of headscarved female actors along with the rise of Islamic movements in the 1970s generated (and still generates) an intense anxiety over the relation between modern civilization and the female body. For many secular circles, women's veiling cannot be confined to a religious practice but indicates a "reactionary" challenge to Turkey's progress. It also misrepresents Turkey in "front" of modern European countries. Some secular groups consider the headscarf to be a threat to the secular republic and deny that wearing the headscarf can be a civil and democratic right.[22]

In parallel with secular actors then, Islamists also conceive of the female body as a site of challenge to the imperialism of the West and as a body on which to present their alternative project of modernity. Women in several Islamist texts of the Arab world are "relegated to the task of being the last bastion against foreign penetration" (Haddad 1998, 21). The *hijâb* is considered the last border against Western cultural imperialism. This is also valid for Turkish Islamists who, as salvation novelists show, present women's headcovering as the "sign of

Islamic identity." The covered female body thus is the most important sign through which '80s Islamists contest the Kemalist civilization process. Islamic morality, order, and alternative modernity are all narrated, symbolized, and embodied through women's veiling, chastity and decency.

The centrality of women in both Kemalist and Islamist conceptions of modernity explains the construction of the main plots of salvation novels around women's issues. Even in novels like *Boşluk* which revolve around the problems of a male character, the author makes references to the headscarf issue, leads women characters to adopt the headscarf, and imagines an ideal Islamic order via women's transformation. Many other salvation novels such as *Müslüman Kadının Adı Var*, on the other hand, are directly based on women characters who, with their Islamic visibility, challenge the current order and represent the collective and communitarian morality of an ideal Islamic order.

Women's role as the backbone of communitarian morality is mainly worked out through their adoption of Islamic veiling. Dress in Muslim contexts, as in all cultures, is not only a means of bodily protection. It is, as Giddens notes, "a means of symbolic display, a way of giving external form to narratives of self-identity" (1991, 62). Veiling, however, in an Islamist frame, does more than provide an external form for self-identity. It is considered one indispensable component of the "moral issue." Dilara's explanation of her veiling to her friends in Ankara mirrors such a framing of Islamic veiling. In response to one of her friends' question, "Why should young girls not older cover their heads?" she says,

This is because all kinds of molestation occur to young women…. Why do not young men flirt with old women? Why is it young girls and young women who end up in brothels? Even if they [old women] doll themselves up, or dress up immodestly, nobody cares about it. There are so many points bearing wisdom in every command of God. *Veiling reduces prostitution and its instigation. It protects women from dangers.* (88; emphasis added)

These sentences are repeated in many novels in explaining the reason for women's veiling. Such an explanation implies that "women have to be veiled to avoid the male gaze in public spaces." It assumes that the "public sphere is under the domination of the male gaze" (Çınar 2005, 76). Veiling is presented as a requirement to protect the female body from danger and to ensure public morality, as the author of *Müslüman Kadının Adı Var* does. Through the mouth of Dilara, the author gives voice to the dominant Islamist discourse of the 1980s that frames women's visibility on the basis of communitarian morality. Notions of communitarian morality provide Islamists with a *habitus* around which not only collective identities are shaped but also an ideal Islamic society is built. Women's headcovering and conduct in such a frame are thought to constitute the basis of an idealized moral Islamic order.

Communitarian morality, which revolves around gender issues—i.e., women's headcovering and modesty—is central to Islamist politics' desire to differentiate itself from modernist liberal politics (Göle 1997a, 63). This also explains why policies and measures pertaining to gender relations are often the first to be introduced by Islamic regimes or demanded by oppositional Islamist movements (Taraki 1995, 644). This is because the position of women in an Islamic vision of the world expresses what an ideal Islamic society both fears—*fitne* (disorder)—and needs—order. It is generally women, with their "unveiled outlook" and "potential to seduce men," that arise as the source of *fitne* not only in Islamic novels but also in general Islamic discourse. In other words, *fitne* originates when women do not respect the boundaries of Islamic moral conduct provided with Islamic veiling. Veiling, as in the Dilara's accounts, is framed as the basis of Islamic moral codes and communitarian morality. The veiling of women, in other words, is represented as a major moral opponent against *fitne* and degeneracy.

What is interesting regarding the position of Islamist women is that in many academic and nonacademic works, Islamist women are represented as passive and submissive members of Islamist movements (Saktanber 1994, 103). What is implied in these works is that veiled women are subservient objects within an Islamic discourse that is shaped by a male vision, and it is true that the male voice was dominant in Islamic circles throughout the 1980s. In the case of *Müslüman Kadının Adı Var*, however, it is an Islamist woman novelist who posits Islamic headcovering and an Islamic framing of women as the basis of communitarian morality. She not only frames women in this way, but also conveys messages about the necessity of women's modesty and chastity for an ideal Islamic society. Therefore, it can be argued that it is a collective Islamic subjectivity in the 1980s that gave voice to Islamic discourse in a way that internally disallowed any politics of gender. Put differently, collective Islamism of the 1980s disregarded all particularities and differentiations regarding gender, class, or ethnicity within the Islamist movement. Muslim agents shared a common discourse based on the collective representations of Islamism and the role of women in ensuring communitarian morality.[23]

Islamic novelists, who frame women in terms of the morality of general society, also criticize the current secular order via women. In order to present an alternative vision of women as promoted by Islam, novelists portray modern society as it "exploits" women by turning them into a "commodity in the name of modernity." Katırcı Turhal depicts an image of women as promoted by secular conceptions of civilization:

Women have been made so cheap that advertisers use women when they are selling engine oil and tire. They exhibit women's bodies in addition to every kind of commodity. Women merchants worshipping the world have made our women modern slaves…. Women voluntarily adopted this captivity for the sake of some money they would make. And they called this equality, freedom and women's rights. But women have been mistaken. They have been enslaved in two ways. Women have begun working outside in order not to be under the command of their husband at home. This time however they became slaves of their professions and supervisors. Housework, children and their office work squeezed them almost to death. Women could neither become a perfect mother and wife nor a businesswoman. House and business life made women burn out. And children were carried to day nurseries early in the morning. They could neither see a cuddle of a mother nor the warmth of a house in a period when they needed both. And a new generation has grown up in unhappiness. What about unemployed men? An army of thousands of unemployed men with their jobs occupied by women, ... I think it will be very costly to the country. Unemployed fathers, burnt out mothers, street-trained children. (146)

This paragraph illustrates the way Islamic actors picture modern society and the position of women in it in the early years of the Islamic movements during the 1970s and 1980s. Katırcı Turhal challenges modern conceptions of equality and women's right to work outside the house that, according to her, signify the enslavement of women rather than their emancipation. She gives voice to a common Islamic discourse that posits modern society's burdening of women's shoulders with a double cross: housework and business life. Islamic discourse does not, however, let women choose from one of them. Rather it promotes a vision in which women are defined by their domestic roles. Women's domestic roles, as in the case of their veiling and chastity, are again related to the fate of the community. The cost of women's working lives is paid by unattended children and unemployed men, and thus by the whole social order.[24] In ensuring social order, women are relegated to the role of mother.[25]

This Islamic alternative vision of the position of women is based on a critique of "modern secular women." The opponents with whom novelists engage in a discursive struggle over the representation of women in contemporary Turkey are represented homogeneously as "feminists." Katırcı Turhal as a salvation novelist employs an alternative "feminist discourse" in order to differentiate the position of Islam on women. The title of her novel, Müslüman Kadının Adı Var (The Muslim Woman Has a Name) represents a challenge to another well-known book, *Kadının Adı Yok* (The Woman Has No Name), by liberal feminist Duygu Asena (1987). Asena's book was a major work from those women who, as "defiant daughters" of the older Kemalist generation, challenged the patriarchal framing of women by Kemalist circles and demanded substantive equality while expressing their will to control their own sexuality in the 1980s (Arat 1997 and 2000).[26] As Islamists take every opportunity to criticize the basic tenets of secular civilization and convey their Islamic messages, Katırcı Turhal's title, *Müslüman Kadının Adı Var* (The Muslim Woman Has a Name) signifies Islamists' criticism of secular and feminist conceptions of women. Katırcı Turhal presents the following criticisms throughout her novel:

> Now I ask those who deceive women in the name of the Modern Turkish Rights of Women:
> Does protection of women mean to display them like products that are shown to customers?
> Does it mean to push them to assume so many appearances, so they are slaves of fashion?
> Does it mean to abuse them day and night as mother, wife, and business women all at once in the name of freedom of women? Does it mean to make them lose their energy by imposing upon them work proper for men? [...]
> Those who want to protect women should first take care of these problems. Those who say that "the woman has no name" refer only to the woman who is annihilated in the world which they have produced. Those who say that woman has no name tell only their own story. (160)

This passage represents a re-narration of homogeneously perceived feminist discourse within an Islamist frame by a woman novelist.[27] The novelist attributes several qualities to feminists, such as being "slaves of fashion," in order to present her Islamic conception of women in contradistinction to feminism. She homogenizes feminists as her opponents and narrates the position of woman in feminist movements in compliance with the dominant collective assertions of Islamism of the 1980s. She claims that it is the modern and secular way of life promoted by feminism that has led to the destruction of women. Hence she invokes a language of "us" and "them" in line with a politics of the differentiation of Islamism. She constructs the Muslim woman's identity in response to her perception of feminist opponents. The following sentences represent the way feminism is perceived by Islamist actors of the period:

> Faithful women know that feminists who compete with men for superiority are chasing after illusions; faithful women are not interested in such unreasonable games. Those who claim superiority are those who are wretched people, ignorant of God's laws. (157–58)

Thus the author contributes to the '80s Islamist discourse on the role and status of women in Islam that has been shaped in response to what one Islamist writer calls the "modern egalitarianism" of Western modernity (Hatemi 1988). Specifically on the women question, Islamist writings of the 1980s by both male and female actors share a common position against, in their words, "equity feminism" (Abedin 1996), which they claim inevitably foregrounds hostility and antagonism as a necessary co-condition between the sexes. In feminism, according to Islamists, men and women are locked into adversarial positions and matched against each other in a "perennial gender structure" (Abedin 1996, 75). Feminism is sometimes identified as a "new brand of male chauvinism" since it puts a high value on the roles of providing financial support and achieving success in one's career, while devaluing, on the other hand, the domestic roles of women. Thus "egalitarian feminism," according to Islamic writers, denies the differentiation of male and female roles and demands a move toward a "unisex society" (Faruqi 1983) in which the empowerment of women could only be won on the battlefield of men's territory.

Islamist writers of the 1980s argue that Islam respects women's position by replacing the element of "power" with "responsibility" in gender relations within a framework of "mutual responsibilities." They claim that men and women should be defined with their distinct functions in a way that generates harmony and interdependence, not conflict. In other words, in the collectivist discourse of Islamism, men and women are placed in complementary positions that are regarded as the backbone of a "healthy" (Islamic) society (Hatemi 1988; Dilipak 1995).[28] Such a positioning is promoted not only by the intellectual works but also by the literary narratives of the period. Against a "feminist" claim—represented by Duygu Asena's title, *Kadının Adı Yok* (*Woman Has No Name*)—Katırcı Turhal replies in her title that *Müslüman Kadının Adı Var* (*The Muslim Woman Has a Name*). In Islam, she argues, the woman shares a complementary and harmonious position with men:

> Muslim women have always been there, since the creation of mankind for the first time. And they have always taken their places alongside their men.
>
> They have always stood shoulder to shoulder with men; they have struggled for the cause they believed.
>
> Our noble Lord who says that 'we created you as a pair of man and woman' described faithful women alongside faithful men as following: 'Faithful men are supporters of faithful women, and faithful women are supporters of faithful men.'
>
> God has identified their duties in the best manner, in accordance with their creation.
>
> A faithful woman knows the limits drawn by God, and she does not compete for superiority with her husband who is made superior to her by creation in some respects. Man and woman are halves of a whole. Neither can a man be without a woman, nor can a woman be without a man. (157)

Islamists assert that "full equality" between men and women will be reached only when the issue is understood as one of humanity. That men and women are equal in their humanity is recognized by an Islam that places on them equal rewards and duties in matters of faith. In terms of social roles and obligations, however, Islamists claim a division of labor to be the functional basis of an ideal society. In this division, because of natural or created differences, it is asserted that males in some matters are *primus inter pares* (first among equals) (Hatemi 1988, 32). In the above quotation, Katırcı Turhal gives voice to this dominant Islamist discourse and combats modern egalitarianism in the name of social functions based upon natural physiological and temperamental differences between the sexes. In this functional division of labor, what is primarily valued is the domestic role of women as mothers who would raise a "faithful generation." Far from *oppressed*, this line of argument paves the way for authenticating arguments that claim that the position and role of woman is *elevated* in "real Islam":

> In Islam woman is held with high esteem. Woman is one half of a whole, the other half of which is man … if today no scholars of high caliber emerge from Muslims, this is because there are no mothers who breed such scholars. [...]
>
> Muslim women are respectable ladies of warm and pure homes. Women may demand a fee in return to the housework they do. They also have the right to demand a servant. Of course if a Muslim woman does not ask for it, she will be given a greater reward by God. (145–47)

In *Müslüman Kadının Adı Var*, this promotion of domestic roles and the simultaneous rhetorical support given to Dilara to attend university to be a doctor may seem conflicting at first glance. At a rhetorical level, however, Islamist discourse of the 1980s involves assertions regarding the public roles of woman: "A woman can do anything she likes, including earning money. The money she earns belongs to her alone" (Dilipak 1995; Hatemi 1988). Furthermore, there are some occupations, such as those in the field of medicine, that are considered especially appropriate for women. This is caused by moral concerns that women need women doctors in an Islamist framework.

What is salient in the Islamism of the 1980s is the collective ideals that shape any individualistic or worldly demand.

Accordingly, education and occupation were framed within a collectivist discourse of Islamism in a way that made them merely a means for attaining greater Islamic ideals. Literary narratives address and critique every detail of gender convention and idiom within such a framework. As an outstanding example, toward the end of her novel, Katırcı Turhal speaks to young women as follows: "You, young girls.... You will demolish the idols of dowry. You should be the bride of Islam, not the brides of a piece of cloth" (151). One therefore has to become a "bride of Islam," "a mother of Islam," and "a doctor of Islam" to cure, as Islamism asserts, a morally degenerate society to pave the way for an ideal Islamic society.

Accordingly, both Dilara and Cihan indeed become "doctors for Islam"[29] via the process of acquiring a collective Islamic consciousness. The construction of social identity, however, requires more than the mere adoption of particular religious idioms. As theorists of social identity point out, social identity is never unilateral. Social identity "is primarily a matter of the stories people tell others about themselves, plus stories others tell those persons and/or other stories in which those persons are involved" (Whitebrook 2001, 4). It is not enough, in other words, to assert an identity. It must also be validated by other actors at an intersubjective level. Identity formation always involves a dynamic between "how we have been represented and how that bears on how we represent ourselves" (Hall and du Gay 1996, 4). This suggests that politicized identities in particular are continually negotiated via their challenging at an intersubjective level. Cihan declares that "he believes," and Dilara becomes a true believer with her Islamic veiling. But simultaneously they are now transformed into activists engaging in a struggle with their opponents in their process of constructing an ideal Islamic society. They are taught that Islam is not a religion limited to either the private or metaphysical realm. As Katırcı Turhal reminds the reader through Dilara, "Islam was a missionary religion. One who has learned it is obliged to inform the other. Islam would spread in this way" (45). Dilara and Cihan thus are led to adopt an

Islamist version of Islam that is reconceived by contemporary actors as a system of belief organizing all spheres of life. Islam is presented as the only solution whose message should be conveyed to all humanity. In sum, the plot of '80s Islamist novels always involves the transformation of westernized protagonists into Islamist actors struggling for collective salvation.

Islamic Identity in the Path
to Collective Salvation

Dilara adopts Islamic veiling in Kayseri where she spends her summer holiday. "Difficult days," however, begin for her when she decides to return to Ankara to get her diploma. She prepares herself for the task ahead by telling herself that "it was easy to live Islam here [in Kayseri], but now I will go to a different context" (77). Negotiation of her Islamic identity takes place in a big city, Ankara. This signifies an important dimension of Islamist movements: Islamist actors are urban actors, whose will it is to live in modern urban contexts and to participate in modern spaces. Accordingly, in contrast to several Islamic village novels of the pre-1980 period, the salvation novels of the 1980s narrate the struggle of Muslim characters in modern urban spaces. Large sections of the novels are constituted by narratives spelling out the sad stories of headscarved students who are not allowed to attend universities.[30] They narrate the tears and sufferings of Muslim characters, mostly headscarved girls, who are excluded from public life since veiling and whose practices are regarded as contrary to proper civility and ethics. Dilara, who is expelled from the dormitory and is not allowed to receive her diploma in the graduation ceremony, and Cihan, who is sent into exile in another city accused of "struggling for *sharia*" (203), typify such stigmatized and excluded Muslim characters.

Islamist novelists challenge these stigmatizing representations of Islamic identity and develop a positive identity through self-stereotyping. The first dimension of self-stereotyping appears in the presentation of Muslims as victims. The following titles of novels represent this situation: *Kurban* (*Victim*), *Ozyurdunda Garipsin* (*You Are a Stranger in Your Own Land*), *Senin İçin Ağlayacağım* (*I Will Cry for You*), *Şimdi Ağlamak Vakti* (*Now Is the Time to Weep*), *Bacımın Gözyaşları Ne Zaman Dinecek* (*When Will the Tears of My Sister End*), *Dinmeyen Gözyaşları* (*Unceasing Tears*), *Dokunmayın Bacıma* (*Do Not Touch My Sister*), *İşitilmeyen Feryat* (*Unheard Cry*), and so on.

Dilara is depicted as one of these victims of the age. She exemplifies Islamic figures who, as has been demonstrated by various ethnographic studies of the period, feel that they have not been treated as "equal" under Turkey's "secular democracy" (Houston 2001; Navaro-Yashin 2002). They feel that they are discriminated against and victimized because of their Islamic views or lifestyle. Dilara, as one of these Muslim agents, is depicted as having little space to realize her potential since headcovering is banned in schools and headscarved women are not allowed to carry out their professions in official institutions. The novelist portrays Muslim women in the context of this stigmatization as akin to "negroes in America or second class citizens due to the etiquette on their heads" (101).

What is striking here is that Dilara, in the foreword of the novel, is introduced to readers as one of thousands of girls with the same experience: "Dilara's disappointment as an honors degree student is lived and is still being lived by hundreds of thousands of girls in our country" (6). Salvation novels' forewords advise readers how to understand the novel they are about to read. Introducing their texts, novelists often state that the current story narrates the experiences of many believers or many veiled girls. In this sense, Islamic novels are collective stories that relay Muslim agents' stories by narrating the experiences of the social category to which they belong. The novels address Muslims by stating the following: "this is your story and you are not alone." Therefore they seek to emotionally bind Muslims who have the same experience so that they can overcome the sense of isolation, alienation and social stigma extended toward them by a repressive secular milieu. As collective stories, to use Richardson's terms, Islamic novels link separate Muslim selves into a "shared consciousness" and provide the basis for "collective action" (Richardson 1990, 9).

Nevertheless, the representation of this collective Muslim identity does not remain at an apologetic level centered on a discourse of being victimized. Muslim characters in salvation novels are turned into self-assertive personalities who speak with a language of pride reinforced by an Islamic collective idiom.[31] Dilara, as an "awakened" and "conscious" Muslim, begins to speak in a collective tone that endorses a politics of differentiation in her Ankara days. When she first encounters her classmates with her new identity, she is unable to decide whether to greet them in "their language" or as a "Muslim" (*Müslümanca*). Then she reminds herself the following:

> No compromise Dilara. Either all or nothing.... If you do not want to be a quasi-Muslim, then put Islam into practice completely. They spoiled Islam by discarding this and that aspect of it. Even your greeting is useless, if it is not in a manner proper to a Muslim. (102)

On committing to living Islam in every detail of her life, Dilara is made to engage in a discursive struggle with her friends and professors over the meaning of "being modern" and the position of religion in a contemporary age. Her friends and professors voice an oppositional discourse that labels her Islamic veiling "backward" or "not suitable for this age" (103). Dilara, in discussion with one of her mini-skirt-wearing friends, questions the meaning of "contemporary" (*çağdaş*) and of "being civilized," and asserts that, "indeed your [her opponents] style of dress seems to belong to the Middle Ages" (103). The authorial voice intervenes by declaring Dilara to be "more contemporaneous" than these "semi-naked" girls:

> Since it was the fashion, a few years ago, [Dilara too] wore a mini-skirt and put an overcoat on, nobody objected. What they did not like was the fact that she dressed up according to what God prescribed, but not the fact that

she followed what fashion prescribed. Indeed, the modern age and things like that were simply excuses. If whether one is civilized is decided on the basis of dressing manners, then she would be more modern. This is because those who go out half-naked were simply imitating people whom primary school books describe to be the people of the Stone Age.... So, *are not those who walk around half-naked more backward?* (98; emphasis added)

Apart from its very bad evolutionary anthropology, this passage exemplifies Islamists' endeavor not only to challenge secular narratives but also to make the terms of modernity and civilization their own. This aim necessarily brings Muslims into a contradictory situation with westernist agents, since the meaning of these terms is determined by their previous context of use. One common striking strategy of salvation novels is that the westernized female protagonist who is Islamized and veiled in the course of the narrative usually comes from a rich family or "high society."[32] In this sense Islamic novels challenge secular narratives that position headcovered girls as either of rural origin or lower class. The Islamization of rich, urbanite, and cultured girls asserts that the proposed Islamic way of life does not have an inherent conflict with modern identities per se, nor does it signify "backwardness" in any sense. Rather, novelists employ a progressive language. The Muslim woman is presented as modern, forward-looking, yet moral and authentic. Research on headcovered woman also demonstrates that they are careful not to be labeled as backward or narrow-minded. On the contrary, headcovered woman try to construct sociocultural practices that register modernity in a way that does not violate selected Islamic rules (Saktanber 1994). Islamic actors, including salvation novelists, assert that the headscarf does not constitute an obstacle to attending modern urban spaces or to studying modern science. Thus the "modern" emerges in Islamic narratives not merely as compatible with Islam but also as desirable for Islamic subjects. Not only in literary discourse, but also in many accounts of Islamists, headscarved girls appear as "modern *mahrem*" (the forbidden modern) (Göle 1999), signifying veiled girls' aims to selectively appropriate the products of modernity. Salvation novels in this sense represent the search of Islamist actors to develop a coherent "modern Islamic identity" in contrast to secular circles' representation of Islamists as "non-modern" and "backward."

In order to challenge the story that secular actors tell about Islam and Muslims, Islamist novelists stereotype secular characters as their opponents and engage in a discursive struggle with them from their own refracted angle. These opponents are represented by Dilara's professors in *Müslüman Kadının Adı Var*. Her professors are portrayed as characters who are not totally opposed to Islam or religious belief in general. Rather, they are depicted as belonging to a category of what we may call "Muslim Kemalists," a group who claims to believe in Islam, practices some of its prescriptions, yet argues that any public manifestation of Islam is contrary to secularism and modern civilization. One of Dilara's professors is made to identify her own position on Islam: "Look, we are Muslims too. I feast and have a memorial ceremony by reciting *mevlid* once a year. But you are exaggerating" (90). Another statement by a professor who tries to convince Dilara to unveil better clarifies how Islamist authors portray secular discourse on religion. This professor speaks to Dilara about her headscarf as follows:

> There is a big difference between the past and present. People have changed. Their lifestyles, needs and necessities are now different. What you wanted to do is a custom of a thousand and five hundred years ago. Look, are the laws of today the same as those of that epoch? Were there such faculties and universities at that time? Women could not even find a comb for their hair; they had to cover their hair in order to hide how bad it looked. Thanks to God, we too are Muslims, but we should think logically. We are in an age of space. It makes us really sorry that you make scientists like us busy with that kind of nonsense. (114)

This paragraph is indicative of the way Islamists "ventriloquize" the Kemalist conception of civilization. Professors are depicted as secular civilizers, products of the modernization of Turkey in the form of Westernization. They are not against Islam but promote an "enlightened version" of Islam in which religion is lived in private life and is not taken into the public sphere via symbols like the headscarf. The secular civilizing position of university professors is encapsulated by the statement of a professor when she sees headscarved girls at the university campus: "[As I see these veiled girls] I say let me gather these and give them a lecture on our religion" (113). Thus the secular opponents according to Islamist novelists are those who do not take a neutral stance on religion but rather adopt an active posture to "modernize" religion and Muslims. These opponents are made to adopt the basic claims of the secularization theses and an evolutionary perception of modernization that posits that the role of religious belief will decline as history progresses. Dilara's father, who is depicted as a secular professor of biology, exemplifies characters that were inculcated with such a modernist ideology. Katırcı Turhal sets up several scenes between Dilara and her father to delineate the positions of secularists and Islamists. A religious preacher, for instance, tells Dilara's father about the benefits of religious practice for the human body proven by scientific research and argues that "one day scientists will find out the virtues of Islam and all humanity will return to Islam." Surprised, the father is made to ask Dilara about the preacher's contention: "Science and religion? How could they come together?" Dilara replies:

Why not daddy? Science (*ilim*) is one of God's names. God is He who orders both science and religion. Is not intellect a blessing granted to human beings by God? Look, God did not ask children and madman to fulfill the commands of His religion. It means that religion addresses itself to human beings with intellect.... The old father was hearing such words for the first time. So far he has been taught that religion was a factor preventing progress. He has been provided with examples, always from Europe.... [He has been thinking that] when the European countries threw religion away, then they developed knowledge and science. Was not religion the opium of the people? (71–72)

The position of Dilara's father represents modern secular characters in contemporary Turkey who, according to Islamist novelists, have grown up on the basis of Western conceptions of civilization. This refers to a Kemalist "republican epistemology"[33] in which Islam was perceived as a phenomenon that should have been left behind, as the author spells out in the case of Dilara's father. Muslims in salvation novels, as mentioned above, are illustrated as victims of such a modernization process. However, the real victims for Islamists are those westernized/secular characters for whom modernization means imitating Europe. They are victims since they misunderstood modern civilization and are doomed to unhappiness upon expelling religion from their lives. These secular opponents appear as those who "base their reflections on appeals to science and reason alone," exclude the category of faith, and suffer from the "symptomatic illness" of Westernization (Meeker 1991, 192). Thus Dilara's father and her professor at the university are presented as those who need the true message of Islam. The category of secular opponents provides Islamists with a ground to negotiate identity at an intersubjective level.

The equation of civilization with Europe in the Kemalist imaginary leads Islamist novelists to develop an Islamic discourse against Kemalist perceptions of the universality of the West. This discourse involves an assertive claim for authenticity. Dilara's response to her secular professors, who are depicted as "being similar to the Middle Age's priests who were against science" (101), is a mirror image of claims to authenticity:

We would leave the West way behind us, if we ceased imitating the West and read the works of Muslim scholars. Why do we have no scholars who are respected around the world? Let me give you a few examples of your forefathers of whom you are embarrassed, so that you may acknowledge that I am right. It is Biruni, who is a Muslim scholar, who proved that the world revolves six hundred years before Galileo, and who counted the diameter of the world seven hundred years before Newton.

The person who drew the map of the moon for the first time is Ali Kuşçu, another Muslim scholar. It is Harzemi who has blazed a trail in Mathematics.... Those who, for the first time, made cancer surgery and who discovered the cure of leprosy and that the plague is contagious are Muslim scholars. (117)

This passage exemplifies the Islamist position that posits that it is not because of Islam but because of a misconception of modern civilization by secular actors that Turkey (and the Muslim world) is today behind the West. Secular characters, as Dilara's father in the novel, are made to treat Islam as if it was similar to the Christianity of Europe. They compare Islam to "the religion of Europe which was old and distorted."[34] They misread Europe where Christianity, as Islamist actors argue, was considered an obstacle for development, and thus imported a secular modernization with its exclusionary stance on religion. Islamist actors argue that Islam should not be compared to other religions since Islam is the only undistorted alternative to the disruption of the Western modernity. This is because, as Islamist intellectual Ali Bulaç argues, Asian religions such as Buddhism, Shintoism, and Confucianism did not resist the West, while "modernized" Christianity and Judaism could not provide an alternative for the emancipation of the world. Islam, on the other hand, is still a strong alternative with its rich cultural, scientific, and artistic background, and more importantly with its "undistorted authentic sources" (Bulaç 1990, 25).

Islamic actors claim to derive the solution based on Islam's "authentic sources" from the Islamic historical past. This historical past is invariably limited to the period of *Asr-ı Saadet*, the time of the Prophet and four Caliphs, in the discourse of many Islamic groups of the 1980s. It is, however, extended sometimes to include the Ottoman period by Islamic salvation novelists. Both cases, however, involve a claim to authenticity through which Islamic actors invoke historical figures and practices, and present them as models for the present and future.

Islamic claims to authenticity, as Al-Ahmeh notes, involve "references to past events" that imply that they are "repeatable" since they are still "somehow alive at the core of the invariant historical subject" (Al-Azmeh 1993, 56).[35] This claim to authenticity characterizes the fundamentalist nature of Islamism that suggests that Islam's virtues derive from its fundamentals. The employment of authentic language provides Islamists with a sense of strength and pride as well as a "firm ground" to challenge collectively the secular narratives of civilization. It endows "Muslims with a collective identity that works critically against both traditional subjugation of Muslim identity and monocivilizational impositions of Western modernity" (Göle 2000, 93).

The rhetoric of authenticity signifies not only Islamic actors' will to revive the past as a model for the present and the future, but also to question the boundaries of a secular/westernist project of modernity. In other words, Islamist actors challenge secular impositions and boundaries with their aspirations to attend modern institutions and urban spaces with their Islamic values, practices, and outlook. Dilara, in this sense, represents a category of veiled girls who make their way into the spaces of modernity and strive to acquire a public visibility. She defiantly objects to her stigmatization and exclusion as follows: "As if God does not exist in state buildings. If you are veiled, either you would stay at home or you would do lower grade jobs like being a doorkeeper or maidservant" (101). Therefore what characterizes Islamic identity is not a withdrawal but a will to participate in the modern world collectively and critically (Göle 2000, 98). Dilara is depicted as one of those critical Muslim agents by the authorial voice, who warns her opponents that these Muslims will increase in numbers in the struggle for Islam as follows: "They should know this well.... Dilaras, Ayşes, Fatmas will increase in numbers. They will become legion ... and the girls of this country, who were silent and did not see Islam's light, will awaken from their sleep one by one" (147).

The author turns Dilara into a character who struggles to convey the message of Islam to other girls and thus to "increase them in number." She is depicted as a role model with her Islamic way of life that is represented as totally different from ordinary people in its every detail. After her graduation Dilara rents an apartment in Ankara. The author conveys her message through Dilara's mind about how a house and a woman in an Islamic frame should be:

Dilara wanted to furnish her house as she dreamed. She did not want to be a slave to the furniture. She did not want to serve the furniture but wanted it to serve her. What strange bookshelves covering the whole walls, huge armchairs for one person, tables, lampshades, sofas.... Poor women with dustclothes in their hands were servants of their furniture. (132)

Similar descriptions of the ideal house signifying an Islamic politics of distinction are also maintained by the non-literary texts of Islamism in the 1980s (Şenlikoğlu 1993). These ideal houses are usually imagined as spaces where Islam is studied together with friends or neighbors on the way to collective salvation. In Dilara's case it is her school friends who are made to visit Dilara in her new apartment. Her friends who do not tolerate her new veiled Islamic identity on the university campus are later led to visit Dilara's house where Dilara reads the Koran and explains the basic issues of Islam to them. The author depicts the scene as follows:

Girls who used not to get out of the disco and who tolerated alcoholic drinks, cigarettes and all kind of weakness have now made this place [Dilara's house] their resort. But they were no longer those girls as they were in the past. They were reciting the Koran, studying Islamic history and debating important issues. Every session was a source of pleasure for them, opening new horizons for their empty souls. (144)

The author, as is common toward the end of all salvation novels, prepares the ground for everyone to adopt an Islamic way of life and thus imagine a collective salvation. Before achieving this salvation, however, novelists aim to resolve several issues relating Islam and modernity. One crucial issue that emerges is the relation between faith and science. Excluded from the university because of her headscarf, Dilara is made to convey her message to the girls in her house that veiling and studying science do not conflict. The modern Muslim is presented as one who seeks both: "Veiling is one of God's definite commands. Seeking knowledge is also obligatory. Can a Muslim exercise discretion between these two commands of God? A Muslim should struggle to observe both of them, this is what *jihâd* is" (78). The term *jihâd*, which is often associated with Muslim extremism and violent terrorist attacks in the current global agenda, is presented by the author as an Islamic duty to seek knowledge of science without renouncing an Islamic outfit and identity. Her conception of this idealized Islamic identity involves a coexistence of Islam and science. Thus she encourages veiled girls with a collective language, stating that "girls were resolute. They wanted to observe both of God's commands: SCIENCE (İLİM) AND VEILING" (147; capitals original).

This passage is indicative of Islamists' challenge toward the secular narratives of civilization that are accused of endorsing an inherent conflict between science and religion. In rejecting the stigmatizing representations that secularists have of Muslims, conscious Muslim characters in novels argue that their beliefs and visibilities are not an obstacle to the study of *ilim*. Their preference for *ilim*, rather than the republican term for science, *bilim*, however, signifies their intention to appropriate modern science in Islamic terms. The term *ilim* derives from Arabic and has Islamic connotations, in contrast to *bilim*, which refers to modern secular science as adopted by secular circles.[36] This term signifies Islamist agents' attempt to discredit secularism, the ideology which aligns itself with faith in reason (Toprak 1993, 247). What Islamists do, in other words, is to draw a limit to secular rationality in their search for harmony between faith and science.

This example also illustrates that Islamic novels engage in struggle with secular idioms. Islamic novels in this sense are narratives of conflict. A narrative of conflict serves a double function for social movements: It allows the members of a social movement to identify an "opponent," while simultaneously aiding members to establish a shared identity and a sense of "we-ness" among themselves (Steward et al. 2002, 125). Islamic novels as narratives of conflict serve both to identify "opponents," while their discourse of "we-ness" plays a significant role in constructing ideological boundaries for the Islamic collective identity. "We-ness" or collective Muslim identity, is represented by conscious Muslim characters, such as Dilara and Cihan, who reappropriate religion and revive it via the claim to authenticity, and convey Islamic messages to people.[37]

It is not, however, easy for Islamic characters to narrate Islam to the masses because such speech, as novelists depict, is considered a threat to the republic. Cihan, for instance, is exiled to a small town since he is accused of conveying Islamic messages and criticizing the existing order. Invariably, toward the end of salvation novels, authors depict Muslim protagonists as "conferencing characters" that allow the authors to convey their messages more directly to readers. This is a general strategy of Islamist authors since depicting characters as "conferencing" provides them with a device to write monologues that last for pages. Conversation thus disappears at the end of novels. The authorial voice is heard more as omnipresent narrators. In this vein, Günbay Yıldız turns Cihan into a character lecturing to the masses on critical issues such as the role of Islam in modern world, the meaning of modernity, and the dangers of foreign ideologies (like materialism) for youth. The author devises several scenes that allow Cihan to make public speeches. One day, for instance, while he sits in a café with some people from the town, a young man talks to an old man in a condescending and indecent manner. Cihan is asked to comment on the behavior of such young people. The author thus creates a chance to preach on the plight of youth and degeneration of current Turkish society:

> Is not it we who cut their [youngsters'] links with their traditions, customs and moral bases? I was like them until recently.… I lived in a vacuum and I am now living in exile since my parents have not done their duties properly. We should provide our children with firm ground.… [Our ancestors] were powerful since they never let the fear of God disappear from their hearts. What about now? The sick mentality of this age began with fostering godless generations. Fathers disrespected their ancestors and sons disrespected their fathers. Nations that lose their moral values are no different from ships without a captain. (202)

This paragraph constitutes an introduction to the main character's long conference in which he speaks in detail on the problems of modern society. In the last scene, the author makes Cihan give a conference whose subject, as he says, is "the illness our age has fallen in." He continues, "I am going to talk about the swamp our time has sunk into and about our humanity that has been led to a state of aimlessness. And most importantly I will talk about youth" (286). Following his introduction he makes his main point that "religion has gone bankrupt for youth." He portrays current youth as those who have fallen into "meaninglessness" because of "this de-civilized age." He presents his diagnosis as follows:

> If they tried a scientifically approved educational system which also respects religion, if respectable figures constructed ideas of nationality and fatherland, and if ruined foundations were replaced by new ones, then the youth would be a stronghold and would protect itself from anarchy.
>
> Unfortunately, some young people, seeking to serve the country, are not even aware of the fact that they pursue the same cause as the betrayers, since they are unbelievers.…

Certainly, the youth, whose spiritual bonds are cut off, despise themselves.... If we do not respect the religion and beliefs of this country's people.... then we become destined to remain an unimportant society. (286–87)

Günbay Yıldız's messages are not limited to the importance of religious values. He also warns youth about what he calls dangerous "foreign ideologies." One of his topics is Marxism as a "doctrine that led the world to destruction":

For Marx, there is no place for possessions.... For Marx, religion is opium. For Marx, a housewife is an ornament with illness.... For Marx, love for offspring does not exist.... Before all else it was necessary to criticize religion in order to reform societies. He said, "Man created religion, and religion did not create man." Exterminating religion is a prerequisite in order for people to attain true happiness. (287)

Günbay Yıldız—as part of the first generation of novelists who experienced the political conflicts of the pre-1980 period between rightist and leftist groups—often directs his criticism toward Marxism in his novels. To this end, he presents a simplified and caricaturized interpretation of Marxism. What he takes as a measure for his criticism of Marx is again a religious vision of the world to which, he stresses, Marx was hostile. At the end of his speech, he warns youth not to be "seduced" by foreign ideologies (besides Marxism, Zionism is also often cited), but to rely on the true message of Islam. What is emphasized at the end of the novels, therefore, is that Islam is a solution to all malaises of the modern age. The problem as enunciated by novelists is not Islam but de-Islamization in the name of modernity that led to the plight of the current society. In this regard Muslims should struggle to narrate to people the goodness of Islam. Messages of salvation novels are encapsulated by the dominant motto of Islamists of the 1980s: "Peace is in Islam."

As with Cihan, Dilara also transforms into an activist aspiring to convey the message of Islam to people. What is common in both cases (and in the salvation novels of the period), is that Islam not only defines Islamic identity, but also constitutes the only way to salvation for everyone. Inflamed by such a preconception, Dilara, who begins to work as a pediatrician in a hospital, is not satisfied merely performing her occupation. She continually thinks of new ways to serve Islam and humanity. She begins to develop "ways of raising children according to Islam" (18). This is because Dilara

> came to believe that every pediatrician must know the character of their [children's] soul as much as they know how their bodies function. She understood that to cure their body was not sufficient, unless it is accompanied with filling up their spiritual void by addressing their souls. (138)

She begins to address "empty souls" of children coming to the hospital for their physical illness. She asks them the following:

> —Tell me little kid, do you believe in God?
> —Yes.
> —Can we see Allah?
> —No.
> —Why? … No answer, this is because Allah has not been taught to and settled in the heart of this child.
> Dilara explains the existence of Allah by using analogy of microbes and goes on to narrate the following:
> —Then where shall we learn about our creator?
> —No answer.
> —From Koran that Allah sent us, from nature and our Prophet….
> —Now, will you promise me that you will take medicine I will prescribe for you and learn that book [Koran]? (139)

Dilara's enthusiasm to explain Islam to her patients exemplifies the socially committed and authoritarian position of Islamists who think that Islam should permeate every sphere of life. In other words, they know the "good life" and impose it on others. According to this vision of the "good life," it is necessary to live Islam in every detail and to indoctrinate it in youth since "the children, who have grown uninformed about Islam, would become either anarchists or form masses of people who had no interests except eating and drinking" (140). Therefore, precisely as these novels do, it is claimed that the Islamic message, in every instance, should be conveyed to humanity.

In the dominant Islamic discourse of the 1980s, Islam is seen as the basis of every social act, social relation, vocation, and imagination. Islamists are firm in their assertion that "they have the solution." This is also valid for Islamist novelists. As one of them states: "Many philosophers, writers and thinkers searched for the answers to questions such as 'where do we come from? Why are we living? And where are we going?' We have found the answers of these questions…. We are narrating these in our novels" (Aksoy and Kaplan 1997). The answer is clearly spelled out by another novelist as follows: "It is Islam that determines the only true and perfect way of life" (Aksoy and Kaplan 1997).

Islamic novels narrate the realization of this "true way of life" through the privileged, dominant voice of novelists as third person commentators. Islamist authors have a clear "authority" over the meaning of what has been written. In this regard, Islamic novels are what Kristeva calls "bounded texts" (Kristeva 1980). This is to say that before Islamist novelists put pen to paper and set down the first word, they know what the last word will be and almost where the last word will fall.

All salvation novels conclude with similar scenes in which not only westernized characters (like Cihan and Dilara) but also their close circles (fathers, mothers, and friends) are blessed with the true message of Islam. These characters (for instance, the fathers of both Cihan and Dilara) are made to immediately question their beliefs (as a result of their interaction with Muslim protagonists) and to adopt Islamic idioms. Such a fixed happy ending explains why these novels are identified in Islamic circles as "salvation novels." Happy endings involve the message that salvation, being Muslim, and living an Islamic way of life bring peace and happiness to newly converted protagonists. Accordingly, at the end of *Boşluk* and *Müslüman Kadının Adı Var*, Cihan meets the pious character Tuba who had rejected his proposal before and marries him, whereas Dilara is rewarded by going to Mecca during *hajj* as a doctor where she receives a marriage proposal from İbrahim.

The marriages at the end of novels, however, are not only depicted as scenes in which individual characters receive happiness. Rather, novelists emphasize that they are "ideological marriages" in the service of collective salvation. Dilara, for instance, thanks God when she receives her marriage proposal and thinks that the following:

> O my God, thanks be to you, please make our marriage good for Islam. You granted me a life companion who will accompany me during my struggle for your cause. Let this house, which is being established, be a source for generations of hope, which will grow. Let Mus'abs and Zaynabs grow up. (156)

This representation of Dilara's marriage encapsulates the dominant Islamist vision of the world in which love and marriage do not simply refer to a relationship between two persons but are conceived of as a reflection of ideological commitment to religion.[38] This emphasizes that Islamic collective ideals should be prioritized over individual desires and taken as the measure in constructing every aspect of life.

Islamic novels in this regard are closed texts with identical narrative closures. Narrative closure is one of the most significant elements of the narrative through which "the events of the story become fully intelligible to the reader" (Belsey cited by Webster 1990, 55). By their very form, all narratives involve a conclusion. The nature of the ending, however, varies from apparently open to unresolved or ambiguous. The ideological dimension of Islamic novels in this sense is once more displayed by their overt narrative closure in which collective

salvation is achieved. The common closure of these novels signifies the "completion" which Islamism as an ideological system of thought aspires to have. In sum, the narrative closure of
Islamic novels mirrors the Islamic ideal of the collective transformation of society.

The Concrete Performances of Salvation Novels on the Path to Collective and Epic Islamism

I have been arguing that there are close relations between the salvation novels of the 1980s and the social and political processes of the period in which they are embedded. These Islamic narratives can be seen, to use Zeraffa's terms, as a "language bespeaking society as much as spoken by society" (1973, 38). In this way, society (and thus history) enters the salvation novel not in a transparently reflected sense but in a refracted way. The novels' thematization and representation of Islam, modernity, secularism, and related social actors in contemporary Turkey is not, in Lehtonen's terminology, a "transparent reproduction," but a "symbolically coded reconstruction" (2000, 13) of various material, social, political, economic, and subjective aspects of life.

Indeed, the interaction between novels and "real life" does not take shape as a simple representational reflex of life within the novel, but instead involves a struggle for the configuration and reconstruction of it by creating a symbolic dimension of its own. Literature, in this sense, does not only refigure society but also takes part in its formation. It is affected by processes operating in economic, political, and cultural fields while simultaneously influencing these very processes.[1] The meanings generated by the novel as a literary genre, thus, have social influence, political consequences, and cultural power. The literature of nationalism, in this sense, provides rich evidence that there is a direct link between "nation and narration" (Bhabha 1990).[2] Benedict Anderson has shown that the national consciousness is something that is "imagined" through political and cultural projects. The novel, as he notes, has played an important role in the nation-formation processes as cultural artifacts interpreting experiences and presenting new subject positions. The time and space of the modern nation, according to Anderson, is embodied in the narrative culture of the realist novel that functioned for the legitimization of national identities (1991). Novels (in the form of national identity narratives) are special cases of "group defining story" (Feldman 2001, 18) that provide a framework through which national ideologies and personal autobiographies gain shape and meaning. Viewed this way, literature has a "concrete performance" (Eagleton 1996, 179) with its capacity to transgress restrictions, to imagine identities, and to search for possibilities of action and options of agency.[3] What are, then, the "concrete performances" of Islamic salvation novels?

The Islamic salvation novels of the 1980s, with their main plot revolving around Islamic and westernized visions of the world represented by Islamic and secularist/westernized characters, signify a new arena for the cultural politics of Islamism. These novels form a "discursive literary movement"[4] based on an ideology of representation deriving from and contributing to the production of a broader Islamist discourse. Via these novels, Islamist writers challenge the modernization process of the Republican period that, in their words, led to the negative stigmatization and exclusion of Muslim agents at the same time as it paved the way for the rise of a "materialistic," "immoral," and "degenerate" civilization. The salvation novel, as a genre emerging in the 1980s, represents a renewed questioning of the secular narratives of Kemalist modernization through a literary medium.[5]

Whitebrook suggests that not only persons but also political bodies or regimes construct narratives to order and explain themselves. Order for both persons and political regimes depends upon their telling a coherent story. Any political order, in this sense, needs to tell a "compelling story" to convince the "readers" and to establish its identity. The legitimacy of political order is provided by this "storytelling." To ensure a valid legitimacy, the story must be credible and listeners should understand the connection of events in the story (Whitebrook 2001, 135–40). Viewed this way, the political language of the Kemalist project of modernity can be reconsidered in narrative terms. The framing device of the dominant secular narrative of civilization is formed around a conflict between modern Western and Islamic values. The Kemalist elite claimed the universal validity of Western modernity as the way to build modern Turkey. Kemalist modernization based its will to civilize on populism, nationalism, and secularism—in the process producing new boundaries, and excluding and marginalizing Islamic identity (Keyman 1995). On the way to modern civilization, Islamic values—those that condition the way people dress or organize their daily lives—were recounted as a retrograde force that must be left behind. In other words, the narrative of Turkey's secular political regime assigned a "threatening" role to the public assertion of Islam that must always be kept under control.[6]

The rise of Islamist movements in the 1980s and their challenge to the project of modernization/westernization reveal that Turkey's secular democratic political regime could not sustain a mutually understandable and credible narrative for some of its Muslim subjects anymore.[7] In this context, the appearance of Islamic novels, as a site of struggle over the definition of civilization and Islam, can be apprehended as an act of telling new stories by Islamist subjects based on their criticism of the hegemonic secular narratives of civilization. What Islamist novelists aspire for, then, is a re-narration of the process of civilization. They do so by situating their narratives within the larger narrative of civilization, and by attempting to re-narrate the past and present of Turkey, as well as the political context in which they live.

Islamist novelists, then, give historicity and relationality to their narratives while seeking to order and impose a new pattern on events. What distinguishes the narrative forms of salvation novels from mere description is that they involve the arrangement of events, time, and characters in a particular order. They go beyond description to shape and order events through the eyes of Islamist narrators. Islamist novelists, as narrators, define and connect the events, and thus impose an alternative structure on the world.[8] The novel as narrative[9] emerges in Islamic circles not only as a literary form but as an important means of making sense of Muslims and their milieu. This contention assumes an analogy/correspondence between the constituent features of novels and the narrative construction of life. Put differently, the novel's dialogical nature, orchestration of events and themes, and arrangement of spatial and temporal material suggest a certain parallelism with the basic characteristics of the narrative construction of a life. This is because people make sense of the world by integrating events in a temporal and sequential plot. Human beings link events surrounding themselves narratively and organize their experiences into temporally meaningful episodes and stories.

Underpinning these contentions is a claim that people understand their lives in the form of a narrative that provides them with the means to order events with a beginning and an end (Benhabib 1996; MacIntyre 1984; Taylor 1992).[10] People construct their identities through narratives since the construction of a stable identity entails telling a story and thus ordering and imposing a pattern of oneself in the world. Subjects, as Taylor argues, determine the direction of their lives inescapably in a narrative form that allows them to understand who they are and how they became so. As he puts it, "making sense of one's life as a story is also, like an orientation to the good, not an optional extra; … our lives exist also in this space of questions which only a coherent narrative can answer. In order to have a sense of who we are, we have to have a notion of how we have become and of where we are going" (1992, 47). Similarly, MacIntyre suggests that "we all live out narratives in our lives … because we understand our own lives in terms of narratives" (1985, 208–12).[11] Human life for MacIntyre involves a narrative unity within which humans attempt to make rational choices concerning the conflicting demands of different practices.[12] The narrative, in this sense, is the basic condition and essential genre for human beings to be able to make sense of themselves in relation to others and surrounding contexts.

Islamic salvation novels can be conceptualized as narratives representing the longing of Islamist actors to develop a coherent sense of self in the relational context of modern Turkey. They provide information on how Islamist actors contemplate their own and others' lives and actions since these narratives emerge as an activity with direct relationship to political processes—specifically the process of modernization in the form of westernization. Through salvation narratives, Islamist novelists aim to impose a new order and a meaning to events that took place—and that still surround them presently—in this process of modernization. Islamist authors, to use Bakhtin's terminology, orchestrate various voices in the social and historical context of Turkey in a way that displays their goals and intentions in a web of social relationships. They have political implications, since narrating endows the agent with the quality of having a point of view in relation to listeners in a certain public setting.

The Islamic stance adopted by the novelists and the messages conveyed by the salvation novels of the 1980s are indicative of a dominant Islamist understanding of the period that was polemical and oppositional to Western and Kemalist narratives of civilization. Islamist novelists aimed not only to cope with negative representations of Muslim identities, but also to present new ways of being Muslim on the basis of representative ideal Islamic characters. The novel, in other words, is employed by Islamists as a discursive strategy not only to combat the negative effects that, they believe, are produced by secular narratives, but also to imagine and form new social relations, gender roles, and emotions.

The Quest for a New Repertoire
of Action and Emotion for
Islamists through the Novel

On the basis of their promotion of ideal Muslim identities, it can be argued that Islamic salvation narratives do not only organize the symbolic fabric of social life around the negotiation of Islamic and Western lifestyles, but are also formative of identities, social relations, gender roles, and emotions. The Islamic identities promoted by fictional narratives signify the endeavor of Islamists to form new (young) Muslim subjects that "have been excluded from modernist [Western] definitions of civilization and history-making" (Göle 1996, 26). Novel writing, in novelists' words, is construed as an important means to provide the young generation with knowledge and orientation, so they might be able to play an active role in the making of history. Günbay Yıldız, who says that he writes his novels for youth, stresses that,

> [This is] because they need to be raised decent and honest. This is because milestones (*işaret taşları*) in this society have been removed and youngsters are running to a tragic end through roads without signs. I am trying to demonstrate the places of removed milestones. (Aksoy and Kaplan 1997)

The analogy of revealing milestones in this quote is reminiscent of the title of Sayyid Qutb's *Milestones* (1990), which had a great influence on Muslim youth in the 1980s. This analogy is also indicative of the assertive claims of Islamists who posit that they know "the truth" that needs no claim to legitimacy. Literary narratives, in this vein, appear as a means to convey this "absolute truth," or, the Islamic vision of the world, to the young generation in order to lead the whole of humanity to the "true path of Islam."

Several writings in Islamic and non-Islamic journals demonstrate that Islamic salvation novels do in fact resonate with their "implied readers,"[13] Muslim youthes. According to a survey, these salvation novels are widely read by students in Koran courses, *imam hatip* (religious high schools), and university youthes (Şişman 2001, 66). Fatma Karabıyık Barbarosoğlu, a novelist-sociologist who conducted the survey, notes that these novels are especially widely read among girls. Students revealed that these novels were given to them by their fathers and brothers. Barbarosoğlu contends that Islamic novels present those girls living in enclosed circles with an important "public sphere experience" (Şişman 2001, 66). This suggests that through novels, young readers come across characters that they would never be in contact with otherwise and internalize the answers developed by Islamist protagonists on certain controversial issues. In this sense, salvation novels, through their easily read popular forms, function as educational material as much as artistic products. This also conforms to the perception of literature by novelists themselves who constantly state that their aim is to convey Islamic messages via novels. The authorial intervention that becomes explicit at the end of novels, as exemplified in *Müslüman Kadının Adı Var* and *Boşluk*, serves directly to provide young readers with schematic answers regarding the position of women, polygamy in Islam, "foreign ideologies" like Marxism, and the mission of Muslim youth. Islamic novels, in other words, present "mass production dialogues on potentially conflictual subjects" (Şişman 2001, 60).

Viewed this way, Islamic salvation narratives should be understood not only as a linguistic activity but also as a medium that provides Muslims with answers on practical matters, helps constitute the individual's perception of self, other and social context, and provides a ground for the comprehension of non-fictional reality. Because the novel contains our attempts to imagine and assess possibilities for ourselves and to ask how we might choose to live, it is inseparable from philosophical content and integral to any adequate conception of ethical and political reasoning. The novel thus emerges as an important event in searching for the fundamental question of "how should one live?" (Nussbaum 1992, 95). In the context of Islamic salvation novels, it can be argued that they contribute to the understanding of ethical questions by giving expression to more complex and concrete features of the lives of Islamic actors and by enunciating ethical concepts like duty, rights, and obligations.

The novel's peculiarity in expressing the practical features of life leads Nussbaum to argue for the supplementing of abstract philosophical attempts at self-understanding with concrete narrative fictions.[14] She thus considers novels to be valuable sources of information about the practical as follows:

> for novels, as a genre, directs us to attend to the concrete; they display before us a wealth of richly realized detail, presented as relevant for choice … [and] they speak to us: they ask us to imagine possible relations between our own situations and those of the protagonists, to identify with the characters and/or the situation, thereby perceiving those similarities and differences. In this way their structure suggests, as well, that much of moral relevance is universalizable. (Nussbaum 1992, 95)[15]

Salvation novelists explicitly invite their readers through in-text messages or introductions of novels to relate their experience with that of protagonists. By narrating the experiences of a social identity to which Muslim youthes belong, Islamic novels tell them—as the title of a salvation novel notes—that "You are not Alone (*Yalnız Değilsiniz*)." Islamic novels give readers the sense that Muslim characters live similar experiences to them and vice versa. Thus literary narratives serve as an important means of communication within a social category, i.e., Islamic circles. Literary communication, as McDuffie notes, "is achieved not through a face-to-face relationship between author and beholder, but over spatiotemporal distance, through intermediary text" (1998, 102). Therefore Islamic novels can be understood as intermediary texts linking Muslim subjects living in different parts of Turkey (and the world).

They emotionally bind people who have similar experiences and face similar problems.

Literature for Muslim subjects, as Nussbaum explains, "is an extension of life not only horizontally, bringing the reader into contact with events, or locations or problems he or she has not otherwise met, but also ... vertically, giving the reader experience that is deeper, sharper, and more precise than much of what takes place in life" (1992, 48). In their linking of Muslims horizontally and vertically, novels not only provide Muslims with prearranged answers to which they can give their assent, but also evoke certain emotions. Emotions, as Nussbaum notes,

> are not feelings that well up in some natural and untutored way from our natural selves ... they are in fact, not personal and natural at all ... they are, instead, contrivances, social constructs. We learn how to feel, we learn our emotional repertoire. We learn our emotions in the same way that we learn our beliefs—from our society. But emotions, unlike many of our beliefs, are not taught to us directly through propositional claims about the world, either abstract or concrete. They are taught, above all, through stories. (1992, 287)

Therefore Islamic stories can be taken as one of the important sources in the construction of the emotional repertoire of Islamism.[16] This is because novels speak about Muslims, their lives, choices, and emotions within a web of social relations in a secular context. Novels represent the emotions of "conscious Muslims," their feelings of being victimized and excluded. Yet more important than this, Islamic narratives aim to evoke certain emotions in the reader. In other words, they not only record emotions that are claimed to be experienced by a social category of Muslims, but also serve to construct and promote an emotional strategy that paves the way for the rise of an assertive Islamic identity. Shared emotions, like anger toward antagonists or the common grievances expressed by novels, hold a key place in developing collective movement identities.

Novels, in other words, serve an important task in expressing, or formulating, emotions that in turn help to identify antagonists, create a collective consciousness, and set ideological boundaries (Steward et al 2002, 125–30). Islamic salvation novels that both express the sorrowful stories of headscarved actors or of excluded male characters, and promote an idealized assertive Islamic character, participated in a significant way in the formation of the ideological boundaries of collective Islamism. Salvation novels, in other words, provided Islamist agents with a space in which emotions are transposed and perceptions are reconstructed and constituted as they organize events, characters, and actions in a narrative form. In the face of problems that Muslims experience within a secular context, Islamist novelists told Muslim youthes through narratives—as Katırcı Turhal does through Dilara in *Müslüman Kadının Adı Var*—that "you should not make concessions"; "you should keep on your struggle in the way of Islam"; "all goodness lies in Islam and the Islamic way of life"; and "you should have a feeling of pride since you will be the winner at the end." Based on such premises, Islamic novels teach not only forms of life but also forms of feeling.

In stirring up feelings of pride and (expected) success, novelists regularly assert that the stories of salvation novels are lived out not by individual characters but by many actors sharing the same collective experiences. Therefore they insistently and consistently aim to confirm Muslims' sense of collective identity. In novels of the period actors are made to acquire an Islamic consciousness, and are transformed into collective actors speaking with a language of "we" in a way that overcomes feelings of isolation in the current order and links Muslim actors into a shared consciousness for collective action. Collective representations serve as "scaffolding" for Islamists to construct a positive collective Islamic identity. One of the major framing devices in constructing a positive identity is the emphasis put on collective ideals in transforming the society as a whole. To achieve this end, all Muslim actors are required to give up their worldly pleasures for the sake of this collective ideal. Novelists legitimize this situation by often resorting to Koranic verses and sayings of the Prophet to stress that "this is what Islam dictates."

The construction of a discourse around certain key principles of Islam has sometimes been interpreted in a way that paves the road to an essentialist understanding of Islamism, thus overlooking emerging Muslim subjectivities. Based upon Islamist novelists' frequent references to "God's laws" or "divine law," Dilek Doltaş argues that "political Islamist novelists search for neither an identity nor a cultural background. What they search for is the characteristics of an identity and culture of an imaginative ideal society (that they call *Asr-ı Saadet*, age of happiness) … on the basis of the dictates of fundamentalist Islam" (2001, 23). This interpretation is indicative of essentialist accounts of Islamism that attribute to the Islamist social movements a permanent or fixed political language and practice by which Muslim selves are determined. Such an approach interprets Islamists' recourse to textual sources, as in the case of Islamic novels, in a way that implies that "Muslims do not re-imagine and rearticulate what it means to be a Muslim in rapidly developing societies but only *act on* fixed Islamic principles" (Yavuz 2003, 16). Therefore this approach is blind to the issue of agency since it apprehends Islam as a system of belief that leaves no autonomy for subjectivity.

How, then, can Islamists' invoking of divine law (*sharia*) to make sense of the Muslim self and notions of subjectivity be understood? In other words, if "becoming an Islamist involves a consciously willed conformity to a law formulated outside oneself" (Houston 2004, 31), how can the notion of subjectivity apply to an Islamist? Put differently, how can a Muslim subjectivity arise in the context of an Islamist politics that aspires to introduce religious law whose basic precepts are claimed to be bestowed by God? Searching for the space of autonomy where Muslim subjectivity lies, Houston draws attention to the nature of *sharia*, which, for Muslims, besides its undebatable basic precepts, involves revisable concepts that allow for continuous reinterpretation. This suggests that divine law is not only constituted by divine texts but also involves a "humanly produced and elaborated *sharia*." In other words, it is the "unfinished character of *sharia* jurisprudence" and the acceptance of its mutability by human legal innovation that open up a space for a new reinterpretation of Islam (Houston 2004, 33). Islamism in this respect signifies a re-articulation of Islam by the new actors of Islamism in the 1980s. God's laws, as Islamist novelists state, are specific interpretations of Islamic laws by new Muslim subjectivities in the context of the 1980s. Islamic novels that emerged synchronously with Islamist movements provided Islamists with an important space for a new interpretation of Islam and a certain production of Islamic life. Therefore Islamic literary narratives signify new Muslim agencies that voluntarily reinterpret Islam, differentiate themselves from traditional Muslims, and challenge the secular narratives of Kemalist modernization in Turkey. Literary Islamism represents the construction of new stories based upon the re-imagination of a Muslim subjectivity. The rarity of "I" and the ubiquity of "we" in Islamic salvation novels, however, signify that it was a collective subjectivity that paved the way for a collective Islamist movement with its stress on collective harmony and collective ideals that disregarded any internal conflict among the members of the movement.

Islamic novels can, therefore, be taken as a vital means in the construction of a "frame" through which Islamist movement and its collective identity has been shaped. I use the term "frame" here in Goffman's sense of something that facilitates the interpretation of experiences by ascribing their meaning and enabling individuals to perceive, identify, locate and, organize such experiences (Goffman 1986). Frames are crucial for social movements since they provide participants with shared interpretive schemata to make sense of themselves and the world, and narratives are the key mechanisms through which frames are produced and identities forged (Steward et al. 2002). Islamic salvation novels, in this sense, are narratives that provide Islamists with a shared frame for the construction of Islamic identity, and for the alignment of Islamists with the movement and other participants. More concretely, the frame promoted by Islamic narratives in the 1980s provided Islamists with easy and clear schematic answers of "what is good," "what has been done," and "what ought to be done." It can be said that in the context of the 1980s in which Islamist intellectual and political actors constructed a sharp oppositional discourse with their claim for the collective enforcement of public morals, salvation novels with their didactic forms contributed to the formation and propagation of an assertive and collective Islamic vision of the world.

The distinction made between political Islam and cultural Islam has often been employed as an explanatory tool for understanding the complex nature of Islamist movements (Göle 1999). In this distinction the political refers to Islamist movements that are focused on attaining political power (the state), often through utilizing an oppositional discourse. Cultural Islam, on the other hand, signifies an Islamic vision that does not have an interest in capturing state power per se, but endeavors to convey Islamic messages at an individual level pertaining to the Islamization of daily life. In other words, while political Islam represents a top-down will to vertically *Islamize* the whole society, cultural Islam, which does not revolve around an overt political language, aims to transform social relations horizontally.[17] With reference to this distinction, Islamic novels have sometimes been located on the side of cultural Islam. It was asserted that Islamic novels, with their message-conveying narratives for the Islamization of daily life, signified the voice of cultural Islam (Yılmaz 2000).

This interpretation says little about the nature of cultural Islam as promoted by literary narratives, while it also understates "the political" as an inherent component of Islamic novels. I would argue by contrast that the politics of literary Islamism display a close parallelism with the dominant political discourse of Islamism. The construction of the main plot in salvation novels that centers around the negotiation of Islamic and Western visions of the world is reminiscent of the language employed by Islamist political actors in the political field of the

1980s. So for example, Necmettin Erbakan, the leader of the pro-Islamic Welfare Party (*Refah Partisi*), stated that "the history of mankind is the struggle between two civilizations: one (Western civilization) which prefers 'power' and the other (Islamic civilization) which prefers 'right.'" Within this line of thinking, it was asserted that all otherworldly systems will eventually fade away, leaving space for the Just Order (*Adil Düzen*) (Erbakan 1991, 16–18). The discourse of Islamist politicians therefore can easily be paralleled to the discourse by fictional fellow travelers.

Islamic salvation novels also share the authoritarian stance of the more general Islamic discourse of the 1980s. With regard to the representation of a westernized life style, what is salient in all Islamic narratives is their authoritarian organization that gives priority to an Islamic way of life as the only dominant voice. The authors' overarching concern in salvation novels is to construct a discursive hierarchy with the narrators' (Islamists') discourse at the top speaking the language of unproblematic truth. Accordingly, collective Muslim subjectivities of the 1980s engage in relations with their opponents monologically rather than dialogically in the Bakhtinian sense. Thus Islamic literary narratives give voice to what we might call a collective and monologic Islamism that denies that there exists outside of it other consciousnesses or equal subjectivities, with the same rights and with equally sincerely held convictions. This Islamic discourse of salvation narratives signifies a monologic Islamism that in an authoritarian fashion aims to subordinate or abolish all differences.

Another theory that is useful in explicating the nature of Islamic salvation novels—compared to self-critical novels of the 1990s—is Bakhtin's concept of epic and novelistic discourse. Bakhtin distinguishes these two genres primarily on the basis of their organization of time and characters. The epic, he argues, is an "absolutely completed and finished generic form, whose constitutive feature is the transferal of the world it describes to an absolute past of ... beginnings and peak times" (2000, 15). In the epic, everything is evaluated in light of an absolute past which is construed as the "single source and beginning of everything good for all later times as well" (Bakhtin 2000, 15). Thus the epic world draws on a single and unified world view represented by the absolute past, leaving no room for other possible truths. This absolute past is celebrated through the agency of a hero who is a fully completed being and entirely externalized. He has nothing hidden to be uncovered: "Everything in him is exposed and loudly expressed. His internal world and all his external characteristics, his appearance and his actions all lie on a single plane" (Bakhtin 2000, 35). Since wholeness and completeness characterize the hero of the epic world, he lacks inner conflict or resistance.

By contrast, the novel "comes into contact with the spontaneity of the inconclusive present" (Bakhtin 2000, 27). It reflects the world in the making. When the present becomes the center of human orientation in time and in the world, the epic wholeness of the hero derived from the absolute past disintegrates. While the virtue and ideology of the epic hero is exemplary for the whole community or the whole epic world, protagonists in the novel act in a contested terrain where different characters with different world views interact. The novel represents "the heteroglossia of the period" (Bakhtin 2000, 300), or its different voices.[18] Thus novelistic words are inherently dialogical since they draw on the interaction of various voices populating the language of an era. The novel orchestrates all these different voices in the face of an inconclusive future. Given the existence of the future in the novel as a promise of undeveloped possibilities, the novel's characteristic feature is its eternal rethinking and reevaluating. This suggests that the epic hero and the epic world view disintegrate under the pressure of constant reevaluation or the search for a new point of view on one's own self (Bakhtin 2000, 32–34).

Within this framework, Islamic salvation novels, particularly *Müslüman Kadının Adı Var* and *Boşluk*, display characteristics closer to epic discourse than to novelistic discourse. I do not wish to propose that the literary narratives of the 1980s *correspond* to the epic and that those of the 1990s correspond to the novel as a literary genre. The narratives of both decades are clearly closer to the novel in a literary sense. Nevertheless, using the distinction more analogously, Bakhtin's analysis of characters and time in epic and novelistic texts respectively illuminates some of the differences between the two genres of the novel. This is because despite their representation of the Muslim self in the contemporary world, the plot, characters, and themes of the salvation narratives were all articulated with a particular Islamic past, the *Asr-ı Saadet*, period of the Prophet and four Caliphs. In other words, salvation novels constructed an absolute past, derived role models from it, and presented these role models as authentically replicable in modern times. This authenticity is not something given, but something created via the reflexive activities of the actor (Giddens 1995, 52). Islamic novels, then, played an important role in developing claims to authenticity through a narrative form that allowed the revaluing of contemporary practices in the light of a constructed Islamic golden age.

In such an epic world view, the protagonists of Islamic narratives of the 1980s, as exemplified by Dilara and Cihan, appear more like epic characters than individuals. Not only Islamic characters but also secular opponents were represented as stereotypes. They acted in the novels as heroes or villains, but were always oriented toward great ideals—Islamizing the whole society—or a dramatic destiny. The protagonists of the narratives represented either "truth" or "falsehood" clarified in the light of the absolute Islamic past. Salvation novels celebrated the adventures and achievements of heroic religious figures. Islamic heroes of the narratives were depicted as complete and committed identities oriented toward saving the world. This heroic figure lived an ideal Islamic lifestyle in a materialist world and always triumphed over "corrupt" characters.

Thus in addition to its monologic and collective characters, Islamic discourse of the 1980s can also be framed as an *epic Islamism*. This Islamism promoted an Islamic discourse in which the current order was marked with the "malaise" of Westernization that brought about a morally degenerate society. The only medicine for this "malaise" was Islam. An Islamic way of life was totally separate from and incompatible with other—secular, materialist, and individualist—ways of life. Islam was presented as "true," while "the other" was depicted as absolutely "not true." All solutions and peace were claimed to be found in Islam, and this had to be manifested by uncompromisingly practicing an Islamic way of life: by wearing the headscarf, performing prayers, and promoting morally appropriate behavior in private and public life. Muslims had to save themselves from corrupting spaces and relations. As actors possessing knowledge of true "goodness," Muslims had to endeavor to "illuminate" people with the light of Islam. These others who were deemed wretched had no choice but to adopt the true path of Islam in the end. A holistic salvation or the imaginary creation of an Islamic society marked by a re-moralization of public life was inevitable, leading to a closure in which humanity would live "paradise on earth."

Critique of Salvation
Novels within Islamism

Concurrently with the rise of Islamism in the 1980s, various academic and journalistic circles scrutinized and sought to understand veiled girls, Islamic journals, and Islamic intellectuals. Notwithstanding this intense interrogation, the Islamic literary sphere and literary discourse were rarely debated—as opposed to vilified—outside of Islamic circles. Indeed, by the end of the 1980s it was Islamists themselves who began to criticize the narrative and aesthetic value of Islamic salvation novels.

For example, one Islamic academic, M. Emin Ağar, identified salvation novels as a "green series" (*yeşil dizi*), connoting the Islamic nature of novels with "green" and the aesthetically unsophisticated narratives of Islamic novels with the term "series." In *Suffe Yıllığı*, a literary almanac of Islamic circles, Ağar points out that the presence of series (*dizi romanlar*), with their unsophisticated narratives, was one of the problems in Turkish literature. He went on to say that,

> These series are named according to colors—such as a pink, white, or yellow series—that bear no literary concern. We can collect a great part of the novels published as Islamic novels in our milieu under such a series. We can call this new series a green series. The novels that we can include in this series do not bear any artistic or literary concern. They narrate the lives of people who, while initially living an indecent life, begin immediately to live a true Islamic life along with coincidences one can hardly find in fairy tales (*binbir gece maslları*). On the other hand, many are quickly written drawing on the *exaggeration of the news in dailies*. Indeed most headscarf novels are this kind of book. Üstün İnanç's book entitled *Yalnız Değilsiniz* [You are not Alone], Mehmet Zeren's books of *Öz Yurdunda Garipsin I-II* [You are a Stranger in Your Own Land], are novels that quickly novelized the news in dailies. (Ağar 1987–1988, 75; emphasis original)

Similarly, Miyasoğlu, an Islamist novelist, accused salvation novels of being "clumsily written," handling the issues of salvation or the need for faith in an awkward fashion. He argues that "with these novels neither novel nor religious thought could thrive" (Miyasoğlu 1999, 101). These critiques, which at first glance seem only to focus on the literary value of Islamic novels, extend beyond the aesthetic sphere to include the ways these novels represent Muslim characters. A basic criticism of their depiction of Muslim characters focused on their representation of Muslims as lower class as well as their apologetic language of self-pity. It was asserted that the language used in Islamic novels correlated with an "arabesque discourse" mirroring the grievances and dreams of new migrants or of people originally from rural areas living on the skirts of the cities (Kitap Dergisi 1989, 10). Islamic novels were criticized on the basis that they represented Muslims in "a subordinate position" (Miyasoğlu 1999, 224), with their feelings of subordination as a result of their "non-adaptation to the city" framed with an "Islamic arabesque language" (*Kitap Dergisi* 1989).

This critique might be socially accurate, as it appears that the Islamic novels of the 1980s vivify the experiences of the new Islamic actors who, not only in Turkey but also in other Muslim countries, come from recently urbanized social groups.[19] However, toward the end of the 1980s and in the 1990s, Islamists began to take critical objection to representations of Muslims as subordinate agents belonging only to the lower classes. This suggests that the Islamic narratives of the 1980s included aspects of a collective identity that the generation of Islamic actors in the 1990s could not easily accommodate to their own stories of identity. This is because the new generation of Islamists no longer consisted of newcomers, but of people with modern professions and public roles as doctors, engineers, mayors, TV and radio speakers, businessmen, and businesswomen. Islamists in the 1990s formed a middle class and created their own counter-public spaces like hotels, cinema saloons, kindergartens, and beauty parlors. Accordingly, Islamism is no longer a marginal ideology but one which acquired electoral success in local and general elections in the 1990s. In this decade, salvation novels did not sell as well as they did in the 1980s. Indeed, some publishers in Islamic circles have announced "the death of the ideological books." These books include not only salvation novels but all "ideological books," "books on the Iranian revolution," and works by "radicals [the books of radical thinkers]." Publishers note that books that "attack no one" and books on "personal entrepreneurship and development" are what sell (Eren and öztürk 2004). The new books of Islamic actors also involve self-questioning fiction focusing on a critique of the ideals and salvation narratives of the previous decade. In sum, the 1990s has paved the way for a novel(istic) understanding of Islamism. I will now turn to this development.

Self-Reflexive and Self-Exposing Novels of the 1990s: A Path to Muslim Subjectivity

Islamism and Islamic Actors in the Context of the 1990s

The salvation novels of the 1980s issued a challenge to secular narratives of modernization/Westernization in Turkey. Islamic novels deconstructed and reconstructed the Kemalist process of civilizing the country in the form of Westernization. In their deconstruction, Islamists developed schematic narratives in which the current order and its secular/westernized subjects were represented as products of the "malaise" of Westernization. Islam, on the other hand, was reinterpreted and presented as the source of all goodness and the only remedy for the "degeneracy" brought about by secular modernization. Islamic salvation narratives were based on a dualist, yet interrelated, vision of the world in which Islamic subjects were fated to be in constant struggle with secularist values and identities. Such a perception of the world led to a collective representation of Islamic subjects in contradistinction to a similar homogenization of secular identity. In other words, the Islamic literary narratives of the 1980s promoted a countercollective Islamic identity moving toward a fixed goal, represented by a will for a holistic transformation (Islamization) of society. Accordingly, the collective Islamism of the 1980s conceived of Islamic identity in group terms and spoke with a language of "we" in a way that depersonified and stereotyped distinct Muslim selves and individual characteristics.

This collective representation of Islam led to a particular understanding of Islam and Islamic way of life that was presented as distinct from and incompatible with the hegemonic secular values and vision of the world. In keeping with this radical and exclusionary discourse—in which Muslim actors were oppositional rather than self-reflexive, and focused on future revolutionary ideals more than the present—differences within this constructed Islamist collective self were not problemized. Rather, Islamic identity was presented as collective and homogenous, overlooking internal divisions on gender, ethnic, and national lines. Within this frame, men and women, for instance, were defined according to their supposed complementary functions in a way that stressed harmony and interdependence rather than domination or conflict. Collective Islamism of the 1980s then defined individual identity as congruent with collective identity and ideals. Collective ideals in this decade overshadowed both individual desires and differences.

Nevertheless, despite its critical posture toward modern (westernized) society, what characterized Islamism was not a withdrawal from modern life but a collective will to participate in it. In the literary narratives of the 1980s, Muslim youths, male and female, were encouraged to attend universities and acquire modern professions so as to become pious mothers, doctors, and teachers who would transform society in the name of Islam. The 1980s witnessed an increase of Islamist youth on university campuses symbolized by their distinctive body politics, pursued through the headscarf or the Muslim beard. Although the headscarf was banned in Turkish universities, this censure was not always nationally applied until the late 1990s. Thus many Islamic youths attended university despite ongoing constraints and exclusion.

As the 1980s merged into the '90s, Islamist actors acquired modern professions by skillfully utilizing the educational facilities in Turkey. As this movement gathered momentum, Islamic actors became increasingly visible in newly founded pro-Islamic TV and radios stations and (Islamic or secular) private enterprises.[1] Muslim women, organizing around new civic initiatives or platforms, participated in national and international women's conferences (Şişman 1996). Islamic actors formed various associations to foster their interests in business circles and working life (e.g. Hak-İş).[2] Many Islamic groups benefited from the liberalizing policies of post-1980 Turkey that resulted in the emergence of an "Islamic capital" and "Muslim entrepreneurs" (Yavuz 2003).[3] They also took advantage of processes of globalization that presented opportunities to Islamic actors, such as the expansion of their economic interests in international markets (Kösebalaban 2005; Kuru 2005).[4] In sum, Islamic groups began to form their own middle class and became urban actors and professionals capable of using both secular and Islamic idioms.

In the formation of a connected but simultaneously rival economy to secular companies (in high quality and expensive preschool and childcare centers, cafes and popular music), male Islamists were able to become active in public life and in the labor market rather "less painfully" than headscarved women. Male Islamists cut their beards and wore ties while employed in Islamic and "other" companies. Nevertheless, this professionalization and capitalist organization of work facilitated a challenge to earlier collective ideals and definitions of Islam. Frequenting new spaces and carrying out modern professions clearly led to internal conflicts for many male Islamist actors. These conflicts were sometimes publicly shared in Islamic journals and dailies. For instance, an Islamist journalist-humorist, Hasan Kaçan, commented on his own conflict as follows:

A Muslim is a human being who, "as the night does, hides ugly things, and as the sun does, illuminates beautiful things."[5] But how can we do this? Let's say, for example, you are a journalist. Journalism involves interpretation as well as objective reportage. It is what we do. But what is the thing we interpret? All we do is to seek after the hidden agenda [*çapanoğlu*] behind newspapers and television channels. We are no longer aware of beautiful things. I feel this contradiction on my part. How can a Muslim journalist hide ugly things as the night does, and illuminate beautiful things as does the sun? (Kaçan 1996)

Similarly, Cafer Karaduman, a businessman organizing fashion shows for Islamic dress, replied to Islamist critiques of the incongruity of Islamic veiling with catwalk parades by saying the following:

> Shall I defend something that is prohibited [*haram*]? Of course I know that employing female models in fashion shows is a sin. I am also unable to come up with a satisfactory explanation for the things we have done. Nevertheless, there are many events which Muslims are unable to explain satisfactorily. (Kaçan 1996)

These two accounts might be seen as indicative of Islamic actors with internal conflicts in the 1990s attempting to combine Islamic ideals, Muslim identities, and modern professions.[6] They are also representative of the ability of Islamic actors to live with and accommodate seemingly contradicting values and life choices in an Islamic frame.

For many female Islamist actors, Islamism as a social and economic movement provided them with a vehicle to assert their autonomy and build social networks outside of the home, despite that movement's rhetoric of domesticity and conservatism (Arat 1990, 21). Accordingly, the demands of Islamist women—once graduated from school or university—also began to revolve around transformed practices of work. The complaint of the "victims" of the previous decade—"I want to attend university with my headscarf"—turned into a more self-assertive statement: "I want to practice my job as a doctor or a lawyer wearing my scarf" (çayır 2000, 51). However, Islamist women also experienced bitter conflicts between their professional desires and their assigned roles as keepers of Islamic morality—as framed by the headcovering—that prevented their access to the non-Islamic labor market. Women Islamists felt that they were squeezed between their education, the "real life" discrimination of the republic, and gendered roles and duties still expected of them by their husbands or families. The difficulties in developing coherent narratives of identity that could embody both their domestic and public roles became a prominent theme in Islamist women's discourse of the 1990s. A university graduate who works as a housewife depicts her situation as such:

> If I told people that I am a university graduate and that I have five kids, they would ask which accomplishment I am most proud of. If I had said directly that I was a housewife, I would have the feeling that I was nothing else during the times I did not do housework. If I had added that I am a teacher, I would think with regret "what is the use of saying this" since I could not answer the questions of "where my students and school are." I usually say that I am at home and I have children. However, the answer is always hard for me. (Yıldız 1996, 30)

Similar to Islamic males, but different, as well, given the gendered nature of earlier Islamist discourse, veiled women in the '90s appeared to feel squeezed between the collective and oppositional definitions of Islamism promoted in the 1980s and individual desires to participate more actively in the public sphere. As one Islamist writer commented, when Islamist women voiced their will to work outside and attend public spaces, they converged with feminist discourse; on the other hand when they stayed at home, they approached "ordinary women" (Barbarosoğlu 1996, 23). This was painful because both the male and female actors of Islamism voiced an oppositional discourse that posited that Muslim women should be different from westernized feminists and traditional women. As in the case of *Müslüman Kadının Adı Var* by Katırcı Turhal, Islamic actors radically homogenized and accused feminists of disregarding their maternal roles in the name of a career outside the home. But Muslim women also aimed to differentiate themselves from their traditional mothers. Nevertheless, as the above quotation indicates, Muslim women who once imagined both being a "conscious" mother and having a profession felt themselves squeezed between their individual professional desires and collective Islamic ideals when they graduated from school.

Women Islamists hotly debated the position of women and the meaning of the headscarf in Islam in relation to secular conceptions of modernity in newly published journals, monthlies, and public conferences in the 1990s. Instead of the demonstrations and sit-ins of the previous decade, Islamist women actors began to express their will to participate in modern urban spaces via professional social movements, organizations, platforms, and civil associations. Whereas in the '80s, Islamist circles debated whether the public hearing of women's voices was prohibited in Islam (Azak 1999), in the 1990s Islamist women organized conferences and panels during which they spoke side by side with males and to males without the segregation of sexes in the audience. Here the principle of segregation of the sexes was violated and challenged by Islamist women themselves. Similarly, '80s Islamist appeals to headcovered girls to leave their schools if they had to choose between careers and religious faith no longer found an echo among the younger generation of Muslim students. Regarding the attitudes and aspirations of younger veiled girls, an Islamist columnist writes disapprovingly that "they [veiled girls] want to go to the United States not to Palestine anymore" (*Akit* October 26, 2000). This shows that Palestine, the key symbolic place for the Islamic resurgence of the 1980s, was displaced by the United States as the imagined destination in which to actualize an Islamic self. In other words, in the 1990s professional careers and the lifestyle that such careers were thought to bring emerged as an important component of individual Muslim identities in a way that challenged the collective definitions of Islamism.

The 1990s also witnessed the creation of counter-Islamic public spaces advertised as conforming to the requirements of Islamic morality. Newly founded Islamic hotels, which provided separate sections in which women could swim, invited

Muslim women to holiday with slogans such as "now you can swim" or "you too can enjoy a peaceful (*huzurlu*) holiday" (Kömeçoğlu 2006a). Moreover, new movie theaters (playing Islamic films and censored Western films), restaurants (where alcohol is not served), and beauty salons (where female employers serve veiled female customers) facilitated new experiences for Islamic actors. Cafes renovated or built by the pro-Islamic Istanbul municipality provided novel spaces that hosted novel Islamic actors: here were seen "veiled girls flicking cigarette ash into the wind, bearded men toting mobile phones, conspicuous consumption in high heels, fashion accessories, silk scarves and new cars" (Houston 2001, 87). Another article on Islamic cafes points out the novel experiences of actors enjoying the "unsegregated publicness" of these places, i.e., men and women sitting together and enjoying intimacy and romance within "Islamic limits" (Kömeçoğlu 2006b, 187). Thus despite their claims to observe Islamic morality, these new spaces signified the formation of new experiences that challenged earlier Islamist norms, especially the gender politics of Islamism. Compared to the 1980s, this new period has been described as "a post-Islamist stage" in which Islamism lost "its revolutionary fervor" but steadily infiltrated "social and cultural everyday life practices" (Göle 2000, 94). Besides hotels, movie theaters, cafes, and restaurants, newly formed Islamic institutions such as pro-Islamic radio and TV outlets, newspapers, hospitals, schools, fashions, and commercial companies also signified the infiltration of Islamic practices into daily life and the institutionalization of Islamism in Turkey.

In brief, the relational settings or habitus from which Islamic narratives originated in the 1980s were transformed in the new decade. It is in such a context that a new habitus and new professions, desires, market forces, and institutions led to the emergence of new tensions and literary narratives among Islamic circles. In the 1990s the collective harmony of salvation novels was first challenged by dissatisfied female Muslim actors. New critical narratives voiced the frustrations of head-covered women who had acquired modern professions but had little input in public life (Aktaş 1991 and 1995; Toros 1990). The stories of Cihan Aktaş in particular narrated the disappointment of educated Muslim women who were not working outside the home. These women were represented as "neither rural nor urban, neither housewives nor businesswomen, neither ambitious nor relaxed, neither speaking nor silent ... neither existing outside the home nor living at home happily" (Aktaş 1991, 32). In Aktaş's stories, Islamist male actors are heavily criticized for placing the burden of the Islamic movement on the shoulders of women. Male critics claimed in reply that she had forgotten that hundreds of men were "in jail not in the name of manhood but of Islam" (Yanar 2001, 128). In spite of Aktaş's criticism of Islamist male actors, her stories might still be considered only a "partial challenge" to collective definitions of Islam, since she still searches for a "pure" and "preserved" Islamic female identity in the context of modern social relations. However, such narratives and the debates they initiated signified that the epic, collective, and coherent narratives of the 1980s were under dissolution according to the new social positions of Islamist actors in the 1990s.

This younger generation of Islamic actors' new experiences and socialization patterns paved the way for the emergence of more self-reflexive and self-exposing novels challenging the collective ideals of the previous decade. These new self-reflexive novels of the 1990s sharply differed from salvation novels because their narratives and characters questioned Islamic perceptions of self, ideology, and the world. They made the inner conflicts of Islamic identities and conflicts within the group visible. This is not to say, however, that salvation novels have ceased to be published: Islamist authors continue to write salvation novels, although their numbers have decreased and their contents have partly been modified in this decade. For instance, Emine Şenlikoğlu, a prolific writer of salvation novels who employed a discourse of "them and us" in the 1980s, has began to depict injustices within Islamic circles in her new novels. She has especially criticized Islamist men who "oppressed women" with concealed second marriages (see Şenlikoğlu 1995).

Moreover, many of the authors of salvation novels have also given interviews in which they have taken a self-critical stance towards the "schematic" narratives of the previous decade. Yüksel Şenler, for example, who once portrayed unveiled university girls as the "call-girls of Europe" in her influential novel, *Huzur Sokağı*, stated in an interview that "If I had written this novel today, I would use a more moderate discourse.... I now found it schematic" (*Zaman* 2002). Even Günbay Yıldız, the biggest selling salvation novelist, modified his biography in his 1990s novels. The short self-description in his old novels was self-assertive: "The writer dealt with all groups of society.... He wrote on the struggle between right and wrong ... and he *clearly pointed out the solution*" (emphasis added). These biographical notes have been modified in his new novels, which now state, "he wrote on the struggle between right and wrong" and "*he also gave clues towards their solution*." The certainty of Islamic assertions constructed through schematic literary narratives has to some extent been replaced by critical voices in new salvation novels. Nevertheless, they comply with the basic narratives of salvation novels since they still conclude by imposing a good life framed with Islamic salvation on the characters.

By contrast, the self-reflexive and self-exposing novels of the 1990s deconstruct the narratives of salvation novels and of collective Islamism of the 1980s. In terms of sheer numbers, self-reflexive novels are difficult to compare to the salvation novels of the 1980s. In the first place they do not form a coherent genre as do the narratives of the previous decade. Nevertheless, their narratives critiquing Islamic conceptions of the 1980s—via inscriptions of the various voices of the period—provide us with grounds to analyze Islamism and Islamic subjects. In this chapter I will analyze Islamists' perceptions of the self, the other, and the social context in which such selves are composed by drawing on two novels of the period, *Halkaların Ezgisi* (The Melody of Circles) and *Yağmurdan Sonra* (After the Rain). Let me begin by presenting a short summary of both novels.

Halkaların Ezgisi and *Yağmurdan Sonra* as Two
Exemplary Self-Exposing Novels

Halkaların Ezgisi (1997) by Halime Toros[7] is narrated through the inner dialogue of a woman writer who adopts an Islamic way of life by wearing the headscarf in the 1980s yet unveils herself some years later. Nisa, the protagonist of the novel, lives in Ankara in the 1980s and 1990s in an Islamic circle in which she is first seen as "deficient" since she does not don the headscarf (38). In time, she adopts the headscarf with the encouragement of her husband. Upon veiling, Nisa is made to feel that "she is not an ordinary woman anymore" (40) since veiling carries with it new bodily postures, new ways of being looked at, and new modesties, as well as various stigmatizations not only from secular but also from Islamic circles. As a veiled woman, the experience of having new relations with Islamists and secularists makes Nisa realize and question the binary oppositions and formulaic answers employed by both Islamists and secularists. Confused by such a "them and versus us" battle, she refuses to align herself with one side by invoking of prescribed slogans. Nisa begins to hear the voice of her "other self"—which she calls Nisan—that resists the overdetermined position of the headscarf and the burden put by Islamists on women's shoulders to represent Islam. In time Nisa takes a critical stance towards collective, fundamentalist, and revolutionary interpretations of Islam. At the end of a questioning process, she declares that she can no longer bear both the stigmatizations of secularist circles and the prescribed answers of Islamists. In a key passage, the main character says that she is not only Nisa but also Nisan (127). The name "Nisa"—which derives from Arabic, means "woman," and has Koranic connotations regarding veiling—signifies the character's Islamic collective identity, while the name "Nisan" (which in Turkish means "spring") symbolizes her individual identity resisting the constraining dimensions of collective identity. The novel develops through the dramatization of dialogue between Nisa and Nisan as the two sides of her identity. As a result, she decides to leave Nisa "behind the door" (162) and takes her scarf off. This is not, however, an easy process for her. In her internal dialogues, she revises the meaning of the veil, and the role of women in Islam and in general Islamic understandings of the 1980s. After her unveiling she is depicted as a Muslim still performing her prayers. She tries to convince her angry husband that she still "feels veiled" (163). Thus she reconstructs herself along with a re-reading of her experiences in the context of Turkey in the 1980s and 1990s.

Yağmurdan Sonra (1999), written by Ahmet Kekeç,[8] represents a form of public self-exposure different from the unveiling of the body. The novel tells the story of a "lost" Islamist living in Istanbul in the context of the 28 February Process.[9] Murat, the main character of the novel, is an ex-publisher. In an environment where people no longer read books, and as a man who has lost his Islamist ideals, Murat starts to sell stationary. He is presented as a cynic, not interested in politics. However, during the 28 February Process he is taken to court for a book he had published six years ago. In this political environment in which Muslims are scrutinized, he is made to question and revise his past and present life. In the present, Murat has problems in his marriage. He finds his wife boring since she is engaged in the drudgery of housework. He feels that his wife searches for "status" that he cannot provide her with (62). During the evenings when he does not want to go home, he meets "different" friends from secular circles with whom he goes to bars and lies to in order to not drink alcohol. Furthermore, Murat has problems with his father who left his family when Murat was young and married another woman. Despite not seeing him for years, Murat begins to visit his father when he gets old and becomes ill. In one of his visits, Murat sees his stepsister, Hülya, and falls in love with her. His visits to his father's house become more frequent in order to see her. Several times he tries to tell her about his love, but cannot. He is torn between his "sinful" love, and his marriage and faith. The novel concludes with an inner-dialogue on Murat's conflicting and contrasting desires.

These two novels resonate with the Islamic imaginary of Muslim authors who, to use Kristeva's conceptualization, "read history and society as text" (Kristeva 1980, 65) into which they insert themselves by rewriting this history. Here the narratives of a younger generation of Islamic actors—who were born in the 1960s and lived in a milieu in which Islam was no longer a marginalized ideology—express the self-reflexive and self-exposing voice of Muslim actors and their Islamic practices. Narrative as a form provides a way to order events, and allows Muslims to understand "who they are and how they became so." In this sense, the new narratives of the 1990s involve the reconsideration of the practices and understandings of the 1980s as well as perceptions of self and the other in the new political/cultural environment of the 1990s.

Depiction of the Islamist Conceptions of the 1980s

New self-reflexive novels, understood as a manifestation of Islamic actors' will to develop a coherent narrative identity in the context of the 1990s, involve the reexamination of a collective past. Nisa and Murat self-critically depict a social milieu in which Islam is presented as the solution to all malaise. Via the self-reflexive voice of Nisa, Halime Toros in *Halkaların Ezgisi*, portrays the 1980s as a time when "radicalism was religion." Yet somewhat nostalgically, this Islamism and its influence by the ideological discourse of the Iranian Revolution reflected a time when

> the language was changed, new readings were performed and new namings were constructed ... the Koran was taken down from the wall and read ... journals were swallowed ... people dreamed of revolution. [It was a time when] those, who did not have time to wait, were going to the mountains of Afghanistan or Khom. (22–23)

In such a political context, Islamists created the following slogans:

May parents find the straight path, may laic people be damned ... let the *ülkücü* [nationalist] people give up claims to be Muslims.... We all flew to Iran, Pakistan, Egypt and Afghanistan ... Sayyid Qutb was our handbook. Ali Shariati was our rebellion. Books on jihâd were our guidebooks. Life was all about hate and anger. (119–20)

These quotations are dramatic representations of the dominant Islamist conceptions of the 1980s in Turkey. The Iranian Islamic Revolution in 1979 provided Islamists not only with an impetus for the development of a revolutionary interpretation of Islam, but also a revolutionary imaginary that conceived of seizing state power to implement Islamic precepts in secularized Muslim contexts. This decade, as Nisa spells out, encompassed the years "when revolution was dreamed" by Turkish Islamists, too. Similar feelings of an activist ability to remake the world are encapsulated in *Yağmurdan Sonra* in the following words of Murat, who had become an Islamist in his university years as many other actors of Islamism had: "The country was on the verge of disaster. We were going to save it.... We were young, lively, and bold enough to change the world" (29). The repertoire of Islamist groups in Turkey that sought "to save the country" was culled from the works of Middle Eastern Islamist thinkers. Almost all the books by thinkers such as Ali Shariati, Sayyid Qutb, and Abul A'la Mawdudi were translated into Turkish at the beginning of the 1980s, paving the way for the formation of an Islamist vocabulary which, as Nisa self-reflexively points out, was highly clichéd and antagonistic to both secularized regimes and traditional interpretation of Islam. In sum, what characterized the 1980s according to these revisionist novels was a recoding of language and history, and a reinterpretation of faith in a way that led to the rise of a radical/oppositional Islamist discourse.

Nisa lives in such an Islamic milieu and is devoted to living a life in accordance with Islamic principles. However, she does not wear the headscarf. In an environment where "slogans are in the air," life is difficult for her since she is unveiled.

Living "inside" with her "non-Islamic" outlook becomes problematic. This was because, as she says,

> In a time when how others perceive you was more important than how you feel about yourself, when belief had to be manifest (and registered) I was always seen as lacking, deficient, because the Koran commanded "cover your head." When you did it, you were treated as practicing all other precepts. (38–39)

Nisa critically voices the interpretation of veiling in Islamic circles in the 1980s. As promoted by salvation novels of the period, veiling was an indispensable part of the construction of Islamic female identity. While the Koran did not dictate such a strict bodily signifier for males, being Muslim for women meant wearing the headscarf. This was because, as nearly all literary and non-literary accounts of Islamism emphasize, Islamic communitarian morality (and order) was best assured when social interaction between the sexes was strictly controlled. Veiling in such a framework signified not only an Islamic dress code but also the provision of communitarian morality through self-governance and the social control of women. Veiling denoted an Islamist politics of distinction via connotations of women's modesty and chastity.

Brow-beaten by such a discourse, Nisa dons the headscarf with the encouragement of her husband after their marriage. She remembers the day she wore the scarf for the first time as follows:

> Tahsin [her husband] covered me with a cream-color veil ... he wrapped me, he veiled me ... he had kissed me on my forehead and added "*hanım*" to my forename. When I got angry, I could not say "*höst, yavşak, hadi be!*" anymore.... I used to say them. I had to say "*La havle*" [God is enough to us] or lower my eyes and say nothing. I was not an ordinary woman anymore! (25–27)

Thus Nisa narrates her transformation from a Muslim woman to an Islamist through veiling. She self-reflexively exposes her feeling of being "controlled" by her headscarf, as it demands she change her conduct as an ordinary woman. After her veiling she feels that she has to change her look and her language. She should excise impolite words from her vocabulary. This is because veiling carries with it an Islamic praxis that puts on women's shoulders a responsibility to act modestly in daily life. It is impossible to act as an ordinary woman since the headscarf makes woman visible and subject to both Islamist and secularist gazes and control. The act of veiling makes Nisa an "insider" in her Islamic circle, since otherwise she is "always seen as deficient." In other words, she conforms to the defined role of women and the meanings attributed to veiling (such as modesty, distinctiveness and respectability) in Islamist oppositional discourse of the 1980s.

While Halime Toros explains the process of Nisa's Islamization, Ahmet Kekeç does not explicitly narrate Murat's process of being an Islamist actor in *Yağmurdan Sonra*. He indicates, however, that Murat becomes an Islamist in his university years. The scenes in which Murat becomes an Islamist and Nisa adopts an Islamic way of life represented through her veiling correspond to the closing pages of the salvation novels of the 1980s. In other words, the protagonists of salvation novels, who once lived a non-Islamic life, are led to acquire an Islamic consciousness and an Islamic identity towards the end of the story. Accordingly, salvation novels conclude with an imagined peaceful and happy life for newly converted Islamist characters. They are presented as those who have achieved collective salvation. Salvation novels, however, as Fatma Karabıyık Barbarosoğlu, one of their Muslim critics, states, "come to an end where life begins" (Şişman 2001, 55). They end by imagining a blissful Islamic life without connecting this to the experiences of Islamist characters in their daily lives, homes, or workplaces. The new self-reflexive novels of the 1990s, on the other hand, situate key characters in heterosocial urban spaces. Characters acknowledge the difficulty of living in modern urban spaces as Muslims with collective ideals, both in sustaining collective representations of Islamism and in imagining an internal stability of Muslim characters. Nisa's experiences as a veiled woman and Murat's dilemmas in his daily life as a Muslim man become representative of Muslim subjects' conflicting and contrasting desires in the context of the 1990s.

The Veiled Woman between "Islamic Burden" and Secularist Stigmatization

Salvation novels presented veiling not as if it were a "cultural choice" but as "characteristic of an identity" rooted in "human nature" (Doltaş 2001, 26). Accordingly, an Islamic lifestyle was configured as the true "good life" consistent with human nature. Within this constructed association, the characters of salvation novels adopted veiling as the source of a peaceful life and as a means to conform to Islamic claims for authenticity—represented by a lived tradition, i.e., *Asr-ı Saadet*. Nisa, however, makes explicit that as much as the Islamic dress she wore was constructed as a recovery of a sacred tradition, it was also a new practice involving new rules to be learned. As a woman who wears Islamic dress for ten years (52), Nisa critically reflects upon her experience of veiling with a flashback to the 1980s as follows:

> new customs and patterns of behavior were identified [with veiling]. It was an unusual type of feeling. The air we assumed and the comfort we had … as well as the way we nodded and made gestures … with bluejeans, weekend garments, night suits and long and narrow skirts were no longer expressive. Indeed, the new style of dressing brought along its own rules. Modesty [*sakınma*] was the only rule of this new style.… We had not known how to walk, how to live within this new style. We were to learn. Looks directed at us would fashion our attitudes, blames on us would say to us: "stop." (39–40)

This narrative differentiates Nisa from the headscarved characters of salvation novels. While salvation novel characters depict the moment of veiling as a life altering metaphysical event, Nisa describes what veiling means for women in their daily lives. In contrast to salvation novels in which the act of veiling turns characters into stable and assertive women, Nisa spells out that they do not yet know how to walk and live with this new Islamic garment. She becomes aware that veiling is more than wearing a garment; it involves an action system and a mode of praxis framed by "modesty." What imposes such a mode of praxis on veiled women is the social environment in which Muslims and secularists negotiate and define their positions through the headscarf. Secularist circles perceive the headscarf as a threat to secularism and as a garment belonging to the premodern and pre-republic period. Islamist circles, on the other hand, consider the headscarf and headscarved women symbols of Islamic resistance. The headscarf, therefore, equalizes women, abolishing their differences and making them all carriers of Islamic claims. This suggests that headcovering makes women visible and subject to communitarian control not only by secular circles but also by Islamists. Accordingly, Nisa feels that she is subject to the public gaze at every moment of her daily life. Even in a pharmacy, she is asked, "WHY IS YOUR HEAD COVERED?" (capitals original). Nisa hopelessly and silently responds: "Do I have to answer that question in order to get an aspirin?" (32). Nisa feels that when people look at her, they do not look at a woman "who has a name, age, reason, husband and child" (95). What they expect is the presentation of modes of conduct that people connect to headscarved woman: "You should not harm (*halel getirmemelisin*) Muslimness by smoking [in a park]" (95) and "You should behave as if warmth does not disturb you [in this veil]" (92). Social control is so constraining for veiled women, says Nisa, that if they transgress narrowly defined boundaries of Islamic modesty, people,

> would ask, what sort of Muslim is this? They would tolerate your veil, but humiliate the woman inside it. Even if you hide yourself in the deepest folds of your veil, they would find you. They would always warn you that you

> carry a big weight ... they would once more sanctify you. (95)

As Nisa makes explicit later, it was the Islamist interpretation of veiling that sanctified women and made them subject to a public gaze that expected modesty and virtue from them. The visibility and sanctity bestowed on women through the veil, however, means Nisa has limited space in her daily life. She begins to reflect upon her position and that of male Islamists. When she compares her situation with that of Islamist men, she feels that her "feelings of justice" are offended. What is unfair is not "men's comfortable shirts or shaved faces" but the "invisibility" provided by these characteristics. According to Nisa,

> one could do good actions as well as bad ones with such a manner of dressing.... It was enough for a man to walk with his wife on streets so that he could ward off suspicions whether he is a Muslim. In turn, it was enough for a man not to walk with his wife on streets to validate suspicions of other people about his own allegiance to Islam. (111–12)

This quotation illustrates the critical voices of new Muslim actors against a collective definition of the salvation narratives of the 1980s. While the characters of salvation novels promote a discourse of complementarity and harmony between men and women around a collective ideal, this quote reveals a self-reflexive voice questioning the inequality between Islamist men and women on the basis of their bearing a bodily signifier. Nisa does not promote the collective discourse of Katırcı Turhal's *Müslüman Kadının Adı Var*. Turhal presented Islamist women as those who "have always stood shoulder to shoulder with men [in their struggle] for the cause they believed (1999, 157). Halime Toros, on the other hand, makes her character challenge this collective discourse by expressing women's feelings of injustice in public spaces. Toros' novel spells out how veiled women in particular have been humiliated in and excluded from Republican urban space.

Thus Nisa as a headscarved woman is portrayed as the victim of discrimination in many levels of modern urban life in Ankara. One day when she is on a public bus, the driver, who does not see Nisa's face but perceives her Islamic garment from behind asks her, "MOTHER (*HANIM ANNE*), YOUR TICKET?" (capitals original). This hurts Nisa and she feels that "her young body is again humiliated" (46). She believes that the headscarf makes her appear older than she is. On another occasion, Nisa goes to see a play by Shakespeare with her friends. When they arrive at the theatre, they see that there will be a talk by Yusuf Islam (formerly known as Cat Stevens) on his conversion to Islam in a conference hall next to the theatre. When they turn into the corridor that leads to the theatre, young Islamic males warn them that they are going the wrong way. Nisa feels again that she is visible and expected to act similarly to other Islamic males and veiled female actors. When they take their place in the theatre, on the other hand, Nisa feels unveiled "modern looking people" looking at her and her veiled friends, asking, "what are they doing here? Why are they hanging around?" (71).

Finally she encounters a funeral procession on a day when she is alone. The funeral is for a woman from secular circles. While people marched in the procession shouting slogans against Islamic politics, a man shouts at her: "It is because of you! This woman died because of you! You killed her!" Nisa asks herself, "why was this man pointing at me? What did I do? Who was I?" She feels,

so out there and defenseless because of my visibility … as if on the whole earth there was only this one procession, the people waiting at the bus station and me. As if I, alone, was representing everything, as if I alone carried all the responsibility of guilt. The earth split and Muslims slipped into it.… Like everywhere, the assumption of "US" was simply wishful thinking. Although it was useful to talk about "US," it meant nothing when you are left alone on streets. (49–50)

This quote stands in a clear contrast to the discourse employed in salvation novels. What characterized the discourse of characters in salvation novels against secular stigmatization was their assertive and oppositional stance towards secular circles. Protagonists of the Islamism of the 1980s often spoke in the name of a collective "we," along with a discursive hierarchy in which the collective "we" was presented as a solid unity that would achieve holistic salvation at the end. As a result of their experiences in modern urban contexts, however, veiled women in particular felt that they were the ones who were excluded, humiliated, and injured due to their visibility. Nisa makes explicit how Muslim women felt "unprotected" and "weak" in the face of daily experiences in contradistinction to males. She begins to question the use of the collective "we" for veiled women since such a collective identity and discourse does not change the fact that women are alone and subject to the public gaze in modern urban life. This indicates that collective Islamism, in its "postpone[ing] of all problems to the time of post-revolution" (Göle 1992, 159), is unable to hinder the emergence of tensions among female and male Islamist actors in the modern urban context. Nisa's voice is representative of new critical veiled actors who, through their literary and non-literary accounts, disassemble the collective discourse of Islamism of the 1980s.

These new female actors are critical of the roles that collective Islamism attributes to women. As a female character of another self-reflexive novel of the 1990s, *Mızraksız İlmihal*, expresses, collective Islamism places on women's shoulders "the obligation to be a warrior, a guerilla, to take responsibility for a war that would change everything and the world fundamentally" (Efe 1993, 50). In this novel, a veiled female character, a university student in Istanbul in the 1980s, is invited to a campus demonstration against the headscarf ban by a male Islamist protagonist. The female character rejects this offer and objects to Islamist males who act in the name of women, yet who "do not ask women." In contrast to the collective roles attributed to veiled women, these new protagonists' response is encapsulated in the words of the female character of the novel who answers the male character's offer to participate in the demonstration as follows: "I am small. I am weak. I am a girl … GIRL" (Efe 1993, 51). She thus refuses to go along with Islamist political definitions and the Islamist activism of her milieu. This response and Nisa's questioning of collective Islamic identity signifies the resistance of veiled women to collective definitions of Islamism along with their demand to fashion their own individual Muslim self-identities.

Nevertheless, it is not easy for Nisa "to be small" or to rework the boundaries of her individual identity, not merely because of negative stigmatization but also because of Islamic appeals to women "to scare the Satan" (12). She begins to question the framing of woman in Islamist politics that posits women as having to control themselves since otherwise they may seduce men and contribute to disorder (*fitne*) (40). Such an understanding in the last instance grants "rights to men" and "responsibilities for women" (40). She thinks about the Islamist men advocating this discourse as follows:

> We submitted everything to men, even the things we should not have submitted.… This was because men had so many rights over woman… Many men used to read passages from al-Ghazzali's works … "Getting married was very beneficial for men." Of course, getting married is useful for men. Women keep the house in order, serve guests, cook, do the laundry. If men were to be occupied with these tasks, says al-Ghazzali, they would be taken away from studying and worshipping. Then what were women supposed to do? Perhaps, they were supposed to do everything in order for men to be accepted into Paradise. (40)

Nisa criticizes not only the male dominated Islamic discourse of the 1980s, but also challenges the texts of al-Ghazzali, a prominent Muslim thinker and jurist, as sources constituting such a discourse. Her critique thus goes beyond the Islamist male interpretation of Islam to include "sacred" texts that would allow her later to reinterpret them. This Islamist discourse, she says, limits women with their home and advises women to "sit down, listen and be thankful. Read salvation novels. Do not question your existence" (103). Nevertheless, Nisa, as an educated young woman, questions her existence and resists the narratives of salvation novels that tell women—as in the case of *Müslüman Kadının Adı Var*—that "Muslim women are respectable ladies of warm of and pure homes" (Turhal 1999, 145). Despite this rhetoric of domesticity, however, Nisa and her friends represent veiled actors who attended university and acquired modern professions as the 1980s passed into the 1990s. In other words, headscarved women in the 1990s are not depicted as young students struggling to study at the university with their headscarves, but rather as university graduates who wish (as Nisa spells out) "to work and produce" (90). Educated, veiled working women, however, are still treated in Islamic circles with an Islamic rhetoric that identifies women only via their domestic roles and thus overlooks women's desire to work outside. Nisa portrays the perception of women in Islamic circles as follows:

[This educated young woman] surprises people since there exists a certain definition of woman [in Islamic circles]. She has no place here around. Everybody collaborates to push her to her house. But she does resist.... One of her friends who goes to an "Islamic" corporation to ask for a job is offered a blessed husband instead. They say "sister, we'd better offer you a blessed husband instead of a position." Young ladies were left in their very refined melancholy remembering their struggles in their college years. Meanwhile those girls who accept the offer and get married feel cheated since they become ordinary, go back to the kitchen, live different kinds of Muslim lives with their husbands, remember heartaches and wait for their men who wander from one panel to another.... Meanwhile women [preachers] who somehow stayed out of home but believe that women's place should be their houses make speeches: "Ladies, do not go out to the streets. Do not work." They bring and pour every kind of conspiracy theories in front of their houses. (102)

This paragraph represents a sharp criticism of the Islamist framing of women, promoted by both male and female actors of '80s Islamism. This discourse reduces women to domestic servants, failing to notice their individual desires to work. Nisa critically portrays how such an Islamic understanding is humiliating for women since they are made offers that lead them to have a husband, stay at home, and become ordinary and disappointed after their university education. Those who carry out their modern professions, on the other hand, are still treated as inferior to males. The author develops several scenes to exemplify Islamic male characters' perception of working women. For instance, a headscarved reporter working for an Islamic daily goes along with a male photographer to interview an Islamic male officer of a pro-Islamic Welfare Party municipality. Halime Toros depicts the interview as such: "The young lady asks the questions, but the fifty years old man who knows everything chooses the male photographer as the one to speak to" (101). As the sentence suggests, this Islamic framing of women not only shrinks the spaces for women but also denies women's newly acquired modern professions and public visibilities. In the face of male characters' overt denial of their new educated identities, female characters feel that they always have to prove their abilities. Similar difficulties in working in modern settings have also been stated by headscarved women who are presently active in Islamic circles (Sever 2006).[10]

In brief, the difficulties that women face, as Nisa points out in the above quotation, do not only arise from the exclusion of headscarved women from secular spaces. Islamic circles, too, limit women's spaces through their emphasis on women's domestic roles, modesty, and chastity in the Islamic frame. She directs her criticism towards Muslim men who, she says, "push veiled women towards the home" as follows:

Muslims with private business companies could not employ their "sisters" fearing that their honor might be impugned. Muslims working in the public sector used to employ them but re-located them to the farthest rooms of the office. They would then have morning coffee with beautiful girls and elegant women…. But they never failed to greet their sisters. (104–5)

Graduating from university but not working afterwards was particularly problematic for Muslim women. This was because staying at home caused them to merge with the ordinary housewives from whom they were trying to differentiate themselves. Islamist male actors convinced by the Islamist claim that communitarian morality is only assured through the control of women limit the space available for educated female actors. As Nisa states, Islamist males either do not employ women or make them "invisible." Similar objections are also raised by women who are active in party politics. In the political scene, women played an important role in the Welfare Party's electoral successes at the beginning of the 1990s, especially with their voluntary work for grassroots organizations. However, the fact that women were not assigned higher positions in the Party led them to ask, "are we really in politics?" (Taluk 1995). The Welfare Party was criticized as it made use of women before elections but did not nominate any women to stand for election. Moreover, female actors began to publish new journals such as *Kadın Kimliği* (Women's Identity), in which they questioned both the Islamic and secular processes that led to the subordination of veiled women.

Further, veiled actors also began to express a self-critical stance towards their position in Islamic marriages. Islamist women made ideological marriages during the heyday of Islamic activism of the 1980s. Short story writer Cihan Aktaş portrays the situation as such: "We married neither for money nor career…. We would struggle for others, humanity and Islam rather than ourselves. We called it ideological marriage" (Aktaş 1991, 50). In a similar vein, Nisa self-critically revises the ideological marriages of her generation as follows:

We were innocent, young and poor.... As we graduated one after another, we moved out from youth houses, where we had poor but colorful life experiences, into modest places as a family. We did not want jewelry, expensive household goods or a car. We were simply after God's approval.... After getting married we could not understand how marriage turned into seeking the approval of one's husband. We were to learn afterwards that being a woman under such conditions was more harmful than what we suffered during our years at university [by being expelled from it] ... that streets, homes, bureaus and government offices had different moral codes, that it was not true that ninety-nine percent of our population was Muslim ... and many other things. (115–16)

This paragraph is indicative of the disappointment of educated veiled women that was narrated in many stories in the 1990s. Veiled women, who had internalized the "big claims" of Islamism in their university years, began to express frustration at their constrained public and private lives that were determined not only by exclusivist secular politics but also by their Muslim husbands and comrades. Veiling, Nisa begins to feel, led Muslim women to be excluded from public spaces, to stay at home, to leave their schools, and, in sum, "to sacrifice themselves" in the face of difficulties they lived in their marriages and daily lives. While experiencing all of this, they were expected to be patient and to take the women of the Prophet's time as their role models. Nevertheless, Nisa revises her stance to the world by confessing that conditions in real life were different from their Islamic idealistic conceptions:

We had to forget our interrupted schools, dreams and ideals.... If [the men] did not change, then we should. We had to bear everything.... We should have tied boulders to our stomach like the friends of the Prophet had done. But we became pregnant. And the children did not want stones. This life was very different. (116–17)

In radical Islamic understandings of the 1980s, the role and position of women as well as other issues were handled in the context of a romanticized past. Different stories of women from the period of the Prophet were distilled and circulated as ideal role models in both the literary and non-literary texts of Islamism. Nisa's reference to "tying boulders to our stomachs when we are hungry" in order to endure, as well as her confession of the impracticability of these stories for real life, indicates her resistance to the authenticating claims of Islamism. Thus she challenges "the fundamentals" and the fundamentalist interpretation of Islam dominant in the 1980s. What this fundamentalist understanding involved was a desire to return to sacred tradition and to question every religious practice that was "distorted" after the golden age in order to reconstruct them in the modern era. Yet Nisa declares her generation's failure in this project by admitting that the life contemporary Muslims live is totally different from the concepts and stories of the Islamic golden age.

Indeed, Nisa is aware that Muslims began to live "different lives" in the 1990s. She tells how, as idealized Muslims in the previous decade, they "did not have full automatic washing machines, computers ... and foreign currency accounts in banks" (118). By contrast, Nisa notes how in the 1990s, "we were climbing up the ladder of the city. Our bodies were getting thinner and thinner, our garments were new and our clothes were becoming more and more colorful ... people were used to going to restaurants with great food and service and to vacation and entertainment resorts" (118–19). Nisa depicts the process of the formation of a Muslim middle class, and the vertical mobility that Islamic circles achieved in the 1990s. In this new decade,

> Everything, all realities, all truths, all faults and all goals have changed. Radicals became liberal and democratic. They assumed positions in political parties, they cut their black beards. They handed down their shirts without collars to their wives to be kept for special days. Everything was expressed in the phrase, "ah the good, old days!" (24)

Nisa portrays the transformation of Islamism's male actors who, in the face of "real" life, revised their radical stance, gave up on their Islamic ideals, and became visible in transformed urban spaces with new "faces" and new politics.[11] This transformation of Islamism, however, did not involve veiled women. Nisa points out how

> the only thing that has not changed is this woman. The thing on her head. The thing on her body. It is the only thing that does not change. That is not questioned. When the subject is woman, all the groups unify. When the subject is life, all diverge. (25)

Nisa references the transformation of Islamism and the revision of radical conceptions of Islamism by its male actors in the late 1990s from the point of view of a female subject. Those male actors who once dreamed of an Islamic revolution and rejected party politics have turned themselves into liberals pursuing politics in different parties. They transformed their bodies by shaving off their beards and folding up their "Islamic shirts." Yet Nisa observes how the complete exaggeration of the importance of the headscarf is still maintained by all groups despite their rejection of all other radical conceptions of Islamism. Women, in other words, are still perceived on the basis of their assigned role, and are made to represent Islamic identity and Islamic morality. Squeezed between an "Islamic burden" demanding her embodiment of Islam and secularist stigmatization leading to her exclusion from public space, Nisa begins to question her act of veiling and her headscarf. She explores and seeks an answer to the question: "why are we covered?" Her response involves a critical reconsideration of both republican Kemalist and Islamic politics on the body as follows:

> We knew that clothes were provoking, disguising, transmitting, signifying and a center of demonstration. It was very normal for us to try to tell something with our clothes as children of a culture which dealt with peoples'

clothes and bodies and even oppressed and hanged people for [not wearing] clothes. We have learnt to act this
way from those who were in power.... Even if we did not
want it, the veil ... has been our only reference. Perhaps,
signifiers [of our body] are very important in order to
point out who has the authority over one's own body.
Nevertheless it does not happen so. Our bodies turn
themselves into signifiers. Bodies were overloaded with a
MEANING that they cannot carry. Language was not
needed anymore. (92)

In depicting Islamic actors as "children of [Turkish] culture,"
the author contextualizes the Islamic act of veiling within the
history of republican modernization. She refers to republican
reforms banning the fez and imposing new clothes, in particular the Hat Law of 1925. In the lines following the quotation
above, she cites *İskilipli Atıf Efendi*, an idealized figure in
Islamic circles, who was hanged by the Independence Court
(*İstiklal Mahkemesi*) in 1926 for objecting to the Hat Law. The
author portrays the culture in which Islamic actors were inculcated as one with an intense interest in intervening in matters
concerning the body. In response, Islamists contest such a culture via a counterintervention on the body. The emphasis put
on the headscarf by 1980s Islamic texts illustrates this point.
Precisely because the modernist elite considered veiling to be a
symbol of backwardness and discouraged its use in the name of
a new civility and universalism, Islamists responded with the
act of veiling, propagated as the sign of an alternative Islamic
project of modernity and civility. However, this process, as the
author critically points out throughout her narrative, resulted
in an obsession with veiling. She notes in capital letters that
the Islamic headscarf was burdened with an essential meaning that left no space for individual identities, political inter-
ventions, statements, and differences.[12]

In such a context, as a writer willing to tell people "different stories" in her lectures, Nisa feels that Islamic circles invite
"not her" but "it [the veil]" (84). In other words, people invite
her to conferences not to listen to her individual voice but to

hear absolute Islamist truths and prescribed Islamist answers. Squeezed between her individual and collective identity, Nisa begins to hear an inner voice, another self—Nisan—that represents her earthly and nonideological identity. This other self summons Nisa, saying, "veiling hurts me.... I want to work, produce, succeed. I do not want to be despised and humiliated" (90). Her two selves engage in a ferocious and exhausting dialogue to find an exit from the well-guarded borders of the collective definitions of Islamism. In an environment where "people approach the world and others through their absolute truths and their collective goods and wrongs," Nisa declares that "I am not playing" (85). Nisa listens to Nisan and decides to take her scarf off.

Muslim Man between His Religious Faith and Sinful Love

In *Yağmurdan Sonra*, author Ahmet Kekeç gives voice to the experiences of everyday life, contrasting the desires and frustrations of an ex-Islamist in the aftermath of the 28 February Process. The date refers to the first few months of 1997 when the pro-Islamic Welfare Party was head of a governing coalition. This period is an important turning point in the secular polity of Turkey, which has historically sought to produce a controlled, nationalized, and subservient Islam. By contrast, the Welfare Party's first political maneuvers made its coalition partner, the True Path Party, as well as the secular Turkish political establishment, unhappy (Mecham 2004, 343). When Necmettin Erbakan became Prime Minister, his first state visits he made were to Islamic countries such as Libya and Iran, representing his long held desire to establish an Islamic economic bloc against Western powers. Moreover he invited the leaders of religious brotherhoods (*tarikat*) to dinner during Ramadan at his official residence. The appearance of religious leaders at the offical residence and of party members in religious *hajj* dress in the public space of the Istanbul airport occupied TV scenes for several days. Such visible Islamic references were presented by secular media circles as an attack on the presuppositions of Kemalist modernism. The rise of the Welfare Party's power and the increasing visibility of Islamic actors and symbols in public spaces led to an intervention by the military into the civilian and political sphere, supported by the mainstream media and civil associations. This event is popularly referred to as the 28 February Process. In the process, the National Security Council forced Erbakan to adopt several pro-secular measures in order to counter a perceived Islamic threat (*irtica*). The intervention led to a limiting of public space available to Muslim actors. The wearing of the headscarf on university campuses was properly policed, with veiled students forced to uncover to enter campus. The financial transactions of Islamic companies were scrutinized.

Various interpretations and evaluations of these events infiltrate *Yağmurdan Sonra* via the voice of the protagonist Murat. Murat consumes media news and has conversations with people from secular circles. Secularists' perceptions emerge in the novel when Murat engages in the following dialogue with one of his neighbors:

> Look what this man [Erbakan] has done ... you get such terrible insults in the tent of a desert-Bedouin, they show disrespect to your national anthem, and you behave as if nothing happened. O my dear, such events make me fearful. Have you seen those women with black veils at the Sultanahmet area? ... They are encouraged by the government ... they will go down soon by a military coup, let's see. (24–25)

This quote refers to various political events (like Erbakan's trip to Libya) that had already been represented in the media and that were influential building blocks in the case built by the secular media that resulted in the 28 February Process. Murat's neighbor is depicted as someone who takes a critical stance towards the pro-Islamic Welfare Party and looks forward to a military coup. This neighbor, however, make a distinction between Murat and Islamists in general by saying, "but you are not like them Muratçığım" [dear Murat] (29). Although it is not made explicit throughout the novel, his neighbor's response suggests that people assume that Murat has an Islamic sensibility because his wife is veiled. It also appears that Murat does not use any Islamic signifier, like a beard, since the secular characters he meets treat him as if he were secular as well, and speak with a language criticizing Islamists. Murat, on the other hand, does not adopt the assertive and polemical stance against such criticisms taken by the Islamist characters of salvation novels. Although he gets angry with the secular critiques, as a man who is "alone and has lost his ideals for the future" (24), he takes a cynical attitude, responding either by saying, "he does not care about such events [against the visible Islamists]" or by pointing out that "he does not have a paranoia [about Islamists]" (25).

Murat is a man who has lost the confident Islamic language of his university years. One of the reasons underlying this is his "virtuousness," which is expressed in his resistance to changing circumstances and to using his many social networks to get rich. His brother-in-law, for instance, when referring to the Welfare Party government, tells him that "your boys came to power" and encourages him to talk to his old friends in Ankara in order to make new business. Murat rejects his suggestion even as he recalls his wife's complaints that "they do not yet have a car" (62). Problems in his marriage are spelled out as another reason for Murat's frustrations in his daily life. Murat is bored by his wife's complaints about their situation, her praising of his "talented" brother-in-law, Sunday rituals (having breakfast and then reading the newspapers, etc.), and their routine life (74ff).

While confronting these problems in his business and marriage, Murat learns that he is to be taken to court for a book that he had published six years ago. He is informed that he is accused of "inciting the public to hatred and hostility on the basis of class, race and religion."[13] Murat once again recalls his neighbor's response: "but you are not like them Muratçığım," and begins to question his political and apolitical self: "Where do I stand? What am I?" Psychologically oppressed by these problems, Murat begins to spend time in cafes after work since he wants to go home late. One night in a cafe he meets a writer he knew a few years ago and his friends. Among them, Müge, a twenty-six-year-old sociology student, appears extremely attractive to him. Murat looks at her and thinks the following:

> She looks like the VJ girl that he sees in TV in the morning. A beautiful girl. Not beautiful so much as attractive. For the last ten years, all the girls he saw seemed attractive to Murat. They were all so natural, so at ease. Especially girls from Cerrahpaşa [faculty of medicine] who came to his shop. He felt utterly confused and agitated when he saw them. (50)

Murat diverges from the assertive and committed Islamist characters of salvation novels because he makes explicit his feelings about women. Author Kekeç violates the Islamic principle of moral guidance towards the inner self via his self-exposing character that is attracted to Müge and other women. Murat compares Müge with his wife. When he learns that Müge is a widow, he catches himself thinking that Müge might be an "easy girl" (83). Then he is ashamed of his thoughts and asks himself whether thinking of such possibilities "is not immoral and more importantly a sin?" (83). As Murat learns more about Müge, he compares himself with this twenty-six-year-old woman and feels himself "raw, untouched and inexperienced (*toy, el değmemiş ve acemi*)" (80). Interaction with new people outside of his Islamic circle leads Murat to reconsider the experiences he has had so far in his life. As a married Muslim man, he begins to violate an Islamic morality that revolves around controlling the social interaction of the sexes, not only by thinking about Müge but also by going with her to restaurants and pubs where he pretends that doctors prohibit him from consuming alcohol for medical reasons (176).

What differentiates this novel from salvation novels is Murat's perception of "the other." Salvation novels were based on the construction of oppositional characters. They homogenized secular characters as lacking self-consciousness and presented Islamic characters in contradistinction to their secular opponents. By contrast, in *Yağmurdan Sonra*, Kekeç does not totalize and stigmatize all non-Islamic characters. Murat realizes that Müge is different than her secular friends. While her friends speak with a secularist oppositional language and position themselves against Islamists, Müge is portrayed as a character who respects differences. Thus we can specify two types of "other" in the novel. One is the "offensive" secularist character, represented by Müge's friends and Murat's neighbors with whom Murat is in conflict at a discursive level throughout the narrative. The other is Müge, "a democratic liberal other" who respects different views. Murat goes to pubs, to non-Islamic spaces, and discovers "other worlds" with this "other"— while frequently asking himself, "what I am doing here?" (84). New contacts with the "other" and excursions to new spaces shake his singular and well-rooted Muslim identity.

Another event that upsets Murat's Muslim identity is his encounter with his stepsister, Hülya. Murat has had a problematic relationship with his father since his father left his family when Murat was young and married a woman of Italian origin. Murat begins to visit his father when his father gets old and sick. When visiting his sick father, Murat meets Hülya. He is affected by her beauty, as she is a girl in her twenties with "blonde hair and tall legs" (67). Murat is drawn to Hülya and begins to fall in love with her. He visits his father's house more frequently. He waits for Hülya when she goes out of her office. He plans to tell her about his love several times but cannot. When Murat's brother-in-law realizes that Murat is interested in Hülya, he criticizes Murat, saying,

You are siblings, mate! Is it proper for a man to chase after his sister? Shame on you! Even if you do not feel shame, at least know that it is also a sinful act, you rascal! You are an educated, married and furthermore a devout man! Does it suit you? (161)

Even though Murat tries to reject the criticisms by saying, "she is not my sister," he accepts the truth of his brother-in-law's words. Nevertheless, he confesses that

> One can not control his feelings all the time. Hülya is my weakness. I love her. Even though my love is not reciprocated, it is a source of strength and meaning in my life. It may be a dangerous intimacy, an immoral tie but … I love this girl. Let this be my death. Let this be the denial of my whole life, of the order that I have for years struggled to establish. (130)

The character develops a new mode of reasoning in a narrative form that stands opposed to the collective narratives of Islamist subjects of the 1980s. Salvation novels sought imaginatively to construct a notion of communitarian morality that revolved around controlling one's inner and outer selves and thus promoting modesty. Murat diverges from the Islamist characters of these novels. Murat's exposure of his love, especially an "unnatural" love, violates the borders of Islamic morality and constitutes a challenge to the collective understanding of Islamism. More "dangerously" perhaps, his exposition of love signifies his refusal to conform to Islamist social constraints.

By narrating the "indecency" of a Muslim subject, *Yağmurdan Sonra* also constitutes a challenge to the Islamic conception of literature that claims to derive from *edep* (decency) and to the narratives of salvation novels that never depict Islamic characters in non-Islamic places and relations. The polarized discussions about this novel in Islamic circles demonstrated attempts to police the borders and hinterlands of Islamic morality. After its publication, radical circles accused Kekeç of depicting "indecent" and "deviant" relations and asked "how a Muslim personality could write such things" (Değirmenci 2000, 69). Radical circles accused the novel of being autobiographical and asserted that the novel did not portray "us" [Muslims] adequately. A critic wrote that the novel "stabbed us from behind and even bad-mouthed us" (Değirmenci 2000, 70). Kekeç replied to these comments in his column by stating that "the 'We' is not clear I think.... Am I subjective in my writing? Of course. The novel did not bear any mission. I am not a missionary. I have just written a novel. If you write on life, it is inevitable to depict some taboos.... I am not uncomfortable with that (Kekeç 2000). Clearly, Kekeç's understanding of literature and Islamic identity diverges from the authors of collective Islamism. As noted by a novelist in 1989, many Islamist actors of the 1980s "claimed that the novel was a means for expressing our ideals.... It was not enough to write a poem, its content must have been full of belief, ideology and pedagogy.... If in a novel a protagonist stands in front of a brothel, the writer was condemned as if it were he who stood there" (Kitap Dergisi 1989, 11). In this regard, Kekeç's narrative issues a challenge to collective representation of Islamic subjects. The novel presents the inner self of a Muslim character as a site of struggle between conflicting desires. Murat's longing for love, as the above quote demonstrates, leads him to resist the boundaries of communitarian morality and to free himself from the image of Islamic identity. His desire for "dangerous intimacies" in public places constitutes his resistance to the authoritarian tendencies of Islamist politics that depend on monitoring the social interaction of the sexes in public space.

Despite his rejecting of Islamist tenets and his conflicting and contrasting desires, Murat feels that he cannot save himself from being charged as *irticacı* (reactionary) in the context of the 28 February Process since his trial as an ex-publisher continues. When he reads a statement of *Batı Çalışma Grubu*[14] noting that they "scrutinize everything that the reactionaries (*irticacılar*) do," he ridicules both himself and the "secularist regime" that takes him to court by thinking that,

Have they [*Batı Çalışma Grubu*] been watching over me? If so, who knows what they think about me? Vagabond, lover, idle.... He does not take good care of his business, he does not go home, he spends his days and nights on streets. So far we have not come across any backwardist (*irticai*) activity here, but such people are more dangerous. He hides [*takiyye yapıyor*] who he is, by giving the impression that he spends his time with girls and has fun all the time. (154)

Murat criticizes the military elite's essentialist understanding of Islam that interprets every manifestation of Islamism as a threat to the foundations of the republic. He speaks subtly and ironically about his situation and the regime's treatment of his Muslim personality. Significantly, and like Nisa in *Halkaların Ezgisi*, Murat desires to withdraw to more private boundaries, having given up his Islamic assertions and taken a critical stance against collective definitions of Islamism. Similar to Nisa, to achieve this he does not only take an oppositional stance to the fanatical secular harassment of Islamists, but also directs his criticism toward Islamic circles. When Murat chats with a few Muslim publishers about the February 28 Process, one of them notes in passing that the "[February 28] Process runs severe." In response Murat says,

> If the process has gone harshly, we should blame it on not only those who initiated it, but also on people like you who prepared such a process by leading astray the devout majority.... You pretend to be superior by talking about universal democracy, pluralism and law, while you simply repeat what you hear from high ranking military officials.... Why did not you think about [this], when you kept selling cheap salvation stories? (145)

Thus Murat does not invoke the discourse of collective Islamism of salvation narratives that simply accounts for the "victimization" of Muslims because of exclusionary secular politics. Rather, he considers the Islamist understanding of his period as another source of the conflict. In other words, he finds not only secularists but also Islamists responsible for the rise of systemic conflict and distances himself from the understandings of both groups.[15] Despite his reassessment of Islamic politics, the novel concludes with Murat's arrest and jailing as a Muslim man who is unable to both tell Hülya about his love for her and find happiness in his marriage.

Self-Reflexive Narratives and Emerging Muslim Subjectivities

What differentiates *Halkaların Ezgisi* and *Yağmurdan Sonra* from the salvation novels of the 1980s is their self-reflexive and self-exposing narratives. Reflection, as Ricoeur notes as follows, is not intuition: "Reflection is the effort to recomprehend the *ego of the ego cogito* in the mirror of its objects, its works, and ultimately its acts.... Reflection is the appropriation of our effort to exist and our desire to be by means of works which testify to this effort and this desire" (Ricoeur 1974, 327). Reflexivity, in this sense, is the basic process that unites individual and social processes. As Mead points out, "it is by means of reflexiveness—the turning back of the experience upon himself—that the whole social process is brought into the experience of the individual involved in it" (Mead 1934, 134). Islamic literary narratives of the 1990s constitute the self-reflection of Muslim actors as mediated through texts. In other words, the self-reflexivity of actors constructed through novels brings the Islamic experiences of the 1980s and 1990s to the fore. Nisa narrates the exaggerated importance of veiling in Islamic circles as well as the conceptualization of women as the key bearer of Islamic claims in the 1980s. Murat makes the constraining collective definitions of Islamism explicit. In short, both Muslim characters narrate themselves in the mirror of works, texts, and discourses of Islamism derived from the 1980s, seek to reinterpret their earlier experiences, and reconstruct their subjectivities in an intelligible form.

What connects these two characters at the end of their process of self-reflection is their critique—even transgression—of the collective boundaries of Islamism. Nisa transgresses the boundaries by taking her scarf off, while Murat unveils himself and violates Islamic morality by exposing his inner self and sinful love. Boundary-crossing signifies a subject-creating event. It is a "revolutionary element" since it breaks down "accepted classification" (Iser 1993, 9). During the 1980s, the headscarf, salvation novels, and Islamic intellectual works questioned the

Westerncentric Kemalist conception of civilization and performed a transgression of secular boundaries—boundaries that equated "civilization" with the "West"—by Islamic subjects. These subjects, however, were collective subjects speaking in a language of "we" that was oriented towards group ideals promoted by the literary and intellectual narratives of Islamism. New socialization patterns, the acquisition of new professions, the attendance and transformation of urban spaces, and alternative practices of Islamic precepts in daily life resulted in new subject formations in the 1990s. The confession of conflicting desires, the acknowledgment of sinful love, and the removal of the scarf constitute another boundary-crossing that not only breaks with collective definitions of Islamism but also represents the emergence of new Muslim subjectivities along with their new interpretations of the true (or truer) meanings of Islam.

Nisa's act of taking her scarf off and Murat's confession of his sinful love might be interpreted as these characters' forsaking of their Islamic identities. However, they do not reconstruct themselves by adopting Kemalist secular sensibilities or practices. Even though Murat goes to non-Islamic spaces, he does not drink alcohol. He revises his earlier Islamist ideals and disregards the strictly defined boundaries of Islamic morality. The theme of love in his case plays a crucial role in his transgression of such boundaries—as was the case in *Mızraksız İlmihal* by Mehmet Efe (1993), another self-reflexive novel of the period.[16] In this novel, Efe narrates the love story of a young male Islamist student and his subsequent questioning of his revolutionary ideals. Efe's Islamist protagonist is transformed in a process similar to Murat of *Yağmurdan Sonra*. In both cases, the love relationship challenges the characters' revolutionary and collective Islamic ideals. Love, as Touraine notes, "does away with social determinisms and gives the individual a desire to be an actor, to invent a situation, rather than to conform to one.… It is thanks to the relationship with the other as subject that individuals cease to be functional elements of the social system and become their own creators and the producers of society" (1995, 227). It is Murat's love and the commotion it produces in his inner self that leads him to re-examine his situation and reorder his narrative life history. When he realizes that he is not content with his life, his marriage, and the (Islamist) concepts on which he has built his self-narrative, he acts to create a different self. In the process, Murat, who in his university years once sought "to save the country," now confesses that "we realized too late that we had wasted the best years of our youth with impracticable concepts, with a futile attempt to apply an import-substitutional civilizational project" (29). What he refers to by "import-substitutional project" is the importation of the works of Middle Eastern Islamist thinkers such as Sayyid Qutb and Ali Shariati that played a crucial role in shaping the agenda of Turkish Islamists in the 1980s. The criticism is biting, because one key aspect of Islamist discourse in the '80s was its attack on Kemalism as a betrayal of local values in the form of western mimesis. Because of Islamism's adoption of revolutionary and fundamentalist Islamic thinking, Murat goes on to say,

> we did not read our own traditional cultural works. ... We could not read Ahmet Cevdet Paşa, Yahya Kemal and Tanpınar....What we did read, in the name of "universal revolution" were the trivial scholars of Egypt, Pakistan and Afghanistan. (145)

The Middle Eastern Islamist thinkers that were praised by the Islamist Murat in his university years are now treated as "trivial" by the Muslim Murat. We might say that what he rejects is not his Muslim identity, but rather his Islamist identity and his revolutionary understanding of Islam. Revolutionary Islamism involved a radical and negative re-appraisal of previous Islamic manifestations (as traditional) along with its desire to return to *Asr-ı Saadet*. Murat's reference to Yahya Kemal and Hamdi Tanpınar signifies his decision to cut his ties to fundamentalist/revolutionary Islamism while reconciling himself with other figures that had been treated by radical Islamists as "distorted."[17] In short, Murat's case testifies to a process in which a new Muslim self is shaped via the rejection of revolutionary ideals and the reappropriation/invention of despised local particularities, paving the way for novel understandings of Islam.

Similarly, when Nisa takes her scarf off she does not deny her Muslim identity. However, her situation is more difficult than Murat's since she is now unveiled, naked of the symbol considered the "flagship" of Islam by Islamic circles. Furthermore, Islamic veiling, as Nisa pointed out, refers to a garment that imposes its own rules of walking, behaving, and living on women. Thus the act of unveiling involves returning to a different (her pre-veiling) lifestyle for Nisa.[18] Her decision to take off her scarf is accompanied by an internal fragmentation between her religious collective and her individualist worldly identity, represented by the presence of the two characters Nisa and Nisan in the narrative. These two selves engage in an intense and mournful dialogue lasting for days and months even after her unveiling. After ten years of veiling, it is not easy for her to change from Nisa (her veiled self) to Nisan (her unveiled self). This bifurcation sometimes leads Nisan to address Nisa as follows: "please do not leave me, do not give me up! ... O my God why is it [her decision to unveil] hurting me so much?" (175). After her unveiling, Nisan (her unveiled self) feels that she has once again become ordinary, missing the notoriety of Nisa, her veiled self. Nisan talks to Nisa as follows:

> I missed you so much. Your furious walk, your exceptional stance, the mystery of your difference. Look at me, how I approach ordinary people. I am not anymore different from women in the street. You were my dream and story. I no longer have a story to tell. I have nothing to dream. It is also very boring to feel that you are no longer different [from other people]. (169)

Despite this internal bifurcation and mournful dialogue, as a result of her self-critical process Nisan decides to leave her veiled self (Nisa) "outside." Her new unveiled self is determined to succeed, responding to the crying of Nisa at the door as follows: "Do not cry! I will not let you in. I will try to live with this new style" (162). Nisan tries to convince Nisa by saying that "I still feel myself covered with my new style. I believe that I can be protected so [unveiled]. I always felt myself shelterless and defenseless with it [the headscarf]" (163). Nisan desires to be relaxed with her new unveiled self, still considering herself within Islamic practice.

However, one key difference distinguishes Nisa(n) from the male character, Murat. Nisa(n) needs to explain her feelings and transformation to her close circle and husband. After her unveiling, the author notes, "the talisman that kept her husband protected from evil, and constantly reminded [him] of his religion" (57) suddenly disappears. He becomes cold towards Nisa(n) and has frequent crying fits. She tries to make him understand that she still feels "veiled" (163) even though she no longer wears a scarf. She continues to read the Koran and practice other religious rituals. She does not reject the premises of Islamic belief, even headcovering. What she does oppose is the obsessive interest in the headscarf and the related framing of women that it imposes. Her unveiling is a personal choice and constitutes resistance to collective definitions of Islamism.

Like Murat, Nisa also represents a new Muslim subjectivity that rereads the Islamic experiences of the 1980s. Central to her questioning is the position of women. Islamism constructed a category of veiled Islamist woman in contradistinction to traditional Muslim women. Whereas traditional women were portrayed as living religion in their daily life without understanding its "real message," the Islamist woman is distinguished by her desire to lead the whole society to salvation. As mentioned in chapter 2, Dilara of *Müslüman Kadının Adı Var* exemplified the emergence of Islamist characters with her claims of being different from her traditional aunt. Nisa of *Halkaların Ezgisi* can be paralleled to Dilara since in her Islamization process, Nisa is also taught the importance of the veil, of having a distinct Islamic identity on the basis of this veil and, of the role of women in ensuring social morality. Nisa, however, after ten years of veiling, seeks to question the Islamic dichotomy between traditional and Islamist woman. When she thinks of the Islamic understanding of the 1980s, "she is now surprised, how so many young and beautiful girls without falling in love had turned into empty words, slogans and angers" (137). Nisa(n) criticizes their Islamic conception of womanhood that led to the emergence of activists thinking in clichés and displaying anger to serve Islamic purposes. Nisa(n) critically depicts the related binary position between the activist and the traditional woman as such: "We refused everything that this woman [traditional woman] represented. And we replaced them with nothing. We tried to learn manhood and womanhood from books. We lost our souls among the pages of books. I now understood that woman" (31). Nisa(n) thus confesses the failure of the gender politics of Islamism that left them with "ruins, consisting of only concepts after a process of mental construction" (31). She takes a step to reconstruct a new subject position by resigning from the search for big ideals and realigning herself with the image of traditional woman.

Another aspect of her narrative is her critique of the association of veiling with communitarian morality in Islamic frame. The salvation narratives of the 1980s presented veiling as the prerequisite of social order and morality. Being unveiled, on the other hand, was presented as the source of *fitne* (moral disorder). After her unveiling, Nisa(n) asks her husband whether "every woman you see on the street seduces you?" (182). She answers her own question in response to her husband's silence as follows: "Let women not be ashamed of everything. Let men be more modest.... Let everyone be a master of his/her body, morality, eye and ear" (183). This response represents a sharp rebuke to Islamist discourse on veiling as promoted by the characters of salvation novels, demonstrating another way in which Nisa(n) differs from Dilara of *Müslüman Kadının Adı Var*. Dilara, as in the case of all protagonists of salvation novels, explained the reason for her veiling as follows: "because all kinds of molestation occurs to young woman.... Veiling reduces prostitution and instigation. It protects women from dangers" (88). Such an interpretation of the cause of veiling involves an Islamist framing of the public sphere that is based on a "rigid assumption that the public is, by default, male" (çınar 2005, 77). Nisa(n)'s demand that "men be more modest" therefore constitutes a challenge to Islamist definitions associating the veil with public morality. She also resists an Islamist framing that posits veiling as indispensable for women in order to protect themselves from the probing or insulting male gaze. In sum, Nisa(n) challenges the duty given to women of carrying in their body the collective's morality. She resists the framing of woman as a source of disorder.

Finally, Nisa(n) questions the primary characteristic of collective Islamism: its search for re-implementation of the practices of the period of the Prophet and Caliphs in modern times. This led Islamists to question every religious belief and practice after the golden era of the Prophet and Caliphs. Nisa(n) now judges disapprovingly the radical Islamic stance that she sees as despising the present in the name of the purity of the golden era. Questioning the attitude that seeks to revive the golden era she says that it,

> is as blinding as considering everything of the past sacred and indisputable. Because once you start unwinding the yarn of the sacred, you could go as far as the Koran. Such is the rule of the game. You have to play it to the end. And you will return, as every treasure seeker before you, loaded with nothing but defeat and disappointment. You will lose everything that you took on your journey…. This is what we did. We pretended that there were hidden treasures and that we would find them. (212)

This paragraph is indicative of a critique of the authenticating claims of Islamism by new Muslim subjects. Authenticity was a key word of Islamism, as it provided Islamists with the assurance of an Islamic golden age and a model that could be enacted in the present. Authenticity facilitated the search for "treasure," the endeavor to ground practice in the past in the project of Islamizing modern society. It allowed Islamists to construct role models that might be replicated in modern society. Yet Nisa(n) says that "we are fed up with the stories of women investigating the marketplace or going to *jihâd*. We are tired of the trips to the past, of going to the same places and seeing the same things. We want new and unknown stories" (212). Thus Nisa(n) resists both the authenticating claims of Islamism and its role models. Her self-critical and self-reflexive stance leads her to construct a new narrative exemplified by her revision of the Islamist *Asr-ı Saadet*. While Dilara of *Müslüman Kadının Adı Var* claimed that "we have to take not Europe's but *Asr-ı Saadet*'s women as models (Turhal 1999, 78), Nisa(n) objects to this idealization. Referring to the role models of Islamism, she says that,

> we thought that those men and women lived for us to take them as models. We attributed exaggerated meaning to their every word and attitude. As if they had resolved all their problems and found answers to their questions…. We never thought that they were like us, just trying to live. (217)

Following her de-sanctifying posture, Nisa(n) rereads the period of *Asr-ı Saadet* to emphasize that Islamic history, too, is full of violence and injustice—as in the assassination of the third Caliph after the Prophet Mohammed, Osman. She also reinterprets the role of women of this period as active participants of social and political life. Her rereading of Islamic history results in her cutting ties with collective and fundamentalist definitions of Islamism.[19] What characterizes collective Islamism is its certainty and sureness in regard to its Islamic claims to history. However, Nisa(n) concludes by arguing that "perhaps this history was a big lie. What we knew as right was perhaps wrong and what we knew as wrong was perhaps right" (212). She proclaims that "there is no such age that sheds its golden lights!" (215). Finally Nisan argues conclusively with Nisa as follows: "Life cannot be sanctified Nisa! Life cannot be made sacred. It is only for living" (223).

In conclusion, I would argue that Murat's and Nisa's reflexive reinterpretations of Islamic identities constitute new Muslim subjectivities that are not "anti-Islamic" interpretations of Islam, but rather "anti-Islamist." These two characters do not challenge the basic premises of Islam, and they still conceive of themselves as believers. Both object, however, to Islamist collective, fundamentalist, and revolutionary interpretations of Islam. In this sense, their identities might be described schematically as shifting from Islamist to Muslim. Without the headscarf or with a sinful identity, one can still be Muslim—but one cannot, however, easily be considered Islamist. These new self-reflexive and self-exposing characters testify to the emergence of novel understandings of Islam, simultaneously generated and reflected in fiction.

From **Epic** *to* **Novel(istic)** *Conceptions of Islamism*

Throughout this book, I have interpreted Islamic literary narratives of the 1980s and 1990s as an important means of developing a coherent identity—or a narrative (hi)story—in modern Turkish society by Islamic subjects. What make these literary narratives valuable cultural and political texts of the period are not only the authorial intentions presented in the characterization of Muslim characters but also their plots and dialogues into which ongoing political debates of the two decades infiltrate. To put it more concretely, Islamic narratives are political and cultural texts that are intimately linked to contemporary debates and practices of modernity, democracy, secularism, the subject of the headscarf, and an Islamic order—issues that relate not only to Islamism but also to the entire social formation.

The emergence of Islamic novels in the 1980s represents the appropriation of a modern literary genre by Islamists. Islamist novelists wanted novel writing to be an activity that should derive from and aim toward the propagation of an Islamic vision of the world. This "Islamic vision" refers to a new interpretation of Islam and Islamic identity that was produced in tandem with the rise of Islamist movements in the context of the 1980s. This newly emerging Islamism involved a sharp critique of both a more established traditional understanding of Islam and the Kemalist project of modernization.

Literary Islamism in this vein appeared as part of a general Islamic discourse with new Islamic novels characterized by a critical posture toward what Islamist authors called the "westernist" (*batıcı*) novels of the republican period. Islamist novelists possessed a monolithic but productive perception of the republican novel as based on a misrepresentation of religious signs and a promotion of a westernist lifestyle. They argued that the novels of the republican period involved narratives that "misrepresented" religious personalities and "prioritized an assault on belief" (Yardım 2000, 175). Therefore the issues at stake in their conflict with "westernist novels" revolved around these novels' representations of issues concerning religious (Islamic) belief, identity, and morality. Islamic salvation novels by contrast were claimed to make such "misrepresentations" explicit and to narrate "true Islam." Viewed this way, literary Islamism signifies the endeavor of Islamists to develop a discursive strategy to combat "the negative effects" produced by secular narratives. Hence Islamic novels can be construed, to use Eagleton's term, as "signifying practices" (1996, 205) of Islamic actors within a whole field of discursive experiences.

In the production and consumption of Islamic novels, I have argued that there is a mutually determining relation between texts, contexts, and the formation of Muslim selves. This is because, as Fornas points out, "the relations between cultural texts and human subjects run in both directions: texts emanate from interacting subjects who are themselves continuously transformed by using texts" (1995, 227). Islamic literary narratives then not only reflect Islamist actors' endeavor to develop a positive Muslim identity in the secularized context of Turkey, but also are generative of gender roles, attitudes, and emotions. Thus Islamic literary narratives provide us with a ground to explore the perceptions, emotions, intentions, and interactions of Islamic actors of the 1980s and 1990s. This narrative characteristic allows us to overcome the limitations of culturalist and essentialist approaches toward Islamic movements. This is because today's dominant culturalist and essentialist explanations of Islamism speak through a general category of Islam, disregarding the relational and contextual dimensions of Islamic practice and agency. They often attribute a fixed essence to Islamic activism and Islamic identity outside the scope of time and space. Islamic literary narratives, on the other hand, embed characters in contemporary modern urban contexts and represent them as agents responding to other actors and current debates on Islam and modernity. They reveal and contribute to Islamic politics, emotions, conceptualizations, and changing notions of Islamic agency along with its varying responses to historical and political processes in temporal, spatial, and sequential plots.

I have also shown how the Islamic narratives of the 1980s and 1990s display sharp differences in terms of their authorial discourses, organization of plots, and construction of time and characters. The salvation novels of the 1980s were narratives in which relations between an Islamic and secularized order were negotiated, an Islamic counterculture was imagined, and youths were proposed as the ideal Muslim self, necessitating their formation within a collective identity. The more self-reflexive and self-critical novels of the 1990s, on the other hand, interrogated these collective Islamic ideals as they reconstructed Islamic identity in the changing relational context of the period. Based on the analysis of changing Islamic narratives, I would argue that Islamism is transforming itself as Islamic actors reconsider and revise their own conceptions of Islam, democracy, and modernity in contemporary Turkey. In other words, the emergence of the new self-exposing and -critical narratives of the 1990s that questioned the Islamic project of transforming the whole society in the name of Islam reveals significant alteration in Islamic identity over the two decades.

The changing narratives of Islamic actors also suggest that Islamic identity, as with any identity, is always a project. It is not, to use Calhoun's terminology, a settled accomplishment, even though various external ascriptions may be fixed (1994, 27). Islamic identity, in other words, is not a settled, pre-relational, and pre-political position, as it is often charged with being by the essentialist claims of both Republican and Islamist activists. It is influenced by its theoretical context as well as by its attempts to reconstruct that context. The Islamic literary narratives of the 1980s and 1990s present changing practices, experiences, and conceptions of Islamic actors in the relational context of Turkey. These narratives are not mere descriptions of cultural and political processes in Turkey, but rather are part of these processes. Islamic narratives, in other words, do not only reconfigure these processes but also take part in the formation of these processes.

Finally I would argue that the collective representations of Muslims and Islamic ideals in the salvation novels of the 1980s and in the new self-critical and self-exposing narratives of the 1990s extend beyond the page and inform us about the changing practices and characteristics of Islamic actors and discourses in the two decades. Salvation novels are representative of what I called in this book the "collective and epic Islamism" of the 1980s. Self-critical novels, on the other hand, signify the newly emerging *novel Islamism* that began in the late 1990s. These two kinds of narratives refer to two strands of the Islamic movement dominant in the 1980s and 1990s respectively.

Epic Islamism: A Monologic and Collective Interpretation of Islam

The Islamic salvation narratives of the 1980s, exemplified by *Müslüman Kadının Adı Var* and *Boşluk*, are characterized by their epic discourse in a Bakhtinian sense. This is because their main plots and characters were articulated in an epic Islamic past, the period of the Prophet Mohammed and the first four Caliphs—the "age of happiness" in Islamic imagery. Both *Müslüman Kadının Adı Var* and *Boşluk* derived their Islamic conceptions and imagery from reconstructions of this past and presented them to their readers as solutions to problems brought about by Western modernity. Accordingly, the protagonists of salvation novels, Dilara and Cihan in our examples, were represented as epic characters oriented toward the great ideal of

Islamizing all of society. As ideal Islamic characters, they were depicted as heroic figures devoid of personal inconsistencies or internal conflicts. These ideal Islamic characters acted, studied, got married, wrote novels, and sacrificed their individual desires in the name of Islam.[1]

The type of world conceived of and presented by Islamic salvation narratives was an epic world, resting on a single and unitary Islamic plane that disallowed the existence of other (secularist opponents') possible lifeworlds. Characters that did not live an Islamic lifestyle were always characterized by their wretchedness and unhappiness. Their wretchedness, as portrayed by Islamist authors, derived mainly from Republican processes of modernization in the form of Westernization that led them to pursue a materialist life uninformed by Islam. Dilara of *Müslüman Kadının Adı Var* and Cihan of *Boşluk* were first portrayed as Westernized and degenerate characters in need of the true message of Islam. In the course of the narrative, they were taught about basic principles of Islam and were led to salvation, as represented by female characters' adoption of the headscarf. They were then turned into Islamic activists seeking collective salvation. Islamic salvation narratives in this regard were dominantly "pedagogical" rather than "performative."[2] They were pedagogical in the sense that all characters (and the novel itself as a genre) served as ciphers to convey Islamic messages. Their authors developed scenes and characters for their own pedagogical purposes. Even Dilara's secular professors were made to serve as objects of Islamic pedagogy, devoid of any personal content.

What characterized pedagogical Islamic discourse was its single truth presented in a single voice. For this reason, and though it might appear that Islamist and secular conceptions of civilization are negotiated in the salvation novels and nonliterary texts of the period in a dialogical way, this is more, to use Bakhtin's term, a "dialogized monologue" (1996, 345). The two voices, Islamist and westernist/secularist, are not *intersubjec-tively* related, as the latter voice is parodied and allowed no reflexivity to respond to the claims, styles, and metaphors of the former. This makes itself explicit through the authoritarian organization of Islamic texts which remove all other voices at the end and reach an epic closure represented by the holistic transformation of all characters. Typically, this authoritarian organization of the narrative is indicative of the authoritative discourse of what we may call monologic and collective Islamism of the 1980s as an idiom and form of politics.[3]

It should be noted, however, that the Islamic discourse of the 1980s that emerged via an oppositional posture toward Western forms of capitalism, democracy, and Kemalist secular visions of the world, developed interactively with secular actors and values. This is because Islamic actors were characterized not by a desire to isolate themselves from modern urban spaces but rather by a collective will to participate in them. Despite their critical stance toward republican processes of modernization, the salvation novels of the 1980s portrayed Islamic characters studying at universities or working in modern professions. Islamic literary narratives presented ideal role models as pious and virtuous yet willing to take part in modern urban spaces, even if in search for their Islamic transformation. Islamic actors' attendance at modern spaces and their interaction with modern secular values increased as the university student characters of salvation novels graduated and turned into actors active in politics, the economy, and modern professions in the 1990s.

The increasing participation of Islamists in public life since the 1990s—via their acquisition of new modern professions, the formation of Islamic middle classes, and their changing consumption patterns—raised new ethical questions that the oppositional Islamist discourse of the 1980s appeared to be unable to answer. Put another way, Islamic actors' presence at heterosocial spaces, universities, cafes, and restaurants, and thus their interaction with the secular public and the "other," clashed with the epic truth and protective framework of 1980s Islamism. New professions, new interactions with the "other", and the new settings of modern social life led Islamists to reflect upon the ideological "life-planning" of the 1980s.

Lifestyles are not separated from social context but rather are "characteristically attached to and expressive of specific milieu of action" (Giddens 1995, 83). Thus since the relational context of Islamists' action has changed in the 1990s, the idealized/imagined/lived Islamic lifestyle of the previous decade has been fractured by the proliferation of lifestyle choices.

Accordingly, the pedagogical salvation narratives of the 1980s began to be questioned by Islamic actors themselves. New actors, exemplified by Nisa of *Halkaların Ezgisi* and Murat of *Yağmurdan Sonra*, appeared on the scene challenging the schematic answers to "Westernization" that Islamism provided in the salvation novels. They critically reflected upon their Islamic ideals and Islamic practices to revise them in the light of new experiences, paving the way for the emergence of the "performative narratives" of the 1990s. "Performative narratives" presented Muslim characters in search of a new sense of self, disconnected from the constraining Islamic conceptions of the 1980s. The inner turn or interior search of the characters of these new novels resisted typification and general labels. To put it in the context of our exemplary characters, Nisa resisted and challenged the Islamic teaching about the headscarf and the collective role assigned to women of representing Islamic morality. Murat, on the other hand, exposed his "sinful" inner self in his search for love despite being a married Muslim man.

The new self-critical novels of the 1990s, with their emphasis on the interiority of characters and their focus on the present, are no longer able to be interpreted in light of an (Islamic) absolute past, and thus are closer to "novelistic discourse" in the Bakhtinian sense. They are novel(istic) in the sense that the protagonists of these narratives act in a contested terrain where they interact with different world views, in contrast to the single and unitary terrain of salvation novels. While the heroes of salvation novels lacked personal depth and their narratives received no dynamism from protagonists' internal conflict, the self-critical novels represented Muslim characters in the uncertainties of their daily lives, with doubts, insecurities, and conflicting desires. In contrast to the idealized and epic characters Dilara and Cihan, the self-reflexive postures of Nisa and Murat illustrate that the epic wholeness of the Islamic subject of collective Islamism disintegrated in the 1990s, and the unity of the governing ideology was undermined by the hero's interiority or self-reflexivity.

Self-reflexivity is not taken here as a quality that led to the emergence of (Muslim) subjectivity in the 1990s and which Islamists lacked in the previous decade. The novels of the 1980s—and Islamism itself—were also products of the reflexive action of Islamists. However, the representation of Islamic salvation characters with their unitary Islamic affiliations was singular and undifferentiated in order to form a collective "we." In that sense, Islamic subjectivity in the 1980s might be described as a "collective subjectivity," constructed mainly through the mediating contexts of publicity, including novels. The Islamist movement attempted to develop as a singular collective subject, censoring fragmenting tendencies on ethnic or gender lines, and criticizing both established Islamic understandings and secular moral codes—points that differentiate Islamists from traditional Muslims and secularists. The new narratives of the 1990s are products of self-reflexivity in a more individual sense, mirroring conflicts within Islamic selves and collective Islamic identity. Therefore 1990s narratives signify that a crucial tension has developed between the collective and individual Islamic subjects, and that as a result, the subjectivity of the individual has become an object of experimentation and representation in the 1990s. In new novels, in other words, the epic characters tend toward introspection, and epic truth (the sacred Islamic tradition) is subjected to a new re-evaluation.

Novel Islamism: New Critical Faces and Interpretations of Islam

The critique of epic representations of Islamism initiated by Islamic actors themselves paved the way for novel interpretations of Islam. This critical stance arose as Islamist actors reflected upon and revised their experiences of the two decades, renarrating the collective and revolutionary ideals of Islamism, Islamic conceptions of women and veiling, party politics, governmental practice during the February 28 Process, and the role and position of Islam in public and private life. The confession by Islamic actors of their logical flaws, their mistakes, and their inner conflicts constitutes key developments that differentiate novel understandings of Islam from the epic conceptions of the 1980s. Previously, Islamic signs of difference were constituted via the submission of self to religious faith, modesty, and the moral guidance of the community and individual. These signs, as Göle argues, characterize Islamic "religious conceptions of self and society in contradistinction to the public exposure of self, the confessional culture and the quest for transparency (2000, 103). Novels of the 1990s, on the other hand, represent a voluntary self-revelation or public self-disclosure by new critical actors. The confessional act of Muslim actors—the revelation of inner conflicts, non-Islamic thoughts, and non-Islamic experiences—constitutes a challenge to Islamic conceptions of self and morality, and undermines the collective definitions of Islamism.

These confessional and self-exposing acts challenging Islamic understandings of the 1980s are not restricted to the literary field but have extended into the practices of Islamic intellectuals and politicians since the late 1990s. A recent phenomenon among Islamic circles is the emergence of autobiographical accounts of Islamic actors who critically revise their Islamic past. The autobiography of Mehmet Metiner, a prominent Islamic figure of the 1980s and 1990s, provides an invaluable inner observation of an actor and his understandings of the period. Metiner, who was a member of the National Outlook Movement in his youth and then served as a consultant to the Welfare Party, can be characterized as one of many newly emerging self-critical figures of the 1990s. Paralleling the characters of self-critical novels, Metiner depicts the 1980s as follows:

> We were in a political struggle. We used to believe that working for the party was a requirement of Islamic jihâd.

> We used to call Erbakan *hodja* "the unique leader of Islamic world". Our party would come to power, erase all obstacles in front of Islam and reach our goal.... Our goal was to re-Islamisize society by establishing the Islamic state (2004, 47).

He then critically reflects upon Islamic party politics, its government experience during the February 28 Process, and the trajectory of Islamic movements in general, including the Afghanistan and Iran cases. He states that Islam in power in different cases "reduced Islam solely to a political ideology through authoritarian republican nation states" (Metiner 2004, 376). Such an Islam, according to Metiner, is "Jacobin Islamism" that leaves no space for nonIslamic actors, and is not in this sense different from what he calls the "secular Kemalist Jacobinism" criticized by Islamic actors. He confesses that Islamic actors in the 1980s were critical of Western democracy but he goes on to state, "they had learned democracy from Mohammed Qutb who was neither a political scientist nor social scientist" (Metiner 2004, 216). He then states that he and his friends have now "given up political Islam" and expresses the idea that Islam aims at capturing the state as follows: "Islam is not an ideology or religion of a state, and the Koran is not a constitution" (Metiner 2004, 216). He identifies his new position as someone who is in favor of democracy and "democratic secularism."[4]

In a similar vein, the new self-critical novels and self-exposing autobiographical accounts of Islamic actors are characterized by common references to the inadequacies of collective and revolutionary representations of Islamism of the 1980s in handling the "real world." Praxis often conflicted with and transformed utopian Islamic visions of the past, making Islamic actors draw lessons from their experiences and revise their life narratives. One group who drew lessons from their experiences, particularly after the February 28 Process, was the reformists within the National Outlook Movement (NOM) who founded the Justice and Development Party (JDP). The resignation of a younger generation of politicians from the movement was based on the awareness that given Turkey's secular public configuration, a perennially contradictory and polarizing Islamic discourse could not remain in power, as illustrated by the closing down of all NOM parties. Declaring that "they have changed," this younger generation of Muslim politicians have also stated that "Islam did not advocate a system to be implemented through seizure of the state," and they have recently criticized the concept of an "Islamic economy" (in contrast to the NOM's attempt to build economic cooperation between Islamic countries). Politicians of the JDP distanced themselves from the NOM by announcing that "they have taken off their National Outlook shirt." They moderated their discourse and announced that they are not an Islamic but a "conservative democrat" party.

New Muslim politicians are reminiscent of İrfan, the self-critical character of Mehmet Efe's novel, *Mızraksız İlmihal*, who also states that "he wants to take of his militant uniform" (1993, 171). Self-critical politicians and literary figures are new Muslim actors who resist epic, collective, and utopian interpretations of Islam. They also make a novel interpretation of a "new Islamism."[5] "New Islamism" was presented as a repositioning of the "traditional political Islamism" of the Welfare Party according to new national and international realities. According to Kadir Canatan, an anthropologist author of the journal *Bilgi ve Düşünce*, the main difference between "new" and "traditional Islamism" involves a vital conflict over the method and aim of Islamizing society as follows: "Traditional Islamism aims at transforming society through the state, and thus focuses on capturing state power.... New Islamism on the other hand has changed its ideological stance as a result of its political experience and it does not anymore see society as an object that has to be transformed" (2003, 23–27). These statements can be paralleled to the dialogue of self-reflexive characters with their new self-limiting Islamic stance on state and society.

These self-critical novelistic, intellectual, and autobiographical accounts all indicate a common social and political experience: professional Islamic actors who engaged in capitalistic economic activities, interacted with secular actors and modern forms of life, and became active in politics in the relatively democratic context of Turkey from the 1980s onward have developed a novel interpretation of Islam that is distinct from the collective definitions of an earlier Islamism. What characterizes these Muslim actors is not only their critical attitude toward revolutionary interpretations of Islam, but also their overt will to withdraw Islam to private boundaries. The female characters of the 1990s novels who resist the excess of meanings given to the headscarf, the male characters (or politicians) willing to take off their ideological blinkers represent Muslim actors that have renounced Islamist political ideals. This point is personified by an ex-Islamist character of Şakird, a recently published self-critical novel, who claims that he does not want to save people's faith anymore, but rather just wants to be an "ordinary man" (Müstecaplıoğlu 2006, 27). This new position is also captured by a headscarved female actor's comment in a recent interview as follows: "When I die, Allah will not ask me, 'did you Islamize the state?' Allah will ask me, 'what did you do to protect your self (*nafs*)?' I think I am solely responsible for myself" (Sever 2006, 226).

Recent research both in Muslim and non-Muslim contexts demonstrates that there is a "process of individualization of faith" among Muslims (Roy 2002, 181). For Göle, Islamism undergoes major changes connected to the transformative forces of a more liberal market, the agency of women, self-reflexivity, and individuation (Göle 2000). Individualization does not necessarily mean the emergence of more liberal interpretations of faith. It can also lead to "fundamentalism, as witnessed in contemporary Protestantism" (Roy 2002, 181). However, in the case of Turkey, Islamic actors' will to retreat into individual borders is accompanied by a liberal interpretation of Islam. What characterizes the new discourses of Islamic actors is the disappearance of a discursive hierarchy toward other life options. To put it differently, while the salvation discourse of Islamism engages in authoritative relations with and leaves no space for other discourses, a novel understanding of Islam provides a ground on which Islamic and other discourses might potentially condition each other. The younger generation of Muslim politicians who identifies themselves as "conservative democrats," the new headcovered female actors who state that they "benefit from and employ the concepts of feminist movements" (*Birgün* 5 May 2004), and the protagonists of new novels who search for the possibility of an Islamic life without the headscarf or through the friendship of people from non-Islamic circles are all indicative of new Muslim subjects who develop a discourse in which Islam is reinterpreted as a practice compatible with democracy, secularism, and feminism.

In a parallel vein, Yeşim Arat's study on educated headcovered women shows how these women reinterpret Islamic law in keeping with their modern identities and practices, since they reject "polygamy, unilateral divorce, or unequal inheritance rights that are generally attributed to Islam and viewed as restrictive of women's liberties." According to Arat, these new interpretations of Islam demonstrate "the infiltration of secular values of equality into the religious frameworks" of a new generation of Muslim women (2001, 43). As Muslim actors intrude into the heterosocial spaces of modern urban life and interact with secular republican values, they develop different interpretations of Islam and negotiate lifestyle choices from different options. Their novel interpretations of life choices display a potential to transform secular public life in Turkey to make it more diverse and democratic, as they practice an Islam more compatible with other worldviews.

My portrayal of 1980s epic Islamism and 1990s novel(istic) Islamism is not, however, restricted to the chronological transformation of Islamic discourse over the two decades. Epic and novel Islamism also refer to two different strands of Islamism that still coexist and clash in the present. The very debates presented above on the role of Islam in the modern world are indicative of the cleavages among Islamic circles. The most severe criticism of those who state that "they have changed" derives from other Islamic circles (particularly the National Outlook members and some radical groups), who still voice a collectivist discourse of Islamism. They accuse the new generation of Muslim politicians and critical intellectuals of "bitter betrayal," identify them as infected with the "westernization disease" and comment on their situation as a "backward transformation" (Alan 2004). Predicting the relative influence of epic and novel(istic) Islamism in the midterm future is difficult, although the electoral success of the Justice and Development Party and the rise of self-critical autobiographies and literary narratives suggest the possibility of a permanent shift in appeal.

Finally, then, in this transformation of Islamism, I would argue that the novel as a genre appears to be the most important tool of the new actors of Islamism in their reappropriation of religion and modern forms of life. The narrative form of the novel allows Muslims to make sense of life and of themselves as they attempt to reorder events and renarrate their life history. Writers use the novel as a tool of self-reflexivity, criticizing the restraint of the collective definitions of Islamic identity and "giving voice to and subjectivizing the Muslim" (Göle 1997a, 80). New novels provide Muslim actors with a rhetorical means of negotiating both individual and collective identity rather than expressing prescriptions for an Islamic community. The rhetoric allows for the narrative "cultures in contact" rather than "cultures in conflict." By reinterpreting the golden age of Islam, questioning their ideals, fashioning their inner conflicts as a struggle between the homogeneity of faith and the heterogeneity of practice, and establishing horizontal relations with the "other," the characters of the new novels represent a potential hybrid Muslim identity. New novels, with their narratives of the intimate relations and internal worlds of Muslim actors, manifest both the way in which experience is re-narrated over time and the way in which the perceiving subject itself is transformed. These transformed subjects refer to newly emerging Islamic imaginaries in the public sphere, which create a tension within the Islamist movement and signal in turn the transformation of Islamism.

Notes

Introduction

1. As an example of the production of such a discourse, see Bernard Lewis' article titled "The Roots of Muslim Rage: Why So Many Muslims Deeply Resent the West and Why Their Bitterness Will Not Easily Be Mollified" (1990).

2. According to Nilüfer Göle, Huntington's conception of Western modernity as distinct from and particularly in conflict with Islamic civilization disregards the universalistic pretentions of Western modernity. She writes that his thesis "calls for the abandonment of the universalistic stand of Western modernity and reaffirmation of Western identity and civilization as particular and unique. This accounts for the widespread echo his 'clash of civilizations' thesis has created both in conservative Western circles and amongst hard-line Islamists" (Göle 2006, 21).

3. I am using the term "imaginary" in the way that Castoriadis defines it: as the central and essentially arbitrary values through which any society institutes itself (Castoriadis 1997).

4. See, for instance, Qutb 1992; Mawdudi 1986; Bulaç 1987.

5. The following discussion between Emran Qureshi (journalist and expert in the fields of Islam and human rights) and Heba Raouf Ezzat (political science lecturer and womens' rights activist) on *sharia* and human rights can be taken as representative of this "compatibility" debate. For Qureshi, "The Sharia law, as is practiced in many Muslim countries today, is clearly incompatible with the Universal Declaration of Human Rights. Today Sharia is a source of injustice that profanes Islam and shames Muslims who adhere to a compassionate and merciful interpretation of their faith." By contrast, for Ezzat, "The Sharia law is not only compatible with human rights but also the most effective way to achieve human rights. Human rights violations in Muslim countries—whose regimes are usually supported by Western allies—are not due to Sharia law." Available at http://www.qantara.de/webcom/show_article.php/_c-373/_nr-6/i.html (accessed 10 September 2006).

6. On the historical pecularities of Ottoman/Turkish Islam in the sphere of politics, see Mardin 2006.

7. For an analysis of women and gender in an Islamic novel, see İlyasoğlu 1994. For analysis of selected stories written by Islamic authors, see Çalışkan (1996). Adem Çalışkan, in his unpublished PhD thesis (2002), presents an anthology of Islamic literature, and V. Ertan Yılmaz, in an unpublished MA thesis (2000), explores Islamic popular novels as sources of identity construction for Islamic actors. Herkül Milas, in his study on *Türk Romanı ve "öteki": Ulusal Kimlikte Yunan İmajı* (2000) (Turkish Novel and the "Other": Greek Images and Turkish National

Identity), refers to some Islamic novels in terms of their representation of the "other." Lastly, H. Bülent Kahraman, in an article reviewing the changing patterns of Turkish literature, alludes to the importance of Islamic literature in challenging republican epistemology (2000).

8. Such arguments are common to Islamic intellectual accounts, films, or novels of the period. See, for instance, Miyasoğlu 1999; Bulaç 1995.

9. For instance, the position of the *mustaz'af* (victimized), with which Islamic actors identified themselves in the 1980s, was defined with revolutionary content as follows: "A *mustaz'af* who accepts and does not object to his position is like a *mustakbir* (tyrant). In that case he contributes to the ongoing oppression and as a result goes to hell together with mustakbir" (ünal 1986, 417–18).

10. On the role of Islamic civil associations in the socialization of Islamic youth, see Türkmen 2006.

11. Ali Bulaç's seminal book *Çağdaş Kavramlar ve Düzenler* (1987) (Contemporary Concepts and Orders; first published in 1976), which was one of the earliest and most influential texts on Islamic youth, is a manifesto that theorizes "real Islam" in contradistinction to capitalism, Marxism, fascism, and secularism. He argues that this book is also a response to modernist Muslims who contend that "Islam is not an obstacle to attaining the level of Western civilization, development and modern science," in the process both misrepresenting Western modernity and making Islam identical with capitalism, socialism, or fascism (1987, 14). Bulaç was not alone in his search to distinguish the Islamic solution from the Western solution as his position was also shared by many prominent Turkish Islamist intellectuals of the period. Abdurrahman Dilipak for instance also stated that "The Islamic state does not promise wealth and prosperity to the Muslim community.… [To expect such a thing] would be to mistakenly expect that a goal promised by Capitalism could be reached via the Islamic route" (quoted by Gülalp 1997, 422).

12. On Islamic novelists' conceptions of literature, see the collected interviews in Yardım 2000.

13. See, for example, Mustafa Miyasoğlu's *Kaybolmuş Günler* (1975) and *Dönemeç* (1980).

14. For examples of such readings of Islam, see Tanyol 1999; Tuşalp 1994.

15. The concept of *takiyye*, which has been taken from Shia Islam and was adapted to describe the agenda of Islamic movements in Turkey by some secular groups in the 1990s, is often endorsed to signify the hidden intent of Islamic actors and thus to fix the meaning of Islamic movements. *Takiyye* is a tenet of Shia Muslims that refers to the concealment of their faith, if necessary, from non-Shias, especially Sunni Muslims. Historically, Shia Muslims have been in the minority and persecuted by some Sunnis since they have been considered heretics. Thus *takiyye* has been used as a method of self-preservation for Shia Muslims (Donzel 1998).

16. This interpretation, however, involves logical flaws. On the one hand, it denies the agency of Islamic actors, who are presented as driven or fixed by their Islamic faith, and hence explains Islamic social action by invoking an ideological determinism. On the other hand, it attributes a malignant form of agency to Islamic actors who are construed as capable of producing different narratives to disguise their real intentions in seeking to attain political power.

17. Notoriously literature was, for instance, regarded as an obstacle to "true" citizenship as enunciated in Plato's *Republic*. What underlies Plato's suspicion is a conviction that literature deals with image-making in a world of fiction. It, therefore, turns citizens' minds from the good to the corrupt by blurring the distinction between the true and the false (Plato 1996). This "ancient quarrel" between literature and philosophy has contemporary disputants, and literature has customarily been distinguished from "fact" on the basis that it "invents" or "makes up" reality (Mendus 1996).

18. As Eagleton notes, this modernist vision of science from the eighteenth century onward has shaped a great part of the intellectual world, producing a tacit knowledge on the scientific and nonscientific, organized by "plain, objective," and "fictional" languages respectively. In this division, literature has been consigned to the nonscientific realm since it is inherently regarded as fictional (Eagleton 1996, 2ff).

19. Bakhtin's conceptualization of literature displays close parallelism to that of Eagleton and Bourdieu. Literature for Bakhtin "is an inseparable part of culture and it cannot be understood outside the total context of the entire culture of a given epoch. It must not be severed from the rest of culture, nor, as is frequently done, can it be correlated with socioeconomic factors, as it were, behind culture's back. These factors affect culture as a whole and only through it and in conjunction with it do they affect literature" (1996, 2).

20. The emergence of the novel as a genre demonstrates the relation between literature and socioeconomic processes since the novel's history is closely linked with the creation of an industrial economy and a middle classes. The novel emerged as a specific genre in response to a new kind of audience that was literate, self-conscious in its manners and morals, and aware of itself as a class distinct from other sections of society (Stevick 1967). It arose in the eighteenth century as a middle class cultural product depicting individuals freed from the pre-industrial constraints of society. In an age when the ideology of individualism and a secular worldview were gaining currency with a developing middle class, the novel, writes Ian Watt in *The Rise of Novel*, "could only concentrate on personal relations once most writers and readers believed that individual human beings, not collectivities such as the church, or transcendent actors such as the Persons of the Trinity, were allotted the supreme role on the earthly stage" (1995, 87). The basic narratives of early novels, imbued with scenes depicting conflict between the individual and society, were not in this regard arbitrary, but reflected the ideology of relevant actors that sought the freedom of individual over community.

21. The novel selects, combines, and organizes certain events in a narrative form having a beginning and an end. The very process of the construction of narratives implies important points about people both collectively and individually since narratives are the central mechanisms through which emotions are expressed and identities are forged. In this regard, narrative theory as a way of looking at the organization and structuring of human experiences or language into larger units (novels for instance) is a helpful way of understanding the way that literature functions (Whitebrook 1996).

22. Geoffrey Harpam, in *Language, Literature and Ethics*, delineates this interplay between narrative, identity, and politics succinctly as follows: "Literature… articulates goals, instructs people on how to picture and understand human situations, moralizes action by showing its ends, provides models of motivations and a

set of character types and decisional models, structures an opportunity for the reader to test his or her capacity for discovering and acknowledging the moral law, holds the mirror up to the community so that it can identify and judge itself, represents negotiations between the community and the individual, engenders a relation between author and reader, promotes explanatory models that help make sense of different situations and that shelter the subject from the threat of inchoate, fixes the past and so makes possible free action in the future, and models the 'unity' that might be desirable in a human life" (cited by Whitebrook 1996, 39). Harpam's conceptualization of literature can be taken as a succinct résumé of Taylor's, MacIntyre's, and Nussbaum's approaches to literary narratives that are seen as embodying fundamental moral and political ideas relating theory and form through which people make sense of themselves and the world.

23. The novel as a genre has the capacity to explore emotions and motives, to demonstrate how choices are arrived at, and to examine the effects of those choices on individuals and communities (Whitebrook 1996, 44). The novel, in this sense, brings certain aspects of human life to the fore for theoretical attention. Furthermore, by presenting choices and the consequences of those choices, as Whitebrook suggests, it offers political theory some insight into the Machiavellian problem (1996, 33). This is because what the novel depicts, in the last instance, are individuals as political agents making choices within the context of particular political dilemmas. It expands political theory by dealing with particularities that often resist political theorizing.

Chapter 1

1. Eagleton argues that "pure" literary theory is an academic myth and claims that the "history of modern literary theory is part of the political history of our epoch" (1996, 170). It is therefore irrelevant to approach literature through the distinction between "fact" and "fiction," since there is no essence of literature as such. For Eagleton, the category of "literature" should be demystified in order to open up a new space to consider its relation with social ideologies and its political implications.

2. The case of Shakespeare illustrates the point as follows: "Shakespeare was not great literature....which the literary institution then happily discovered: He is great literature because the [literary] institution constitutes him as such. This does not mean that he is not 'really' great literature because there is no such thing as literature which is 'really' great or 'really' anything, independent of the ways in which that writing is treated within specific forms of social and institutional life" (Eagleton 1996, 176). The novel *Satanic Verses* by Salman Rushdie can be taken as another example. It might be thought—by the author and many readers—that this novel portrays the life of Mohammed and his epoch in a fictional language. It received, however, its meaning in a "real" context of historic power relations involving Western and Islamic cultural, political, and literary institutions.

3. Bourdieu's arguments regarding how struggle over the formation of meaning and social status is displaced onto the cultural field have profoundly influenced the sociology of literature. Bourdieu's theory first and foremost emphasizes that the

symbolic aspects of life are inseparably linked to the material conditions of existence. Social distinctions (and the power relations in them) are produced not only through material conditions but also in all areas of cultural life including groups' preferences in music, art, and literature. The production and consumption of cultural artifacts, he argues, contributes to the process of social reproduction. His basic concern in this regard emerges as the analysis of the role of culture in the reproduction of social relations of power (Bourdieu 1995 and 1996).

4. In his analysis of the social relations of power, Bourdieu situates actors within the context of different "fields" (art, law, or education) within which social action is organized. The organization of social life through different fields suggests that competition in social life is not necessarily over material resources but also involves the struggle over cultural resources in the cultural field. In each field, agents occupying diverse available positions engage in a struggle to control the interests or resources which are specific to the field in question (Bourdieu 1995).

5. Writing literature, then, can be conceptualized as a practice in the literary field that is an "independent social universe with its own laws of functioning, its specific relations of force, its dominants and its dominated and so forth" (Bourdieu 1995, 163). The autonomy of the literary field, however, does not negate its relation to other fields or to overall power relations. Rather, the literary field is relatively autonomous but structurally homologous with others. The relationality of different fields emerges in the way that a specific form of capital acquired through struggle in one particular field can be converted into other fields. Cultural capital (or prestige), for instance, can be a means to attain material property (economic capital).

6. On the origins and development of the Turkish novel see Evin 1983.

7. Namık Kemal states that "the Europeans have made so much progress in the way of the novel that it is possible to find in the language of each civilized nation thousands of stories from which moral, and even to a large extent educational benefits can be derived. Among them, especially some novels by such famous writers as Walter Scott, Charles Dickens, Victor Hugo and Alexandre Dumas are immortal works that are a source of pride for the civilization of our time.... In our country, however, the novel is the most deficient among the types of literature produced. Perhaps not even three stories can be found that could be read with pleasure" (translated and cited by Evin 1983, 16).

8. On the Young Ottoman movement see Mardin 2000.

9. For a discussion of the themes of love and free marriage choice in late nineteenth century Turkish literature in relation to changing family patterns, see Alan Duben and Cem Behar 1991, 87–121. For an interrogation of the construction of femininity and masculinity in the early novels of the late Ottoman Empire, see Sirman 2000.

10. In a society where communitarian values of modesty prevailed, the novel's expository quality of individual lives and love was sometimes considered dangerous for women by some novelists. For instance, according to Mehmet Celal, a novelist of the late Ottoman period, "since almost all novels narrate a love affair, they confuse women's minds, who are weak and sensitive by their very nature" (cited by Andı 1996, 42). Aijaz Ahmad mentions a similar attitude in another Muslim context. He states that during the formation of the Urdu novel, much of the debate revolved around "issues of femininity in a very conservative way" (Ahmad 1987, 20).

11. For instance, Ahmet Mithat calls Beşir Fuat and his circle "decadents" who, according to Mithat, were atheists, materialists, and alienated figures of the period (Berkes 2002, 379).

12. By referring to the political context in which the Turkish novel emerged, Murat Belge notes that "Turkish novelists are more political than their Western colleagues," (Belge 1994, 68).

13. Ömer Seyfettin, a nationalist storywriter, explains the absence of the novel as such: "Literature is an art of love and imagination. A great part of poetry deals with the love affair. But [exposing] love is forbidden in our tradition.... Women cannot even be seen because of their veil" (1989, 61).

14. However, Köksal argues that the literature of the early republican period should not be construed in too much of a homogeneous way. Although what she calls an "official nationalist" literary stance dominated the cultural realm during the nation formation process, there were also two other literary stances, represented by "cultural nationalists" such as Yahya Kemal and Ahmet Hamdi Tanpınar and "social realists" such as Suat Derviş and Hüsamettin Bozok (Köksal 2003, 209–12).

15. On the representation of religion and religious personalities in Turkish literature, see Gülendam 2002.

16. There are of course exceptions to these types of village novels, such as the novels of Yaşar Kemal.

17. Sometimes as a sharp critique, all literary products other than the Koran, *hadith* (sayings of the Prophet), and *evliya menkibeleri* (narrative of the merits and virtues of Islamic Saints) were rejected. In one of the daily Islamic journals, a columnist writes, "If the Westerners had the stories of our Saints, they would never write novels. If Tolstoy, Dostoyevsky, and Balzac knew Islamic Saints they would quit writing novels and become immediately their disciples.... Today reading books of those who claim to be writer is futile and wrong, since it prevents us reading Koran, *hadith* and *evliya menkibeleri*" (Altay 1995).

18. For a detailed analysis of Bulaç's thoughts in relation to literature, see Meeker 1991.

19. For a similar comment on the possibilities opened up by the 1961 Constitution, see *Kitap Dergisi*, 1989.

20. See, for instance, Davies 1991 and Yunus 1988.

21. Miyasoğlu (1999) argues that in his novels he consciously uses figures from traditional narratives like *Aslı ile Kerem*. Such an endeavour, besides a search for developing an original narrative, signifies Islamist novelists' aim to differentiate their narratives from those of the republican period. Miyasoğlu's reference to Islamic/Ottoman traditional narratives differentiates Islamic literary discourse from the radical Islamic stance that was critical of all Ottoman tradition in the name of a return to fundamentals, i.e., to the period of *Asr-ı Saadet*.

22. Another novelist, Mustafa Miyasoğlu, defines Islamic literature as "the emergence of Islamic content with literary quality." The prefix "Islamic," as he argues in the following quote, shapes the conception of literature as it does in any sphere of life: "Islamic literature is a literature reflecting Islam's attitude towards humanity and things. The stance of a man of letter will naturally be like the stance of a Muslim towards contemporary life and the world. A contemporary Muslim artist, whether he talks about the past Islamic life or on the constraints of current lifestyle, will naturally take an Islamic stance" (1999, 118).

23. Hekimoğlu (b. 1932) is a pseudonym of the author whose real name is Ömer Okçu. He published his novel under this pseudonym since he was a military officer (*ast subay*) at that time. As he states in an interview, he grows up in a non-Islamic circle until his twenties. His adoption of the Islamic worldview occurs through his encounter with the writings of Said Nursi (Kalyoncu 2002). He is currently one of the important members of the Gülen movement, an influential Turkish Islamic group with its international educational, economic, and media activities. On the Gülen movement, see Yavuz and Esposito 2003.

24. Said Nursi is an important Islamic figure of the twentieth century as the founder of the Nur movement. On Nursi, see Mardin 1989.

25. Despite the confrontational narrative of this novel, its popularity, according to Şerif Mardin, is due to the fact that it merges both traditional and modern themes. As Mardin argues, "Minyeli Abdullah provides links with modernity both in the genre used, but also by including items of daily life in a Muslim agenda that are necessarily drawn from modernity and the way modernity impinges upon everyday life. The radio for instance is taken for granted in the narrative" (1994, xi).

26. This scenario is first and foremost about Turkey, since, as the author makes explicit in an interview, "the location of the novel (Egypt) resembles Turkey and Minyeli Abdullah is a man like me" (Yardım 2000, 126). Islamist authors prefer to narrate current situations in Turkey through the example of Egypt or other countries in order to escape from state officials' monitoring. Science fiction was also employed to narrate Islamic issues, as in Ali Nar's *Uzay çiftçileri* (Space Farmers). For an analysis of this novel, see Szyka 1995. Besides Turkish novelist Ali Nar's work, Szyka also refers to Egyptian novelist Ahmad Raif's *Al-bu'd al-kamis* (The Fifth Dimension), claiming that both novels present forms of Islamic utopia. The development of characters in Raif's work, Szyka notes, may be "regarded as a fictionalization of the Qutbian model for forming an Islamic society" (1995; 102). He therefore underlines the close parallel between the literary and intellectual discourse of Islamism.

27. Şenler (b. 1937) is known as the first woman who covered her head in the "turban style" while she was taking university education in 1965.

28. Farzaneh Milani notes that in a meeting with members of the Writers Associations of Iran two weeks after the revolution, Ayatollah Khomeini adressed his audience as such: "What I request from the writers is that they be as committed as we clerics are. You gentlemen writers must be committed. Now, you should use your pen for the welfare of these people and write for the welfare of this society" (Milani 1992, 232).

29. Even for those such as Miyasoğlu, who states that they *are* concerned with the literary quality of texts, literature, too, is construed as a tool to convey messages. Miyasoğlu, who argues that he does not write novels with a clear thesis, admits that "my protagonists have a message. This is because I want to narrate a mentality (*zihniyet*). Sometimes several mentalities conflict and engage in a dialogue with each other. What determines my choice in these conflicts is my own worldview. Without doubt, I am writing with an Islamic worldview" (Miyasoğlu 1999).

30. In Turkish, the terms *edep* (decency) and edebiyat (literature) derive from the same origin.

31. http://www.users.pandora.be/avrupaturk/sohbet/ahmet.htm. (10 January 2004).

32. There are several definitions of *roman à these* as a genre. S. Rubin Suleiman proposes the following definition: "A *roman à these* is a novel written in the realistic mode (that is based on aesthetic verisimilitude and representation), which signals itself to the reader as primarily didactic in intent, seeking to demonstrate the validity of a political, philosophical, or religious doctrine" (Suleiman 1983, 7).

33. Altough it is claimed that this almanac involves a collection of the works of writers "sharing the same belief," many authors of salvation novels of the period are not cited in the *Suffe Kültür ve Sanat Yıllığı*. As I will show in the third chapter, salvation novels were first clearly criticized in the pages of this almanac in 1988, on the basis that they do not have any aesthetic content. Thus despite Islamist novelists' apparent collective voice on the function of literature, this almanac reveals cleavages among Islamist novelists over the content and the literary quality of their novels.

34. After evaluating the Islamic novels of 1986–1988, Emin Ağar wrote that "several more novels have been written during these two years. Yet these are not so important from our perspective. For instance Atilla İlhan in his last novel, *O Karanlıkta Biz*, writes about his experience in the Turkish Communist Party and his struggles within it" (Ağar 1987–1988, 79).

35. This is taken from an English translation by Katherine Woods in 1971. Of course, the politics of translation also apply to this text, but that is not my concern here. The original sentences in French are as follows: "Heuresement pour la réputation de l'astéroide B 612 un dictateur turc imposa a son peuple, sous peine de mort, de s'habiller a l'Européenne. L'astronome refit sa démonstration en 1920, dans un habit trés elegant. Et cette fois-ci tout le monde fut de son avis" (Saint Exupéry 1971, 16). Emphasis added.

36. The Turkish translation is as follows: "Bereket versin, Asteroid B 612'nin onurunu korumak için bir dediği dedik Türk önderi tutmuş bir yasa koymuş: Herkes bundan böyle Avrupalılar gibi giyinecek, uymayanlar ölüm cezasına çarptırılacak. 1920 yılında aynı gökbilimci bu kez çok şık giysiler içinde kurultaya gelmiş. Tabii bütün üyeler görüşüne katılmışlar."

37. The Turkish translation is as follows: "Asteroid B 612'nin şöhreti için, şükür ki bir Türk yönetici halkının Avrupa giysileri giymeleriyle ilgili bir kanun yaptı. Böylece 1920'de astronom delillerini etkili bir biçim ve kibarlıkta giyinmiş olarak yeniden verdi. O zaman herkes onun raporunu kabul etti."

38. The Turkish translation is as follows: "Ama 1920 yılında aynı gökbilimci Avrupalı gibi giyinmiş olarak tezini tekrar ileri sürdüğü vakit, herkes kendisine inanmıştı."

39. The Turkish translation is as follows: "Her ne ise çok iyi bir rastlantı olarak büyük ve değerli kumandan Atatürk bütün Türklerin Avrupalılar gibi giyinmelerini sağladı. Böylelikle daha sonraları Türk astronomu Avrupalılar gibi giyindi ve düşüncesini tekrarladı ve B 612 asteroidinin gerçek olduğu kabul edildi." In another edition, the translator prefers the term "great leader": "Asteroid B 612 is very fortunate because a great leader forced the Turks to dress like Europeans. In 1920, the astronomer, dressed in a very elegant suit, repeated his demonstration. This time everybody agreed with him" (trans. Aygören Dirim, Esin yayınevi, 1989). The original Turkish translation is: "Asteroid B 612'nin talihi varmış ki, büyük bir şef Türkleri Avrupalılar gibi giyinmeye zorladı. Astronom açıklamasını çok şık bir giysi ile 1920'de bir kez daha tekrarladı. Ve bu sefer herkes ona hak verdi."

40. The original Turkish translation of this paragraph is: "Astığı astık kestiği kestik korkunç bir önder geçmiş Türklerin başına. Halkı yasa zoruyla Batılılar (Avrupalı ve Amerikalı) gibi giyinmeye mecbur etmiş. Buna karşı çıkanları öldürtmüş. Fötr şapka giymeyenlere işkence ettirmiş. Kravat takmayan öğrencileri okuldan, memurları dairelerinden attırmış. Sokağa başını örterek çıkan kadınların örtülerini, genç-ihtiyar demeden polis ve jandarma eliyle, zorla açtırmış ... bütün bunlardan sonra B-612'ciğin Türkler tarafından keşfedildiği kabul edilmiş. Türk gökbilimcinin 1920 yılında, ayağında pantolonu, sırtında smokini, sadece kulaklarının üst kısmında kalmış biryantinli saçları ve boynunda papyonuyla bir Batılı gibi giyinmiş olarak yaptığı konuşmak ve kendinin değil Batılıların harfleriyle hazırladığı belgeler, alkışlarla karşılanmış.... İşte (Batılı ve onlara benzemeye çalışan) büyükler böyledir." This edition was collected on a court order. For other examples of translation see Neydim 1998.
41. The editor notes that as a result of criticism they received from their readers, they do not make conscious mistranslations in Western classics anymore (Okay 2001).

Chapter 2

1. On the relation between the author-text-reader axis, the reader is traditionally given a passive status, thought of as a passive receiver of meaning. This derived mainly from author-centred criticism of literary texts which put the reader in a marginal or excluded position. Recent approaches in the sociology of literature, however, have started to regard readers as creative agents rather than passive recepients of what authors write. Proponents of "reception aesthetics" or "reader-response" theories argue that the reader never comes to a text as a blank slate but instead places it against their "horizon of expectations" (Iser 1993 and Webster 1990).
2. Şerife Katırcı Turhal (b. 1955) is a high school graduate who has written four novels. Her other books include *Aslında Aşk Var*, *Kayıp Aranıyor*, and *Adı Müslüman*. For more information, see http://www.serifekatirci.com (accessed on 12 February 2004).
3. Language has long been considered a passive medium to convey ideas. The so-called "linguistic turn" of the 20th century, however, has led to the recognition that meaning is produced by language rather than simply expressed in it. Saussure has been an important figure in this turn with his contention that language is not "natural" in the sense that it fits the world of objects and ideas through its sound patterns and structures, but is an arbitrary and conventional system (1966). As a conventional system, language operates not as a passive medium but as a source of thoughts and ideas. This suggests that one can have meanings not because they are expressible through language, but because one has a language to express them in. Language is a means for creating values, and a great part of the constitution of subjects and objects. Language, in other words, is fundamental to all meaning. Although Saussure makes the point that language is a sign system whose conventions are agreed upon by a particular society, he has been criticized for studying language as an abstract and unified system, in a way that disregards the sociality and historicity of the language. Bakhtinian theory of language, on the other hand, opens up new ways to reflect upon the embeddedness of

language, and upon literature as a linguistic activity. Bakhtin (2000) argues that the study of language as an abstract grammatical system contributes nothing new to the process of meaning formation, except for some scientific abstractions. Language, for Bakhtin, is not a mere and secondary means of expressing ideas. It cannot be conceptualized outside the scope of real verbal interaction since a word or an utterance takes place between people who hold a particular place in a network of social relations. Verbal interaction, in other words, forms the basis of any language, which implies that language does not exist in isolation from but rather in interaction between human beings. Any literary utterance, in this vein, even if fictional, has connections with known reality since otherwise its meanings are incomprehensible. This necessitates the recognition that literary texts are social creations, produced on the basis of a common language between the author and the reader in a certain context.

4. Bakhtin states that "all words have the 'taste' of a genre, a tendency, a party, a particular work, a particular person, a generation, an age group, the day and hour. Each word tastes of the context and contexts in which it has lived its socially charged life; all words and forms are populated by intentions. Contextual overtones (generic, tendentious, individualistic) are inevitable in the word" (2000, 293).

5. The stigmatization of headscarved actors on the basis of a civilizational debate is maintained by secular circles. A columnist in a nationalist and secularist daily, *Cumhuriyet*, for instance, writes the following: "If these young girls must cover their heads then they can quitely stay at home and wait for a bigot husband like themselves! In that case no one would have anything to say against them. In her home she can cover her head, or any part of her body as tightly as she wants. What do we care, what does the society care! But those girls who say 'I want to have an education, I want to become a doctor, a lawyer, an engineer, a chemist, a state official or a teacher,' there is only one way we can shoe them and that is the path of modern civilization" (quoted by çınar 2005, 81–82).

6. Authors often caricature modern characters to depict a decadent personality promoted by modern civilization. For example, Günbay Yıldız portrays Ebru as such: "Ebru became one of the typical moms of the twentieth century.... Although Şahin [her child] has reached his first year, his mother did not suckle him with the excuse that her breasts would be deformed.... She did not change his diaper with the excuse that her fingernail polish would be damaged.... She became a mom who hated her kid ... a mom who is indifferent to any hardship of her kid" (Yıldız 2003, 113).

7. The characterization of a "secular other" with its blind imitation of Western modernity is common to salvation novels of the 1980s. In *Boşluk*, when Cihan disapproves of Tuba's headscarf since he finds it contrary to the modern age, the author makes Tuba refer to the imitative nature of secular characters as follows: "'Bindallı [a traditional garment],' said Tuba. We adopted it after it became the fashion of the year in France. Is it necessary that somebody else should remind us ourselves?" (Yıldız 2003, 86).

8. Günbay Yıldız often intervenes in the text to take a critical stance to secular circles, specifically Dilara's father. When Dilara is influenced by İbrahim's reading of the Koran, she asks her father if they have a Koran at home. Her father could not remember and they both begin to look for a Koran in his library. Then the author conveys his message about this situation as follows: "What a sad situation. Live off the beneficence of God. Study science with an intellect given by God. Collect

books and make libraries on the complex ecosystems of living creatures and throw away the Holy Book. What a great injustice" (Yıldız 2003, 26).

9. This is a striking feature of Islamism of the 1980s whose sources are not only constituted by Islamic texts and practices but also involve several European thinkers. Islamic actors selectively appropriate several European thinkers in order to support their own image of Europe. Although he misspells their names, Günbay Yıldız in *Boşluk* speaks through the mouth of pious Vedat to Cihan as follows: "I will mention the book of famous psychiatrist Carl Young titled Modern Man in Search of a Soul . [In this book he says that] 'I have been a doctor for thirty years. The cause of sickness of my mentally sick patients coming from all over the world is their weakness of their beliefs. And they will not recover unless they turn to the true faith.' Alexi Carel says that: 'Faith is a savior where medecine fails.' Vedat also mentions Bernard Show who says, 'If Europe had accepted the religion of Mohammed, Europeans would have recovered from their illness'" (2003, 162).

10. In Islamic discourse of the 1980s, Japan often emerges as a counterexample of modernization against secular actors' imitative perception of civilization. Islamic writers in both literary and nonliterary texts of Islamism have an image of Japan in which the country modernized itself by preserving its own tradition rather than imitating the West. In *Müslüman Kadının Adı Var*, for instance, the author makes Dilara reply to secularist professors who invoke to the West as follows: "We reached the level of Europe only in immorality.... Japan which was destroyed in Hiroshima now surpasses the West with its own complex writing, without its citizens having to remove their national costumes and while they sit on their own cushions" (Turhal 1999, 116).

11. Such a representation of Christian Europe is not limited to the literary sphere but also extends into the discourse of politicians of the National Outlook Movement who, as mentioned above, identified the European Union in religious terms as the "Christian Club." Parallel to the literary discourse, this political movement has also employed a conspiracy theory in explaining Turkey's backwardness that states that the country has been prevented from developing by "capitalist-Christian interests in the West" (Mardin 1983, 152).

12. On a discussion of the headscarf in relation to political theory, see Arat, 2001; and Moruzzi, 1994.

13. At the beginning, this new veiling was represented by university students. However, this movement has been turned into a mass movement in various Muslim contexts. *Hijâb* has also been a garment adopted by middle and lower middle class women (Macleod 1991).

14. Günbay Yıldız conveys several messages in a scene that leads Tuba to question herself about the headscarf. One day while Tuba lectures in a religion class, she sees that "the class became deserted since religion class has been made an elected course." Tuba became upset and thought the following: "they will be future adults without a goal." Tuba then asks her students, "What do believers do?" Some of Tuba's students respond that "believers pray and fast in ramadan." But one small girl does not sit and asks Tuba if she believes in Islam. "Of course" says Tuba. "But," replies the little girl, "believers should cover *mahrem* (prohibited) parts of their body, that is what mummy said."

Tuba feels affected deeply and says, "you are right." Upon this consideration, the author makes his point about the cause of her veillessness. He puts the blame on secular civilization as follows: "Tuba sighed, wondering about society. A society that promises darkness to generations saying that it is the light. Applauding a mentality that makes the teacher helpless in front of her students. Your shame, not mine" (Yıldız 2003, 83).

15. What this young woman says about her mother can be paralleled to Dilara's words about her aunt: "My mother, though illiterate, says her prayers, but she just repeats the same verse that someone in her family taught her" (Hessini 1994, 49).

16. As will be shown in subsequent sections, in Turkey since the late 1990s, new female figures have emerged in Islamic circles having academic titles and writing nonliterary texts on Islamic matters.

17. Ziya Gökalp, one of the idealogues of Turkish nationalism, writes the following in a poem:

> Women are also human beings, and human beings
> They are equally entitled to the basic rights of human beings
> Education and enlightenment
> So long as she does not work, she will remain unenlightened,
> Which means the country will suffer
> If she does not rise, the country will decline
> No progress is complete without her contribution (Doğramacı 1984, 127).

18. The veiling was discouraged (sometimes outlawed) during the modernization process of many Muslim countries. In Iran, for instance, unveiling became a royal decree on January 7, 1936 and this day was celebrated as the day of liberation for women. After the Iranian Islamic revolution, the same day was labeled as the "day of shame" in which Western values were imposed upon Muslim women (Milani 1992, 34).

19. Moghadam refers to the Kemalist revolution as, "women's emancipation model of revolution" in order to differentiate it from Algerian (1962) and Iranian (1979) revolutions in which veiling and modesty were encouraged for women. She calls these latter cases "women in-the-family models of revolution" (1993, 71–72).

20. The Kemalist female image promoted by reforms, however, as Durakbaşa writes, was basically a combination of conflicting images as follows: "'an educated woman' at work; 'a socially active organizing woman' as a member of social clubs, associations, et cetera; 'a biologically functioning woman" in the family, fulfilling reproductive responsibilities as a mother and wife; 'a feminine woman' entertaining men at the balls and parties" (Durakbaşa 1998, 147).

21. Göle notes that "It is the construction of women as public citizens and women's rights (even more cherished than the construction of citizenship and civil rights) that are the backbone of Turkish modernism" (1997a, 65).

22. The decision of the Constitutional Court in 1991 to ban the headscarf on university campuses is still active today. It reads as follows: "The headscarf and the particular style of clothing that accompanies it, which lacks a modern appearance, is not an exemption but a tool of segregation. This situation, which is the display of a premodern image, is increasingly becoming widespread, and this is unacceptable in terms of the principles of secularism, reformism and the Republic. Using democratic principles to challenge secularism is the absence of freedom of religion" (Çınar 2005, 83).

23. In salvation novels, women are often taught about illicit relations and premarital sexual engagements. "Intimate" matters, such as the importance of virginity for communitarian morality, are conveyed by other female actors. For instance, in

Günbay Yıldız's *Benim çiçeklerim Ateşte Açar*, a female literature student who begins to learn about Islam is made to ask a Muslim woman about the importance of virginity. The old woman replies as follows: "Imagine a close friend of yours sends a letter to your office or school with a note on it, 'private'. A friend opens and reads it before you. Then she tells you that you have a letter. You see the letter, you notice that it has been opened and damaged (*örselenmiş*).... You look at your friend's face. She says: 'I just overlooked what was written'. What do you feel? Can you forgive her?" The student immediately replies: "No!" (Yıldız 2000, 87). This argument is supported with other simple analogies. This is one of the examples that is common in most salvation novels. In their process of becoming "Muslim," all female characters are taught the importance of modesty and chastity. The construction of Islamic identity goes hand in hand with the construction of an external environment where regulations of communitarian morality are learned and internalized. Notions of communitarian morality provide Islamic actors with norms or models that play a role in shaping their collective identities.

24. The point that women's working will be detrimental to men's employment is also made by non-Turkish Islamic actors. One of the Morroccan Islamic female interviewees of Leila Hessini for instance, makes the same point as follows: "Women have invaded all the positions of work and this has created a problem for men who no longer have jobs" (1994, 46).

25. Attending university is legalized on the ground that it allows women the necessary knowledge to raise a new generation. Studying modern science is argued to provide women with an "educative motherhood (*eğitimci annelik*)" (Çayır 2000).

26. Zehra F. Arat writes, "Kemalist reforms were not aimed at liberating women or at promoting the development of female consciousness and feminine identity. Instead, they strove to equip Turkish women with the education and skills that would improve their contributions to the republican patriarchy by making them better wives and mothers" (1994, 58).

27. The homogenous perception of feminist actors is not confined to literary fiction but also extends to the nonliterary texts of Islamism of the 1990s. Cihan Aktaş, for instance, identifies feminists as "the psychologically sick, those in search of adventure, who run after fantasies, dumb socialities who aspire to give color to their lives, and finally those who consider that being a feminist is being enlightened, elite, progressive and Westernist" (Arat 2005, 22).

28. Similar arguments on feminism and the role of women in Islam are replicated by female actors not only in Turkey but also in other Muslim contexts. A Belgian-Moroccan Islamist activist makes the following similar points: "The deadly fault committed by feminists is to have pushed woman to compete with man, to walk in lock-step with him in all domains of life, to run after a mirage of equality on the altar of which she continually sacrifices her right to femininity and motherhood.... It is not competition that must be there between the two sexes, it is complementarity" (Malti-Douglas 2001, 130).

29. The Muslim characters in salvation novels are often portrayed as doctors. Similarly, in intellectual Islamic writings of the 1980s, a Muslim who truly understand the message of Islam is defined as a "doctor of humanity" (ünal 1986, 8). The analogy is striking in both political and literary Islamism, in both of which Muslims are depicted as "doctors" that signify Islamists' will to cure what they call the "morally degenerate society."

30. See especially Zeren 1996.
31. Based on her fieldwork conducted between 1989 and 1993 in Ankara on Muslim women, Saktanber similarly argues that the dichotomy between injury and pride shapes the definitive feature of Muslim women's identity in their daily narratives (2002).
32. Islamist novelists' preference to choose "modern," unveiled girls and their construction of an ideal female identity by making these female characters adopt veiling is sometimes criticized by veiled girls themselves through readers' letters. For instance, a veiled girl writes to novelist İsmail Fatih Ceylan in the following way: "In novels written by Muslims, veilless girls (*açık kızlar*) are always depicted as beautiful, attractive and good-looking. Muslim men, who are affected by novels, now find unveiled girls more attractive…. Why do you depict an unveiled girl as first attractive, and then by making her adopt veiling, promote her as an innocent person? You mean to imply that unveiled girls are beautiful and that veiled girls are less valuable? No, there are many beautiful girls among those veiled. I think you find unveiled girls charming because veiled girls do not expose their beauty. Okay, let's say, Muslim men acquire merit in God's sight because they veil unveiled girls. But what will be the situation of veiled girls? Please do not portray [unveiled] girls as beautiful so as to mislead young boys" (Ceylan 2002, 222). The reader then comments that Muslim men are not interested in veiled girls, but rather chase unveiled girls because of Islamist novelists' depiction of them as beautiful.
33. Kemalist republican epistemology, as Ayşe Kadıoğlu notes, is based on a "managerial attitude" of the Republican elite who employed a process of social engineering that would replace local, religious identities with secular, national idenity (1998).
34. Dilara tells her father, whose mind is confused since he was taught that modern civilized Europe left religion behind, not to compare Islam with Europe's religion. She continues as follows: "While Europe was burning mentally sick people alive since it was thought that they were dominated by Satan, Muslim physicians were treating them with music. They did not even have toilets while Muslims were building public bathhouses. Why are we not proud of Avicenna, Akşemddins, Al-Biruni and Harezms but our children are always taught European scientists…. It is always said that Cristopher Colombus discovered America, but nobody mentions the fact that the map in his hand was drawn by Piri Reis and his guide was a Muslim sailor" (Turhal 1999, 73).
35. *Such claims to authenticity are so common in the Islamic discourse of the 1980s that they also extend into the literary sphere. Accordingly, it is claimed that the origin of Don Quixote belongs to Andalusian philosopher Seyyit Hamit bin Engeli, and that Daniel Defoe pilfered the story of Robinson Crusoe from Hayy ibn-i Yakzan (Okay 2001).*
36. The difference between *ilim* and *bilim* is accounted for by academics from Islamic circles in a book as such: "We should note first of all that those who talk about a conflict between religion and science refer to *bilim* (science) not *ilim*. *İlim* is a word that connotes 'light' and 'religion'…. '*Bilim*' on the other hand is a composition of darkness and chaos on the basis of its assigned role. While *ilim* is born in us [our land] and has got its essence from us, *bilim* is a product of the West with its rationalism, positivism" (Yılmaz et al. 1998, 61).
37. In their presentation of collective identity, authors employ a hierarchical discourse. In *Müslüman Kadının Adı Var*, for instance, Turhal does not allow Dilara's

professors to firmly defend their secular views. Rather they are always represented as weak and inconsistent in their discussion with Dilara. Muslim characters like Dilara, however, are always firm and consistent.

38. As another example, in *Müslüman Savaşçı*, protagonists who marry in the last scene are depicted in the following manner: "They were happy but they were aware that they were not born for such happiness. They knew that this world was an examination. They would be in constant fight with Satan and the friends of Satan" (Tekin 1998, 197).

Chapter 3

1. Recent work in cultural studies suggests that during times of social upheaval, novels with ideological content increase, whereas utopian novels increase in times of economic crisis. These findings seek to substantiate a relation between economic processes and literary texts (Griswold 1993). It is also noted that *roman à these* is likely to emerge in national contexts and historical moments of sharp ideological conflicts. *Roman à these* also emerges within cultural traditions that enable writers to interrogate social and political problems (Suleiman 1983).

2. On the relationship between the rise of the novel and the formation of nation-states, Timothy Brennan writes that "It was the *novel* that historically accompanied the rise of nations by objectifying the 'one, yet many' of national life, and by mimicking the structure of the nation, a clearly bordered jumble of language and styles. Socially, the novel joined the newspaper as the major vehicle of the national print media, helping to standardize language, encourage literacy, and remove mutual incomprehensibility. But it did much more than that. Its manner of presentation allowed people to imagine the special community that was the nation" (1990, 49).

3. Parallel to the literature of nationalism, recent work on social movements has also paid attention to the "concrete performance" of novels in presenting subject positions for the actors. In studies of various social movements, the novel (written by gay or feminist activists, for instance) began to be treated not only as a representational form that solely remains on a subjective emotional level, but also as narrative involving a great role in the identity construction processes. Bildungsroman, for instance, has played an important role in environmentalist movements in the way that it "served to outline possible ecological scenarios of development that a protagonist is expected to go through" (Brockmeier and Harré 2001, 43).

4. I borrow this term from Kamran Talattof, who conceptualizes literary movements in terms of their ideologies of representation, demonstrating affinity with social movements. Talattof notes that "an ideology of representation or ideology in general is not simply a set of ideas associated with certain social classes or a hierarchy of values used to justify human actions. It is rather a discursive element that is determined according to the syntagmatic and paradigmatic rules of expression.... Once established in forms of social, religious, or literary discourses, ideologies motivate political movements and create new semantic systems. The dominant cultural and socio-political discourse of a specific episode determines which ideological issues will be central to its literature" (1997, 532).

5. For an interpretation of the official sources of Kemalism, see Parla 1991 and 1992.
6. In the Kemalist process of modernization, Islam was disestablished and reestablished as a phenomenon not separate from politics. Secularism in the Turkish context did not divorce religion and politics. Rather than benign indifference or strict separation, Kemalism instrumentalized Islam in a "*Hobbesian* fashion: that is the State abrogates to itself the right or duty to command the 'Church' what doctine to preach" (Houston, forthcoming). To this aim, the abolition of the Caliphate was accompanied by the founding of the Directorate of Religious Affairs (*Diyanet İşleri Başkanlığı*) that still serves as a body for monitoring Islam (Davison 2003).
7. During the 1980s, not only Islamists but also feminists and Kurds began to voice their discontent with the consequences of the Kemalist project of modernity. The rise of critical voices reveals that the discrepancy between stories told by the regime and stories told by Islamist, Kurdish, and feminist groups increased in this period (Arat 2000; Kasaba 1997).
8. As Somers and Gibson put it, "narratives are constellations of relationships (connected parts) embedded in time and space, constituted by causal emplotment ... [and] the chief characteristic of the narrative is that it renders understanding only by connecting parts to a constructed configuration composed of symbolic, institutional and material practices" (1994, 59). Configuration of several dimensions of human experience through narratives implies that narratives are not the "externalization" of some kind of "internal" reality through giving it linguistic shape. Rather, narratives are forms inherent in human's ways of obtaining knowledge that structure experience about the world and the people themselves (Brockmeier and Harré 2001). Narratives, in other words, are not only a means of representation but also operate as a "mode of cognition" (Lamarque 1994, 150). The presence of narrative structure and technique in several scientific, historical, and journalistic accounts, as well as in literary fiction, attests to the power of the narrative as a form of cognition in human life.
9. Narratives can be taken as subtypes of discourse, the most general category of human linguistic activity, and literature is one of the categories of narrative. Narrative, however, is not identical to all forms of literature. Much lyric poetry, for instance, lacks the narrative form (Lamarque 1994, 132). The novel, on the other hand, is a genre that conforms to the basic characteristics of a narrative. Time, structure, voice, and a point of view as the basic dimensions of a narrative (Lamarque 1994, 132) appear in some form in all novels. Indeed, the term "novel" in this regard is used synonymously with the term "narrative" in literary contexts. This suggests that the novel involves a narrative form through which it connects events and characters in a sequence of time. It turns events into episodes through emplotment. What distinguishes the novel, in other words, is its narration of events and characters in a plot that evolves over time.
10. The narrative has recently received much attention in the social sciences. Several social scientists appropriate narratives as the core of their theories based on the postulation that people make sense of the world through narratives, and that narratives are the means through which social and cultural life is formed (Taylor 1992; MacIntyre 1985; Rorty 1989; Nussbaum 1992). Such a conceptualization of literary narratives as a means to interrogate identity in social and political life implies a challenge to the traditional understanding of the relation between (political) philosophy and literary narratives. This is because political

philosophy and literature have long been considered two distinct and uncompromising domains of knowledge. The emotions that novelists appeal to and the imagination that literature has drawn on have often been seen as suspect in political philosophy.

The growing interest in the study of narratives as a specific mode of constructing and constituting reality, however, has been argued to symbolize a "narrative turn," a "post-positivist movement," or a "discursive turn" in political philosophy (Brockmeier and Carbaugh 2001; Horton and Baumeister 1996). This suggested "narrative turn" involves breaking down the boundaries between literature and philosophy to rethink them in dialogue. Philosophers such as Charles Taylor, Alasdair MacIntyre, Richard Rorty, and Martha Nussbaum, who are associated with the narrative turn, argue that the incorporation of narrative into political inquiry, and thus a rapprochement of philosophy with literature, might revive political philosophy.

11. It should be noted that the term "narrative" as employed by MacIntyre and Taylor does not only include literary narratives. What MacIntyre refers to as "narrative" is the storytelling act that involves a beginning and an end to make sense of the world. MacIntyre, thus, refers more to the autobiography rather than the novel (Whitebrook 1996, 35). Taylor, Rorty, Nussbaum, and Whitebrook (who relate narrative with political processes), however, use the term "narrative" to refer to novels. In light of their theories of the narrative construction of identity, as Whitebrook suggests, the form of the novel and the way in which modern identity is constituted become inseparable (Whitebrook 1996, 35). Literary narratives, therefore, emerge not only as a linguistic form but also as a mental form that can be used to describe and reconstruct human reality.

12. This contention implies that people are confused when they are not capable of integrating their experiences into an intelligible story. Making an intelligible story represents the quest for narrative unity that allows people to order events that otherwise seems inchoate.

13. Because the novel is addressed to a certain group of readers, the novel as a genre has an "implied reader" (Iser 1993). An author thus has readers' knowledge in mind, leading to the creation of meaning. This suggests that literary narratives are "contextual" because they require readers to be familiar with their contents and forms of presentation (Lehtonen 2000, 82).

14. Rorty goes further in his argument to replace philosophy with narrative since he argues that the latter is a better guide to create solidarity (or Rorty's own liberal utopia). For Rorty, "solidarity is not discovered by reflection, but created. It is created by increasing our sensitivity to the particular details of the pain and humiliation of other, unfamiliar sorts of people. Such increased sensitivity makes it more difficult to marginalize people different from ourselves.... This process of coming to see other human beings as 'one of us' rather than of 'them' is a matter of detailed description of what other people are like and of re-description of what we ourselves are like. This is a task not for theory, but for genres such as ethnography, the comic book, the docudrama and especially for the novel" (1989, xvi).

15. In this vein, Nussbaum bestows on the novel a specific role not only in political but also in ethical theorizing. A true conception of ethical understanding, Nussbaum argues, should give priority not to abstract rules but to particular people and situations. This particularity finds its most adequate expression in literary narratives rather than abstract philosophical accounts. This is because "literary

forms call forth certain specific sorts of practical activity in the reader that can be evoked in no other way ... [and because] we need a story of a certain kind, with characters of a certain type in it, if our own sense of life and of value is to be called forth in the way most appropriate for practical reflection" (1992, 290).

16. It should be noted that social movement theory has long understated the emotional factors generating collective identity and solidarity among group members. Underpinning this disinterest is a more widespread contrast constructed in modern science that considers emotions to be the opposite of rationality. Most emotions, however, as underlined by Jasper in *The Art of Moral Protest*, are part of rational action, not opposed to it (1997, 110). This is because emotions, like moral values, are socially embedded. They do not arise naturally but are social constructs learned from an emotional repertoire. One cannot study emotions without making reference to given contexts. Emotions, thus, present us with clues about the responses of social actors pertaining to the outer world surrounding them. The novel, in this sense, is a genre reformulating, reframing, and expressing emotions; as much research demonstrates, the novel also plays an important role in stirring up emotions and reinforcing a sense of solidarity and "we-ness."

17. The Fethullah Gülen movement and its focus on educational activities at a grassroots level are often associated with the term "cultural Islam." This stance is best exemplified by a character of a recently published self-critical novel, written by Barış Müstecaplıoğlu, an ex-member of the Fethullah Gülen movement. In response to "political" Islamists who seek an implementation of sharia, the author succinctly summarizes the movement's position as follows: "Sharia? Why shall we ask for sharia? What will happen if sharia comes? Are we going to ask people to pray forcefully? Are we going to provide a policeman for everybody? If people were praying and fasting voluntarily, and living according to the principles of sharia, does it matter whether you call the regime a republic or something else, does it make any difference? ... Those who tried to capture the state have always failed, but we have continuously gained strength. It will be enough to gain sufficient power within the state to ease our deeds and clear the way, that is all" (Müstecaplıoğlu 2006, 138–39).

18. A word, for Bakhtin, takes its shape in a dialogic relation and "forms a concept of its own object in a dialogic way" (2000, 279). Words (also texts), in other words, are essentially intersubjective, and exist dialogically between the communicating subjects using them. The social, heteroglot, and dialogic nature of language, as noted by Bakhtin, has certain implications for the novel whose basic material is words. The heteroglot nature of the novel implies that social heteroglossia—the many voices of social life—enters the novel in dialogue through the talk of characters. The novel appears as an artistic representation of these different voices as follows: "The social and historical voices populating language, all its words and all its forms, which provide language with its particular concrete conceptualizations, are organized in the novel into a structured stylistic system that expresses the differentiated socio-ideological position of the author amid the heteroglossia of the epoch" (Bakhtin 2000, 300). The novelistic word, thus, is inherently social since it involves a dialogical interrelation between various voices of the era. That is why Bakhtin identifies the novel as "the encyclopedia of the life of the era" or as "the maximally complete register of all social voices of the era" (2000, 430). The dialogizing background and the heteroglot nature of the novel,

according to Bakhtin, are the most fundamental privileges of novelistic prose, a privilege available neither to epic, dramatic, or poetic genres. According to Bakhtin, "there are no speaking persons in the epic who function as representatives of different languages—in the epic, the speaker is, in essence, solely the author alone, and discourse is a single, unitary authorial discourse" (2000, 334).

19. Göle argues that the new Islamist actors' process of becoming Islamist follows a common pattern in that these actors generally move from small provinces to big cities where, during their high school or university education, they encounter the works of contemporary Islamist thinkers (Göle 2000, 95).

Chapter 4

1. Commenting on the new Islamic generation of the 1990s, Gökhan Bacık notes that this generation "started playing the game via modern institutions, colleges, hospitals and TV channels. Their understanding of the world is different. Their basic point of departure is self-expression, not survival" (2003, 31).

2. On Hak-İş, see Duran and Yıldırım (2005). In this article, the authors argue that Hak-İş, as the "labour wing of the Turkish Islamist movement," articulated its approach to unionism and workers' issues in Islamist terms in its early years. Nevertheless, as a result of its participation in democratic processes of negotiation, Hak-İş was transformed in the 1990s into an organization contributing to the democratization of Islamism in Turkey. The auhors write that "the early Islamist rhetoric of Hak-İş was at first weakened and later transformed into a civil societal and democratic one by the Hak-İş leaders, because they recongnized that Islamism did not contain a frame that adequately reflected the particular demands of workers. At the same time, the Islamist framework was also revealed as unsuitable, due to its anti-European stance, for the integration of Hak-İş into the European labour institutions" (2005, 243).

3. Hakan Yavuz defines the category of "Muslim entrepreneur" in the following terms: "Pious individuals who identify Islam as their identity and formulate their everyday map by using Islamic ideas and history to vernacularize (Islamisize) modern economic relations that promote market forces and cherish a neo-liberal project" (2006, 108).

4. Hasan Kösebalaban notes that Islamist actors "came to realize that globalization presents opportunities that have been denied to them by domestic political and economic establishments. Anatolian [Islamic] capital groups started to expand their interests in international markets, while headscarf-wearing university students initiated a massive wave of educational migration overseas" (2005, 33).

5. This refers to a saying of the Prophet, the application of which is supposed to characterize a Muslim. In Turkish, it says that "Müslüman çirkinlikleri gece gibi örten, güzellikleri gündüz gibi aydınlatan insandır."

6. Anthropologist Yael Navaro-Yashin writes her observation of a fashion show as follows: "As the models walked by, I noticed that much of their body shapes could be discerned through the clothes that they were exhibiting. Their full breasts, slender waists, and thin columns of legs imposed themselves through the clothes that they wore which were marked "Islamic." 'Is this fitting with Islam?' I asked a covered woman who was standing and watching beside me, 'these tightly

sewn, narrow gowns that disclose the contours of one's body?' 'Well,' said the perplexed-looking woman, noticing my uncovered head and for a while unable to find an answer. 'This is homewear, you know, only to be worn beside one's husband and relatives.' 'But all these men are watching these models here,' I said. 'Doesn't that contradict Islamic law?' One covered woman who heard my question nodded in agreement with my stated confusion. The first woman, again perplexed, said: 'They are doing this now to introduce the clothes. Normally people wouldn't wear these clothes in public. I am also a trader, you know. And a trader has to exhibit his products. This man is doing this and he is doing it well' (2002, 101–3).

7. Halime Toros (b. 1960) holds an MA in public administration. Her other works are *Tanımsız* (1990) and *Sahurla Gelen Erkekler* (1993).

8. Ahmet Kekeç (b. 1961) is currently a columnist in a pro-Islamic daily. He has worked as a journalist and editor for several Islamic dailies and his stories have been published in various Islamic journals.

9. On February 28, 1997, the military in Turkey, through the National Security Council, intervened in the political and civilian sphere. The Islamic Welfare Party coalition government was forced to resign. In the process, the Welfare Party was closed down. Its leader and some of its members were taken to court and imprisoned.

10. Ayşe Böhürler, a woman politician who is currently an active member of the Justice and Development Party, points out the difference between Islamic men and women in the labor market. "Men," she says, "do not need to be approved." She goes on to say, "since being headscarved has prejudiced connotations such as 'uneducated, ignorant or villager' at work settings, the working women should always try to prove that she is educated, urban and has a vision. She has always to prove her skills at her profession against the prejudice of her Islamic boss because of her headscarf. For that reason it is very difficult for her to make a career" (Sever 2006, 144).

11. Similar points about the rise and transformation of Islamism have also been made by various ex-Islamists. Ahmet Hakan, a columnist for a mainstream daily who publicly declares himself an ex-Islamist, for instance, portrays the story of Islamism in the 1980s and 1990s as such: "It was twenty years ago. The title of a popular journal of the period, Nokta, was informing people about the rise of an 'Islamic youth.' I am talking about days when Ali Shariati's book *Religion against Religion* was being waved like a flag in university corridors. It was the days when Sayyid Qutb's *Milestones* was turned into a 'youth guide.' … Then something happened. Something strange. Holdings emerged [in Islamic circles]. Everybody made some money. People got higher positions in companies or government offices.… As a result of the spoiling function of money and power, our 'Islamic renaissance' has been 'deflated.' (2006).

12. As Farzeneh Minali notes, the overdetermined position of Islamic veiling is also questioned by the religiously oriented women of Iran. Zahra Rahnavard, a writer married to the Islamic Republic's fifth prime minister, makes the following point: "Unfortunately after the Imam's message about purification of the workplaces and the country in general from the remnants of the imperial regime, a number of administrators, instead of tackling the roots of the problem, have emphasized one aspect out of proportion and have left other aspects in abeyance. The overemphasized aspect is women's clothing and the imposition of hejâb [Islamic

modest dress] on them. But we should remember that in Islam men are also required to observe modest dress and behaviour" (Milani 1992, 43–44).

13. This article became popular in the 28 February Process and was used against Welfare Party members.

14. *Batı Çalışma Grubu* is a group within the military founded to monitor Islamic companies and personalities during the February 28 Process.

15. In the context of the 28 February Process, not only novelists but also various Islamist intellectuals from different circles expressed a more critical attitude toward Islamism rather than parroting a simple ideological response. In order to point out the lack of criticism among Islamic circles, journalist-columnist Ali Bulaç wrote articles such as "Bizim mahallenin hikayesi" (The Story of Our Quarter) and "Bizim mahellede eleştiri yürek ister" (Criticism in Our Quarter Needs Courage) (Zaman, 6–9 May 2000). Nuh Gönültaş from the Fethullah Gülen movement contributed to the debate by using the same phrase, pointing out that "our quarter is not so different in its mistakes than yours" (Zaman, 7 May 2000). These columnists noted that the collective and political ideals of Islamism led to an intolerant attitude toward Muslims who criticized an Islamic party, company, or institution from within. They noted the oppositional Islamic perception that "any critique of Islamism by a member of the movement serves the interests of the enemies." Such a perception led to Islamists' closing their eyes to mistakes and injustices in their own circles. Bulaç also criticized the position of older politicians and Islamic authorities as follows: "They know everything, make plans and want you to obey without questioning." Such critiques signify that the collective "we" of the 1980s was under threat.

16. This novel narrates the transformation of a young Islamist man through his love of an assertive and critical Muslim girl. İrfan, the protagonist who at the beginning of the novel says that "a Muslim does not fall in love with a woman, but only with Allah," finds himself at the end of the novel imagining looking for a job and having the small happiness in his private life of a man who "took off his militant uniform [parka]." Commenting on this novel, Göle points out that this narrative "testifies to and contributes to the development from collective political Islamism toward the emergence of Muslim subjectivities" (Göle 1997a, 77ff).

17 Rejecting and disregarding traditional experiences in order to search for the "truth" in *Asr-ı Saadet* has also been critically assessed by Muslim women in the 1990s. Toros, for instance, notes Islamist women's ignorance of the women's movement in Ottoman times as follows: "In the 1980s, when we sought to criticize a huge [Western] tradition through our intuition and readings, we did not know the women and movements that had already done it before us. This was because this past was kept away from us" (Toros 2000, 206–7).

18. After her unveiling, Nisa is made to think that "I need to learn everything from the very beginning. I know that this body will not undertake a young lady's indifference, throwing back her hair and walking nimbly" (54).

19. Criticism of the Islamist conceptualization of women is not limited to the literary sphere but rather extends to the academic writings of Muslim women in the 1990s (Ramazanoğlu 2000; Tuksal 2000). Tuksal's work *Kadın Karşıtı Söylemin İslam Geleneğindeki İzdüşümü* (The Imprints of Anti-Woman Discourse in Islamic Tradition) has generated a fierce debate in Islamic circles. Tuksal, a veiled Muslim theologian, analyzes the sayings about women that have been accepted as the Prophet's tradition in Islam. She argues that the Prophet's sayings promote

a discourse that "humiliates women" and "prioritizes men over women." These sayings and deep-seated attitudes toward women in Islamic circles, she contends, are not religious dogma but human products deriving from a long tradition of patriarchy.

Conclusion

1. Such a characterization of ideal Islamic identity is not confined only to literary representations of Islamism of the 1980s but also extends into other nonliterary texts of the period. These idealized representations of Islamic identity, in other words, can easily be paralleled in prominent Islamist thinkers' identification of the ideal figure who leads the way in establishing an Islamic society. Both the literary and nonliterary texts of epic Islamism in the 1980s encouraged a personal stance in which individual identities and personal desires should be subordinated to collective Islamic ideals of Islamizing state and society. Dilara and Cihan, for instance, can easily be characterized by Fathi Yakan's depiction of the ideal caller in his influential work originally titled "Problems of the Call and the Caller" (1984). In this study (which was also translated into Turkish), Yakan proposes several principles to build an Islamic personality to achieve an Islamic state. Every aspect of life of the ideal caller, including marriage, is conceived within collective ideals. On marriage, he writes, "Islam requires that the purpose of marriage be to establish the Muslim home as the first solid foundation and cornerstone in establishing a Muslim society" (1984, 45).
2. The "pedagogical" and "performative" functions of a narrative derive from Homi Bhabha. See Bhabha 1995.
3. This authoritative discourse that leaves no space to other life options also informs us of the pro-Islamic Welfare Party politicians' presentation of their program of what they called Just Order (*Adil Düzen*). As party spokesmen repeated on numerous occasions, this program was the only alternative to other worldly systems (such as capitalism and socialism). Similarly it was asserted that Just Order would eventually prevail as other systems would fade away (Yavuz 1997).
4. Metiner summarizes his new stance—that he argues is also held by the leader of the Justice and Development Party, Tayyip Erdoğan, and his party—as follows: "Islam is a religion, not a state. Islam cannot stand for a state. The state cannot adopt an ideology and religion. Secularism is not a state ideology, but a political stance involving the state's neutrality towards all religious groups. Secularism is not an aim but a means aiming at providing social peace and consensus. Democracy is in itself without ideology.... Political secularism is as dangerous for social peace as political Islam. No one should do politics based on religion and secularism (*din ve laiklik siyasete alet edilmemelidir*)" (Metiner 2004, 417–18).
5. After the 28 February Process and the formation of the Justice and Development Party, several intellectuals, including Ali Bulaç, abandoned their oppositional stance of the 1980s, arguing that "in new world order, old discourses have lost their significance. We need a new model that is not contradictory but reconciliatory" (Yüksel 2003). They began to publish a new journal titled *Bilgi ve Düşünce* in 2003 under the editorial management of Ali Bulaç. The term "new Islamism" appeared in this journal and was debated in several issues.

Reference List

Abedin, Saleha M. 1996.Women in search of equality, development and peace: A critical analysis of the platform for action, Fourth World Conference on Women and the Islamic Perspective. *Journal of Muslim Minority Affairs* 16, no. 1:73–89.

Adıvar, Halide Edip. 1999. *Vurun kahpeye.* İstanbul: özgür yayınları. Originally published, 1926.

Ağar, Mehmet E. 1987–1988. Son iki yılda roman ve hikaye. In *Suffe Kültür Sanat Yıllığı.* İstanbul: Suffe Yayınları.

Ahmad, Aijaz. 1987. Jameson's rhetoric of otherness and the national allegory. *Social Text* 17:3–25.

Aktaş, Cihan. 1991. *Üç ihtilal çocuğu.* İstanbul: Nehir.

———. 1995. *Son büyülü günler.* İstanbul: Nehir.

Aksoy, Şebnem, and Pervin Kaplan. 1997. İslamcı aşk bestseller. *Radikal,* November 5–6.

Al-Azmeh, Aziz. 1993. *Islams and modernitites.* London: Verso.

Alan, Bülent. 2004. İslamcı aydınların batılılaşma ihaneti 1, *Milli Gazete,* February 7.

Altay, Abdullah. 1995. Hangi kitapları okuyalım? *Milli Gazete,* June 6.

Anderson Benedict. 1991. *Imagined communities: Reflections on the origin and spread of nationalism.* London: Verso.

Andı, Fatih. 1996. *İnsan toplum edebiyat.* İstanbul: Kitabevi.

Arat, Yeşim. 1990. Islamic fundamentalism and women in Turkey. *Muslim World* 80:17–23.

———. 1997. The project of modernity and women in Turkey. In *Rethinking modernity and national identity in Turkey,* edited by Reşat Kasaba and Sibel Bozdoğan. Seattle: University of Washington Press.

———. 2000. From emancipation to liberation: The changing role of women in Turkey's public realm. *Journal of International Affairs* 54, no. 1:107–23.

———. 2001. Group-differentiated rights and the liberal democratic state: Rethinking the headscarf controversy in Turkey. *New Perspectives on Turkey* (Fall): 31–46.

———. 2005. *Rethinking Islam and liberal democracy: Islamist women in Turkish politics.* New York: State University of New York Press.

Arat, Zehra F. 1994. Turkish women and the republican reconstruction of tradition. In *Reconstructing gender in the Middle East,* edited by Fatma Müge Göcek and Shiva Balaghi. New York: Columbia University Press.

Asena, Duygu. 1987. *Kadının adı yok.* İstanbul: Afa Yayınları.

Asımgil, Sevim. 1993. *Sevda geri dön.* İstanbul. Timaş Yayınları.

Ayoob, Mohammed. 2004. Political Islam: Image or reality? *World Policy Journal* 2, no. 3 (Fall): 1–14.

Ayvazoğlu, Beşir. 1982. Nasıl bir gerçekçilik. In *Suffe Kültür Sanat Yıllığı*. İstanbul: Suffe Yayınları.

Azak, Umut. 1999. İslami radyolar ve türbanlı spikerler. In *İslamın yeni kamusal yüzleri*, edited by Nilüfer Göle. İstanbul: Metis.

Bacık, Gökhan. 2003. The transformation of Muslim self and the development of a new discourse on Europe: The Turkish case. *International Review of Sociology* 13, no. 1:21–38.

Badran, Margot. 1995. *Feminists, Islam and nation: Gender and the making of modern Egypt*. Princeton, NJ: Princeton University Press.

Bakhtin, Mikhail M. 2000. *The dialogical imagination*. Austin: University of Texas Press.

———. 1996. *Speech genres and other late essays*. Edited by Caryl Emerson and Michael Holquist. Translated by Vern W. McGee. Austin: University of Texas Press.

Barbarosoğlu, Fatma K. 1996. Kopan filmler arasında başörtülülerin kısa tarihi. *İzlenim*, no. 37:19–23.

Baykurt, Fakir. 1975. *Onuncu köy*. İstanbul: Remzi Kitapevi.

Benhabib, Seyla. 1996. *Situating the self: Gender, community and postmodernism in contemporary ethics*. Cambridge: Polity.

Belge, Murat. 1994. *Edebiyat üstüne yazılar*. İstanbul: Yapı Kredi yayınları.

Berkes, Niyazi. 2002. *Türkiye'de çağdaşlaşma*. Yay. Haz. Ahmet Kuyaş. İstanbul: Yapı Kredi Yayınları.

Bhabha, Homi K. 1990. Dissemination: Time, narrative and the margins of the modern nation. In *Nation and narration*, edited by Homi K. Bhabha. London: Routledge.

Bourdieu, Pierre. 1995. *The field of cultural production*. Cambridge: Polity.

———. 1996. *The rules of art*. Cambridge: Polity.

Boztoprak, Galip. 1982. Romanımıza doğru. In *Suffe Kültür Sanat Yıllığı*. İstanbul: Suffe Yayınları.

Brennan, Timothy. 1990. The national longing for form. In *Nation and narration*, edited by Homi K. Bhabha. London: Routledge.

Brockmeier, Jens and Rom Harré. 2001. Narrative: Problems and promises of an alternative paradigm." In *Narrative and identity: Studies in autobiography, self and culture*, edited by J. Brockmeier and D. Carbaugh. Philadelphia: John Benjamin's.

Brockmeier, Jens and Donal Carbaugh. 2001. Introduction to *Narrative and identity: Studies in autobiography, self and culture*, edited by J. Brockmeier and D. Carbaugh. Philadelphia: John Benjamin's.

Bulaç, Ali. 1987. *Çağdaş kavramlar ve düzenler*. İstanbul: Beyan Yayınları.

———. 1990. *Din ve modernizm*. İstanbul: Endülüs Yayınları.

———. 1995. *İslam dünyasında düşünce sorunları*. İstanbul: İz Yayıncılık.

Calhoun, Craig. 1994. Social theory and politics of identity. In *Social theory and political identity*, edited by Craig Calhoun. Cambridge, MA: Blackwell.

Canatan, Kadir. 2003. AKP bağlamında "Yeni İslamcılık." *Bilgi ve Düşünce*, no. 4:22–28.

Castoriadis, Cornelius. 1997. *The imaginary institution of society*. Translated by Kathleen Blamey. Cambridge: Polity

Ceylan, İsmail Fatih. 2002. *Kapanmayan yara*. İstanbul: Nesil.

Cilasun, Raif. n.d. *Bir annenin feryadı*. İstanbul: Erhan.

Cizre, ümit, and Menderes çınar. 2003. Turkey 2002: Kemalism, Islamism, and politics in the lights of the February 28 Process. *South Atlantic Quarterly* 102, no. 2/3:309–32.

Clark, Malcolm. 2003. *Islam for dummies*. New York: Wiley.

Çakır, Ruşen. 2000. *Direniş ve itaat*. İstanbul: Metis Yayınları.

Çalışkan, Adem 2002. *Cumhuriyet devri İslami Türk edebiyatı 1960–2000*. PhD diss., Samsun Ondokuz Mayıs üniversitesi Sosyal Bilimler Enstitüsü.

Çalışkan, Koray. 1996. Özenilesi yaşamlar, İslami romanlar üzerine bir inceleme. *Birikim*, no. 91:89–95.

Çayır, Kenan. 2000. İslamcı bir sivil toplum örgütü: Gökkuşağı İstanbul Kadın Platformu. In *İslamın Yeni Kamusal Yüzleri*, edited by Nilüfer Göle. İstanbul: Metis.

Çınar, Alev. 2005. *Modernity, Islam and secularism in Turkey: Bodies, places and time*. Minneapolis: University of Minneapolis Press.

Davies, Merrly Wyn. 1991. *İslami antropolojinin oluşturulması*. Translated by Tayfun Doğukargın. İstanbul: Endülüs Yayınları.

Davison, Andrew. 1998. *Secularism and revivalism in Turkey: A hermeneutic reconsideration*. New Haven, CT: Yale University Press.

———. 2003. Turkey, a secular state? The challenge of description. *South Athlantic Quarterly* 102, no 2/3:333–49.

Değirmenci, Ali. 2000. Bizim öykümüz hangisi? *Haksöz*, no. 109:61–71.

Dilipak, Abdurrahman. 1995. *Bir başka açıdan kadın*. İstanbul: Risale.

Doğramacı, Emel. 1984. *The status of women in Turkey*. Ankara: Meteksan.

Doltaş, Dilek. 2001. Siyasal İslamcı yazında ahlak, yaşam ve kadın kimliği. *Adam* no. 184:22–31.

Donzel, E. J. van. 1998. *The encyclopedia of Islam*. Leiden: E. J. Brill.

Duben, Alan, and Cem Behar. 1991. İstanbul *households: Marriage, family and fertility 1880–1940*. Cambridge: Cambridge University Press.

Durakbaşa, Ayşe. 1998. Kemalism as identity politics in Turkey. In *Deconstructing the images of Turkish woman*, edited by Zehra F. Arat. New York: St. Martin's.

Duran, Burhanettin, and Engin Yıldırım. 2005. Islamism, trade unionism and civil society: The case of Hak-İş labour confederation in Turkey. *Middle Eastern Studies* 41, no. 2:227–47.

Eagleton, Terry. 1996. *Literary theory: An introduction*. Oxford: Blackwell.

Eickelman, Dale F., and James Piscatori. 1996. *Muslim politics*. Princeton, NJ: Princeton University Press.

Efe, Mehmet. 1993. *Mızraksız ilmihal*. İstanbul: Yerli Yayınlar.

Embree, Lester. 1998. A construction of Alfred Schutz's "Sociological aspect of literature. In *Alfred Schutz's sociological aspect of literature: Construction and complementary essays*, edited by Lester Embree. Boston: Kluwer Academic.

Emerick, Yahiya. 2002. *The complete idiot's guide to understanding Islam*. Indianapolis: Alpha.

Erbakan, Necmettin. 1991. *Adil ekonomik düzen*. Ankara: Semih ofset.

Eren, Mehmet Ali, and Muhsin öztürk. 2004. İdeolojik kitapların ölümü. Available at http://www.aksiyon.com.tr/227/pages/dosyalar/dos2/htm.

Eroğlu, Ebubekir. 1982. İslami edebiyat terimi. In *Suffe Kültür Sanat Yıllığı*. İstanbul: Suffe Yayınları.

Eryarsoy, Beşir. 1988. *İslam devlet yapısı*. İstanbul: İşaret Yayınları.

Esposito, John L. 1995. *The Islamic threat: Myth or reality*. New York: Oxford University Press.

———. 1999. Clash of civilizations? Contemporary image of Islam in the west. In *Islam, modernism and the west: Cultural and political relations at the end of the millennium*, edited by G. Martin Munoz. London: I. B. Tauris.

———. 2002. *What everyone needs to know about Islam: Answers to frequently asked questions*. Oxford: Oxford University Press.

Evin, Ahmet ö. 1983. *Origins and development of the Turkish novel*. Minneapolis: Bibliotheca Islamica.

———. 1993. Novelists: New cosmopolitanism versus social pluralism. In *Turkey and the west: Changing political and cultural identities*, edited by Ayşe öncü, Metin Heper, and Heinz Kramer. London: I. B. Tauris.

Faruqi, Lois L. 1983. Islamic traditions and the feminist movements: Confrontation or cooperation. *Islamic Quarterly* 27, no. 3:135–45.

Feldman, Carol Fleisher. 2001. Narratives of national identity as group narratives: Patterns of interpretive cognition. In *Narrative and identity: Studies in autobiography, self and culture*, edited by Jens Brockmeier and Donal Carbaugh. Philadelphia: John Benjamin's.

Faruki, İsmail R. 1985. *Bilginin İslamileştirilmesi*. Translated by F. Koru. İstanbul: Risale.

Fornas, Johan. 1995. *Cultural theory and late modernity*. London: Sage.

Giddens, Anthony. 1995. *Modernity and self-identity*. Stanford, CA: Stanford University Press.

Goffman, Erving. 1986. *Frame analysis: An essay on the organization of experience*. Boston: Northeastern University Press.

Göle, Nilüfer. 1992. *Modern mahrem*. İstanbul: Metis.

———. 1996. Authoritarian secularism and Islamist politics: The case of Turkey. In *Civil society in the Middle East*, edited by Augustus Richard Norton. Leiden: E. J. Brill.

———. 1997a. The gendered nature of the public sphere. *Public Culture* 10, no. 1:61–83.

———. 1997b. The quest for the Islamic self within the context of modernity. In *Rethinking modernity and national identity in Turkey*, edited by Sibel Bozdoğan and Reşat Kasaba. Seattle: University of Washington Press.

———. 1999. *The forbidden modern: Civilization and veiling*. Ann Arbor: University of Michigan Press.

———. 2000. Snapshots of Islamic modernities. *Daedalus* 129, no. 1 (Winter): 91–117.

———. 2002. Close encounters: Islam, modernity and violence. In *Understanding September 11*, edited by Craig Calhoun. New York: New West.

———. 2006. Islamic visibilities and public sphere. In *Islam in public: Turkey, Iran and Europe*, edited by Nilüfer Göle and Ludwig Ammann. İstanbul: İstanbul Bilgi University Press.

Griswold, Wendy. 1993. Recent moves in the sociology of literature. *Annual Review of Sociology* 19:455–67.

Gülalp, Haldun. 1997. Globalizing postmodernism: Islamist and western social theory. *Economy and Society* 26 (August): 419–33.

Gülendam, Ramazan. 2002. Türk romanında dine ve din adamına bakış. *Hece*, no. 65–67:303–13.

Güntekin, Reşat Nuri. 1995. *Yeşil gece*. İstanbul: İnkılap Kitapevi. Originally published, 1926.

Gürçağlar, Şehnaz T. 2001. *The politics and poetics of translation in Turkey 1923–1960.* PhD diss., Boğaziçi University, Institute of Social Sciences.

Haddad, Yvonne. 1998. Islam and gender: Dilemmas in the changing Arab world. In *Islam, gender and social change*, edited by Yvonne Haddad and John L. Esposito. New York: Oxford University Press.

Hakan, Ahmet. 2006. İslamcı aydınların yükselişi ve düşüşü. *Hürriyet*, September 14.

Hall, Stuart, and Paul du Gay, eds. 1996. *Questions of cultural identity.* London: Sage.

Hatemi, Hüseyin. 1988. *Kadının çıkış yolu.* Ankara: Fecr.

Hessini, Leila. 1994. Wearing the hijab in contemporary Morocco: Choice and identity. In *Reconstructing gender in the Middle East*, edited by Fatma Müge Göcek and Shiva Balaghi. New York: Columbia University Press.

Holbrook, Victoria R. 1994. *The unreadable shore of love: Turkish modernity and mystic romance.* Austin: University of Texas Press.

Horton, John, and Andrea T. Baumeister. 1996. Literature, philosophy and political theory. In *Literature and political imagination*, edited by John Horton and Andrea T. Baumester. London: Routledge.

Houston, Christopher. 2001. The brewing of Islamist modernity: Tea gardens and public space in Istanbul. *Theory, Culture and Society* 18, no. 6:77–97.

———. 2001. *Islam, Kurds and the Turkish nation state.* Oxford: Berg.

———.2004. Islamism, Castoriadis and autonomy. *Thesis Eleven*, no. 76:25–45.

———. Forthcoming. *Imagining Kurdistan.* Oxford: Berg.

Huntington, Samuel P. 1993. The clash of civilizations. *Foreign Affairs* 72, no. 3:22–28.

Iser, Wolfgang. 1993. *The fictive and the imaginary: Charting literary anthropology.* Baltimore: Johns Hopkins University Press.

İlyasoğlu, Aynur. 1994. *Örtülü kimlik.* İstanbul: Metis.

İsmail, Hekimoğlu. 1986. *Minyeli Abdullah.* 33rd ed. İstanbul: Timaş Yayınları.

———. 2003. *Minyeli Abdullah.* İstanbul: Timaş Yayınları. Originally published, 1968.

Jasper, James M. 1997. *The art of moral protest: Culture, biography and creativity in social movements.* Chicago: University of Chicago Press.

Kaçan, Hasan. 1996. Çelişkim. *Yeni Şafak*, June 1.

Kadıoğlu, Ayşe. 1998. Republican epistemology and Islamic discourses in Turkey in the 1990s. *The Muslim World* 88, no. 1:1–21.

Kahraman, Hasan Bülent. 2000. "Je suis un autre": Turkish literature in *Transition between national and global self. In Step-mothertongue: From nationalism to multiculturalism: Literatures of Cyprus, Greece and Turkey*, edited by Mehmet Yashin. London: Middlesex University Press.

Kalyoncu, Cemal A. 2002. Hekimoğlu İsmail ile söyleşi. *Aksiyon*, July 1.

Karal, Enver Z. 1956. *Atatürk'ten düşünceler.* Ankara: Türk Tarih Kurumu Yayınları.

Karpat, Kemal. 1962. *Çağdaş Türk edebiyatında sosyal konular.* İstanbul: Varlık.

Kasaba, Reşat. 1997. Kemalist certainties and modern ambiguities. In *Rethinking modernity and national identity in Turkey*, edited by Reşat Kasaba and Sibel Bozdoğan. Seattle: University of Washington Press.

Kasaba, Reşat, and Sibel Bozdoğan, ed. 1997. *Rethinking modernity and national identity in Turkey.* Seattle: University of Washington Press.

Kekeç, Ahmet. 1999. *Yağmurdan sonra.* İstanbul: Şehir Yayınları.

———. 2000. Bir eleştiri. *Yeni Şafak*, May 19.

Kerimoğlu, Yusuf. 1985. *Kelimeler ve kavramlar.* İstanbul: İnkılap Yayınları.

Keyman, Fuat E. 1995. On the relation between global modernity and nationalism: The crisis of hegemony and the rise of (Islamic) identity in Turkey. *New Perspectives on Turkey* 13:93–120.

Kitap Dergisi. 1989. İslami arabesk'in dili. *Kitap Dergisi,* no. 28:8–15.

Köksal, Duygu. 2003. The role of art in early republican modernization in Turkey. In *La multiplication des images en pays d'Islam,* edited by Bernard Heyberger and Sylvia Naef. Wurzburg: Orient Institut der DMG.

Kömeçoğlu, Uğur. 2006a. Islamic patterns of consumption. In *Cultural changes in the Turkic world since 1990,* edited by Barbara Pusch and A. Yumul. İstanbul: Orient Institute.

———. 2006b. New sociabilities: Islamic cafes in Istanbul. In *Islam in public: Turkey, Iran, and Europe,* edited by N. Göle and L. Ammann. İstanbul: İstanbul Bilgi University Press.

Kösebalaban, Hasan. 2005. The impact of globalization on Islamic political identity: The case of Turkey. *World Affairs* 168, no. 1:27–37.

Kristeva, Julia. 1980. *Desire in language: A semiotic approach to literature and art.* Edited by Leon S. Roudiez. Translated by T. Gora, A. Jardine, and L. S. Roudiez. New York: Columbia University Press.

Kuru, Ahmet. 2005. Globalization and diversification of Islamic movements: Three Turkish cases. *Political Science Quarterly* 120, no. 2:253–74.

Lamarque, Peter. 1994. Narrative and invention: The limits of fictionality. In *Narrative in culture,* edited by C. Nash. London: Routledge.

Lehtonen, Mikko. 2000. *The cultural analysis of texts.* London: Sage.

Lewis, Bernard. 1990. The roots of Muslim rage: Why so many Muslims deeply resent the west and why their bitterness will not easily be mollified. *Atlantic Monthly* 266, no. 3:47–60.

MacIntyre, Alasdair C. 1984. *After virtue: A study in moral theory.* Notre Dame, IN: University of Notre Dame Press.

Macleod, Arlene E. 1991. *Accommodating protest: Working women, the new veiling and change in Cairo.* New York: Columbia University Press.

Makal, Mahmut. 1950. *Bizim köy.* İstanbul: Varlık yayınları.

Malti-Douglas, Fedwa. 1994. A literature of Islamic revival: The autobiography of Shaykh Kishk. In *Cultural transitions in the Middle East,* edited by Ş. Mardin. Leiden: E. J. Brill.

———. 2001. *Medicines of the soul: Female bodies and sacred geographies in a transnational Islam.* Berkeley: University of California Press.

Mardin, Şerif. 1974. Super-westernization in urban life in the Ottoman Empire in the last quarter of the nineteenth century. In *Turkey: Geographic and social perspectives,* edited by P. Benedict, E. Tümertekin, and F. Mansur. Leiden: E. J. Brill.

———. 1983. Religion and politics in modern Turkey. In *Islam in the political process,* edited by J. Piscatori. Cambridge: Cambridge University Press.

———. 1989. *Religion and social change in modern Turkey: The case of Bediüzzaman Said Nursi.* New York: State University of New York Press.

———. 1994. Introduction to *Cultural transitions in the Middle East,* edited by Ş. Mardin. Leiden: E. J. Brill.

———. 2000. *The young Ottoman movement: A study in the evolution of Turkish political thought in the nineteenth century.* Syracuse, NY: Syracuse University Press.

————. 2006. Turkish Islamic exceptionalism, yesterday and today: Continuity, rupture and reconstruction in operational codes. In *Religion and politics in Turkey*, edited by A. Çarkoğlu and B. Rubin. London: Routledge.

Mawdudi, S. Abul A'la. 1986. *The Islamic way of life*. Edited by Khursid Ahmad. London: The Islamic Foundation.

McDuffie, Michael. 1998. Literature, music, and the mutual tuning-in relationship. In *Alfred Schutz's sociological aspect of literature: Construction and complementary essays*, edited by L. Embree. Boston: Kluwer Academic.

Mead, George H. 1934. *Mind, self and society: From the standpoint of a social scientist*. Edited by Charles W. Morris. Chicago: University of Chicago Press.

Mecham, R. Quinn. 2004. From the ashes of virtue, a promise of light: the transformation of political Islam in Turkey. *Third World Quarterly* 25, no. 2:339–58.

Meeker, Michael. 1991. The new Muslim intellectuals in the Republic of Turkey. In *Islam in modern Turkey*, edited by Richard Tapper. London: I. B. Tauris.

Mendus, Susan. 1996. What of soul was left, I wonder? The narrative self in political philosophy. In *Literature and political imagination*, edited by J. Horton and A. T. Baumester. London: Routledge.

Meriç, Cemil. 1994. *Bu ülke*, yay.haz. M. Ali Meriç, İstanbul: İletişim yayınları.

Metiner, Mehmet. 2004. *Yemyeşil şeriat, bembeyaz demokrasi*. İstanbul: Doğan.

Milani, Farzaneh. 1992. *Veils and words: Emerging voices of Iranian women writers*. Syracuse, NY: Syracuse University Press.

Milas, Herkül. 2000. *Türk romanı ve "öteki": Ulusal kimlikte Yunan imajı*. İstanbul: Sabancı üniversitesi Yayınevi.

Miyasoğlu, Mustafa. 1975. *Kaybolmuş günler*. İstanbul: Ötüken Neşriyat.

————. 1980. *Dönemeç*. İstanbul: Ötüken Neşriyat.

————. 1999. *Sanat ve edebiyat konuşmaları*. Ankara: Akçağ.

Moghadam, Valentine. 1993. *Modernizing women: Gender and social change in the Middle East*. Boulder, CO: Lynne Reinner.

Moran, Berna. 1983. *Türk romanına eleştirel bir bakış*. Vol. 1. İstanbul: İletişim yayınları.

Moruzzi, Norma C. 1994. A problem with headscarves: Contemporary complexities of political and social identity. *Political Theory* 22, no. 4:653–72.

Müstecaplıoğlu, Barış. 2006. *Şakird*. İstanbul: Metis.

Navaro-Yashin, Yael. 2002. *Faces of the state: Secularism and public life in Turkey*. Princeton. NJ: Princeton University Press.

Neydim, Necdet. 1998. Küçük Prens ve çeviri. *Binbir Kitap* 1, no. 1:34–42.

Nursi, Said. 2000. *The flashes collection, the seventeenth flash, fifth note*. İstanbul: Sözler.

Nussbaum, Martha. 1992. *Love's knowledge: Essays on philosophy and literature*. New York: Oxford University Press.

Okay, Sevda. 2001. Klasiklere dokunduk. *Yeni Şafak*, July 28.

Parla, Jale. 1993. *Babalar ve Oğullar: Tanzimat Romanının Epistemolojik Temelleri*. İstanbul: İletişim yayınları.

Parla, Taha. 1991. *Türkiye'de siyasal kültürün resmi kaynakları*. Vol. 1–2. İstanbul: İletişim.

————. 1992. *Türkiye'de siyasal kültürün resmi kaynakları*. Vol. 3. İstanbul: İletişim.

Plato. 1996. *The republic*. Translated by Richard W. Sterling and William C. Scott. New York: Norton.

Qutb, Sayyid. 1990. *Milestones*. Indianapolis: American Trust.

————. 1992. *The Islamic concept and its characteristics*. Indianapolis: American Trust.

Ramazanoğlu, Yıldız, ed. 2000.*Osmanlıdan Cumhuriyete kadının tarihi dönüşümü*. İstanbul: Pınar yay.

Richardson, Laurel. 1990. Narrative and sociology. *Journal of Contemporary Ethnography* 19, no. 1:116–36.

Ricoeur, Paul. 1974. The *Conflict of interpretations: Essays in hermeneutics*. Evanston, IL: Northwestern University Press.

Rogers, Mary F. 1991. *Novels, novelists and readers: Towards a phenomenological sociology of literature*. New York: State University of New York Press.

Rorty, Richard. 1989. *Contingency, irony and solidarity*. Cambridge: Cambridge University Press.

Roy, Olivier. 2002. *Globalized Islam*. London: Hurst.

Saint Exupéry, Antoine. de. 1971. *The little prince*. New York: Harcourt Brace & World. Originally published, 1943.

Saktanber, Ayşe. 1994. Becoming the "Other" as a Muslim in Turkey: Turkish women vs. Islamist women. *New Perspectives on Turkey*, no. 11:99–134.

———. 2002. *Living Islam: Women, religion and the politicization of culture in Turkey*. London: I. B. Tauris.

Sever, Metin. 2006. *Türban ve kariyer*. İstanbul: Timaş.

Saussure, Ferdinand. 1966. *Course in general linguistics*. Edited by C. Bally and A. Sechehaye. Translated by W. Baskin. New York: McGraw-Hill.

Seyfettin, Ömer. 1989. *Dil konusunda yazılar yay haz. M. Uyguner*. Ankara: Bilgi yayınevi.

Sirman, Nükhet. 2000. Gender construction and nationalist discourse: Dethroning the father in the early Turkish novel. In *Gender and identity construction: Women of central Asia, the Caucasus and Turkey*, edited by Feride Acar and Ayşe Güneş Ayata. Leiden: E. J. Brill.

Sivan, Emmanuel. 2003. The clash within Islam. *Survival* 45, no. 1:25–44.

Somers, Margaret R, and Gloria Gibson. 1994. Reclaiming the epistemological "Other": Narrative and the social construction of reality. In *Social theory and the politics of identity*, edited by C. Calhoun. Cambridge: Blackwell.

Stevick, Philip. 1967. Introduction to *The theory of the novel*, edited by Philip Stevick. New York: Free Press.

Steward, Gary, Thomas E. Shriver, and Amy L. Chasteen. 2002. Participant narratives and collective identity in a metaphysical movement. *Sociological Spectrum* 22:107–35.

Suleiman, Susan Rubin. 1983. *Authoritarian fiction: The ideological novel as a genre*. New York: Columbia University Press.

Swingewood, Alan. 1975. *The novel and the revolution*. London: Macmillan.

Szyka, Christian. 1995. On utopian writing in Nasserist Prison and Laicist Turkey. *Die Welt des Islams* 35, no. 1:95–125.

Şenler, Şule Yüksel. 2003. *Huzur sokağı*. İstanbul: Timaş.

Şenlikoğlu, Emine. 1993. *İslam'da erkek*. İstanbul: Mektup.

———.1995. *Sabıkalı ve dul*. İstanbul: Mektup.

Şişman, Nazife. 2001. *Kamusal Alanda Başörtülüler: Fatma Karabıyık Barbarosoğlu ile Söyleşi*, İstanbul: İz.

———. 1996. *Global Konferanslarda Kadın Politikaları*, İstanbul: İz.

Talattof, Kamran. 1997. Iranian women's literature: From pre-revolutionary social discourse to post-revolutionary feminism. *International Journal of Middle Eastern Studies* 29:531–58.

Taluk, Şeyda. 1995. Biz siyasette gerçekten var mıyız? *Kadın Kimliği*, no. 9:18–19.

Tanyol, Cahit. 1999. *Neden türban, şeriat ve irtica*. İstanbul: Gendaş yayınları.

Taraki, Lisa. 1995. Islam is the solution: Jordanian Islamists and the dilemma of "Modern women." *British Journal of Sociology* 6, no. 4:643–61.

Taylor, Charles. 1991. *The ethics of authenticity*. Cambridge, MA: Harvard University Press.

———. 1992 *Sources of the self: The making of modern identity*. Cambridge: Cambridge University Press.

Tekin, Sadık. 1998. *Müslümansavaşçı*. İstanbul: Bengisu.

Topaloğlu, Bekir. 1977. *İslam'da kadın*. İstanbul: Yağmur.

Toprak, Binnaz. 1993. Islamist intellectuals: Revolt against industry and technology. In *Turkey and the west: Changing political and cultural identities*, edited by Metin Heper, Ayşe Öncü, and Heinz Kramer. London: I. B. Tauris.

———1995. Islam and secular state in Turkey. In *Turkey: Political, economic and social challenges in the 1990s*, edited by Çiğdem Balım, E. Kalaycıoğlu, C. Karataş, and G. Winrow. New York: E. J. Brill.

Toprak, Binnaz, and Ali çarkoğlu. 2000. *Türkiye'de din, toplum ve siyaset*. İstanbul: Tesev.

Toros, Halime. 1990. *Tanımsız*. İstanbul: Damla Yayınları.

———. 1993. *Sahurla gelen erkekler*. Ankara: Vadi Yayınları.

———. 1997. *Halkaların ezgisi*. İstanbul: Kırkambar Yayınları.

———. 2000. Hayat, hikayeler ve suskunluğa dair…. In *Osmanlıdan cumhuriyete kadının tarihi dönüşümü*, edited by Y. Ramazanoğlu, 189–208. İstanbul: Pınar yay.

Touraine, Alain. 1995. *Critique of modernity*. Translated by D. Macey. Oxford: Blackwell.

Tuksal, Hidayet Ş. 2000. *Kadın karşıtı söylemin İslam geleneğindeki izdüşümü*. Ankara: Kitabiyat yayınları.

Turhal, Şerife Katırcı. 1999. *Müslüman kadının adı var*. İstanbul: Adese Yayıncılık.

Türkmen, Buket. 2006. Muslim youth and Islamic NGOs. In *Islam in public: Turkey, Iran and Europe*, edited by N. Göle and L. Ammann. İstanbul: İstanbul Bilgi University Press.

Tuşalp, Erbil. 1994. *Şeriat A.Ş.* Ankara: Bilgi yayınevi.

Ünal, Ali. 1986. *Kur'an'da temel kavramlar*. İstanbul: Beyan Yayınları.

Voloshinov, Valentin. 1971. *Marxism and the philosophy of language*. Translated by L Matejka and I. R. Titunik, Cambridge: Harvard University Press.

Watt, Ian. 1995. *The rise of the novel: Studies in Defoe, Richardson and Fielding*. London: Hogarth.

Webster, Roger. 1990. *Studying literary theory: An introduction*. London: Arnold.

Whitebrook, Maureen. 1996. Taking the narrative turn: What the novel has to offer political theory. In *Literature and political imagination*, edited by J. Horton and A. T. Baumester. London: Routledge.

———. 2001. *Identity, narrative and politics*. London: Routledge.

Yakan, Fathi. 1984. *Islamic movement, problems and perspectives*. Translated by Maneh al-Johani. Indianapolis: American Trust.

Yanar, Işıl. 2001. Özneleşme sürecinde kadın ve iktidar. *Tezkire*, no. 19:119–29.

Yardım, Mehmet N. 2000. *Romancılar konuşuyor*. İstanbul: Kaknüs Yayınları.

Yavuz, M. Hakan. 1997. Political Islam and the welfare (Refah) party in Turkey. *Comparative Politics* 30, no. 1:63–82.

———. 2003. *Islamic political identity in Turkey*. Oxford: Oxford University Press.

———. 2006. The transformation of a Turkish Islamic movement: From identity politics to policy. *American Journal of Islamic Social Sciences* 22, no. 3:105–11.

Yavuz, M. Hakan, and John L. Esposito, ed. 2003. *Turkish Islam and the secular state: The Gülen movement.* Syracuse, NY: Syracuse University Press.

Yıldız, Ahmet Günbay. 1974. *Yanık buğdaylar.* İstanbul: Timaş Yayınları.

———. 2000. *Benim çiçeklerim ateşte açar.* İstanbul: Timaş yayınları.

———. 2003. *Boşluk.* İstanbul: Timaş Yayınları.

Yılldız, Nuray. 1996. üniversite mezunu bir ev kadınının portresi. *İzlenim*, no. 37:30–32.

Yılmaz, İrfan, İ. Hakkı İhsanoğlu, and Selim Aydın. 1998. *Yeni bir bakış açısıyla ilim ve din.* Vol. 1. İstanbul: Feza Gazetecilik A. Ş.

Yılmaz, V. Ertan. 2000. *Bir kimlik oluşturma aracı olarak İslami popüler romanlar.* Master's thesis, Ankara üniversitesi Sosyal Bilimler Enstitüsü.

Yunus, İlyas Ba. 1988. *Niçin İslam sosyolojisi.* Translated by Ilım Güner. İstanbul: Akabe.

Yüksel, Metin. 2003. Siyasal İslam bitti, yaşasın yeni İslamcılık. *Hürriyet*, February 16.

Zaman. 2002. Nuriye Akman'ın Şule Yüksel Şenler söyleşisi. *Zaman gazetesi*, June 16.

Zeraffa, Michel. 1973. The novel as a literary form and as a social institution. In *Sociology of literature and drama*, edited by Elizabeth Burns and Tom Burns. Middlesex: Penguin.

Zeren, Mehmet. 1996. *Öz yurdunda garipsin.* 2 vols. İstanbul: Hazen.

Index